How We Worked, How We Played

Herman Schultheis and Los Angeles in the 1930s

Edited by Christina Rice

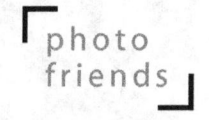

photo
friends

LOS ANGELES PUBLIC LIBRARY

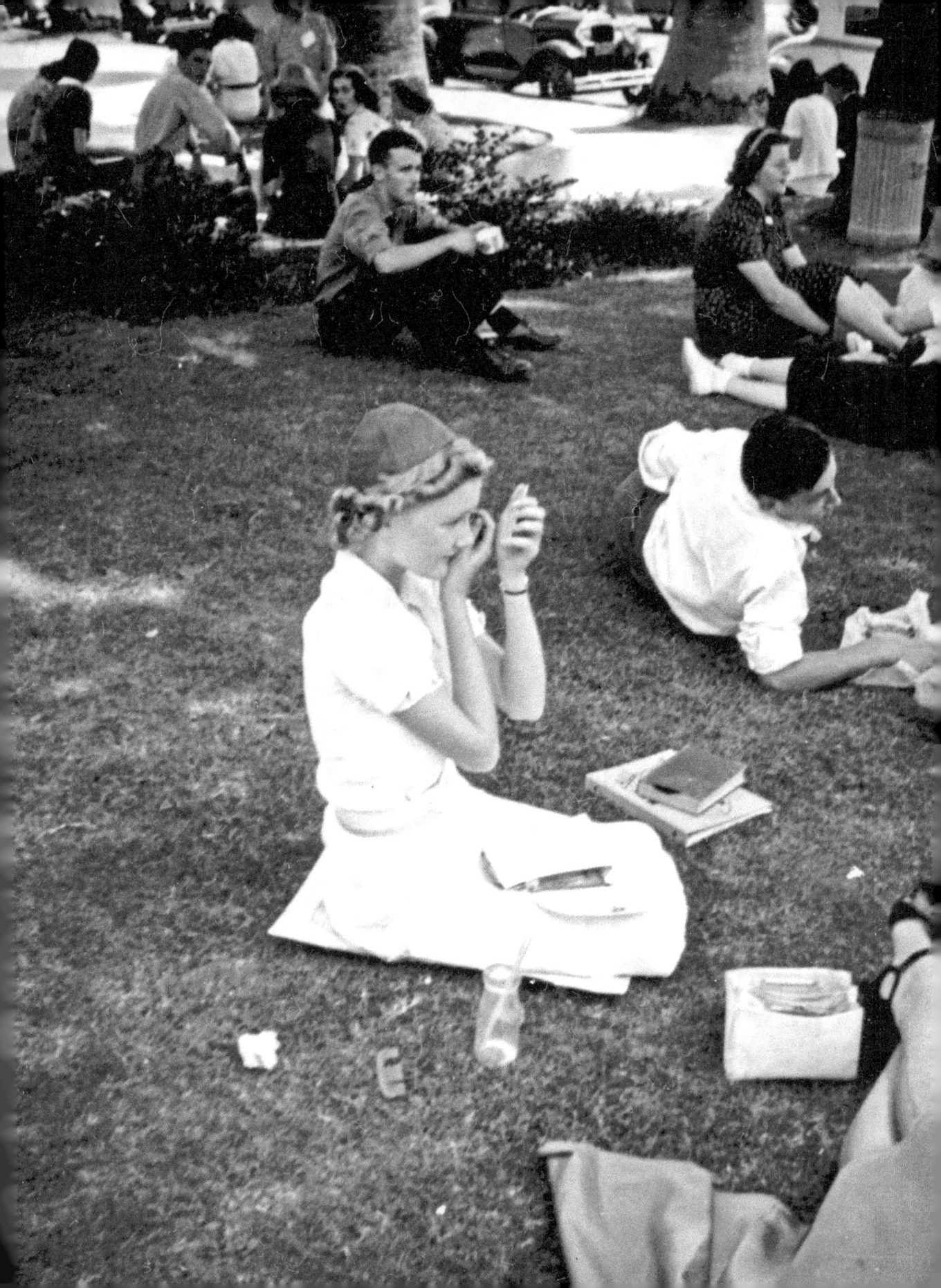

Contents

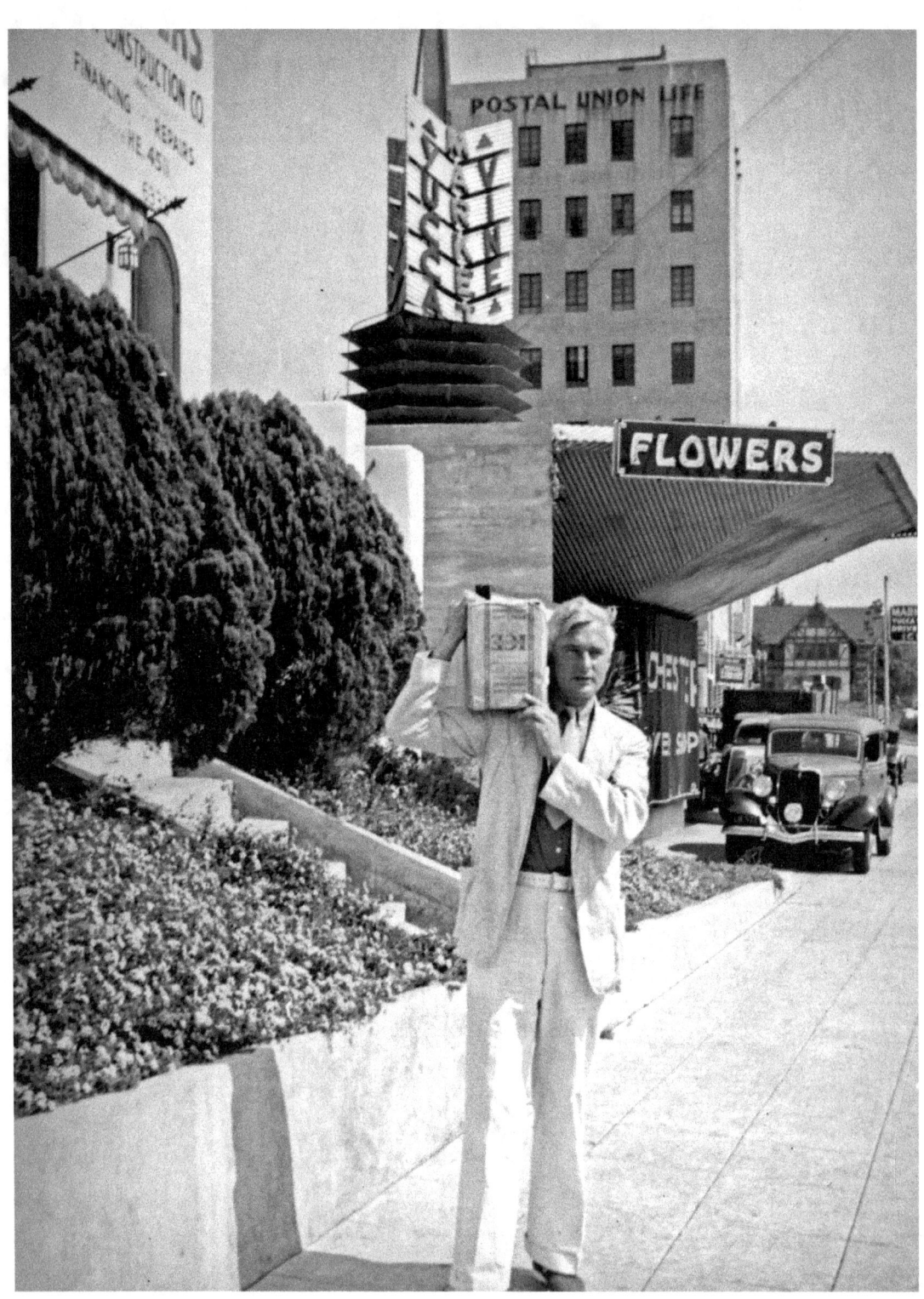

Herman Schultheis heads west towards Ivar Avenue from Yucca–Vine Market
on Yucca Street in Hollywood, ca. 1937. (Order #00097312)

How We Worked, How We Played

Herman Schultheis and Los Angeles in the 1930s

When Herman J. Schultheis disappeared in the jungles of Guatemala in 1955, it seemed any sort of public legacy was destined to vanish with him. His wife, the former Ethel Wisloh, never remarried or made any public statements about her husband following his disappearance. When she died in 1990, the home she had shared with Schultheis in the Los Feliz neighborhood of Los Angeles, along with all its contents, was left to a local Catholic charity. It was only then, over 35 years after his untimely death, that we finally got to meet Herman Schultheis.

What was found inside the house is now the stuff of animation legend. The Disney Studio had employed Schultheis as an engineer around the time of *Fantasia, Pinocchio, Bambi,* and *Dumbo.* A PhD, with a meticulous nature, Schultheis kept a detailed, illustrated notebook documenting how special effects were achieved on the landmark Disney films he worked on. These techniques had become lost over the years, and when the notebook, currently housed at the Walt Disney Family Museum, was discovered inside a Murphy bed, it was an unexpected revelation.

The Schultheis treasure trove also included photographs. Lots of photographs. Thousands of photographs. Schultheis, a German immigrant who arrived in

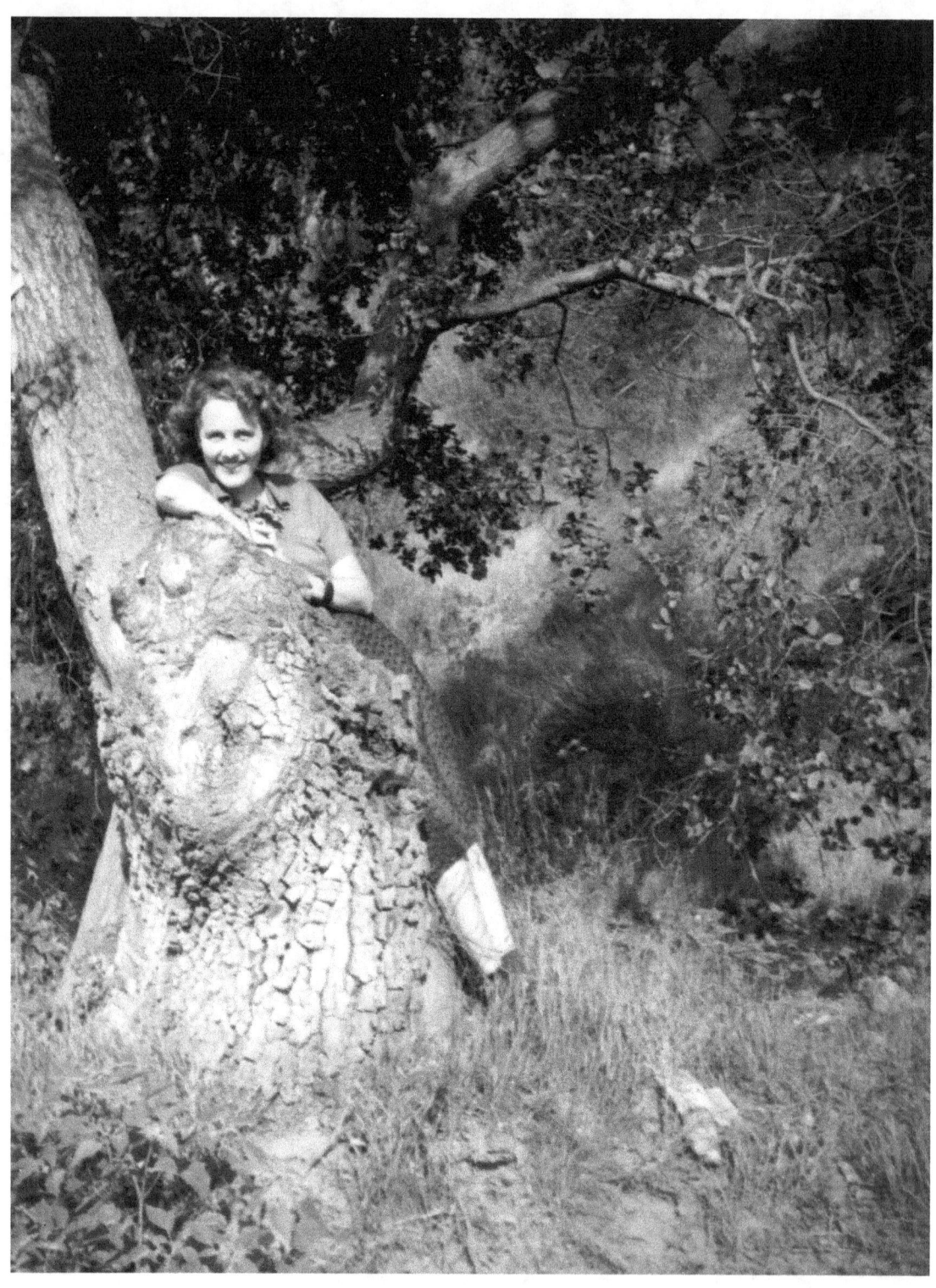

Ethel Schultheis leans against a tree in what appears to be Nibley Park
in the Rossmoyne Historic District of Glendale, ca. 1938. (Order #00082289)

New York in his mid-twenties, was kind of a Renaissance man. Besides the PhD in electrical engineering, he was an accomplished pianist, an amateur archeologist, and an avid photographer who seemed to always carry a camera with him. It was while pursing these latter two interests that he met his untimely demise in the Central American jungles.

Following their marriage, Herman and Ethel left the east coast and headed west, arriving in Los Angeles sometime in 1937. They initially settled into a home in the Hollywood Hills and explored their newly adopted city with a vengeance. With his trusty camera by his side, Schultheis captured a region in the midst of tremendous growth—and one that was also suffering through the Great Depression with the rest of the nation.

Herman Schultheis' Los Angeles isn't always the same one seen in so many picture-perfect postcards of the era with squeaky-clean streets, pristine beaches, movie star homes, and endless fields of orange groves. His Los Angeles tends to be a working class city, beginning to show the signs of urban decay, but forging ahead with progress. A land where beachcombers picnic in the shadows of oil derricks, families work in suburban fields, and minority populations are displaced for the advancement of others.

Schultheis' images also contain the beautiful but bittersweet story of two people, clearly crazy about each other, but whose time together would be cut tragically short. Ethel was often Herman's muse, be it in a field of flowers, at Union Station, the County Fair, or at home. He, in turn, was not afraid to let her turn the camera on him as they discovered their city together.

Following Ethel's death, the Los Angeles Public Library received the extensive collection of Schultheis' photos. Over 5,000 of these images of Southern California have been digitized and are available through the library's website (photos. lapl.org).

Herman J. Schultheis has been gone from almost 60 years but his legacy is now set and will only continue to grow. His photographs serve as a love letter to both his city and his wife, and also provide us with an indelible document of what once was.

Christina Rice
Los Angeles Public Library Photo Collection

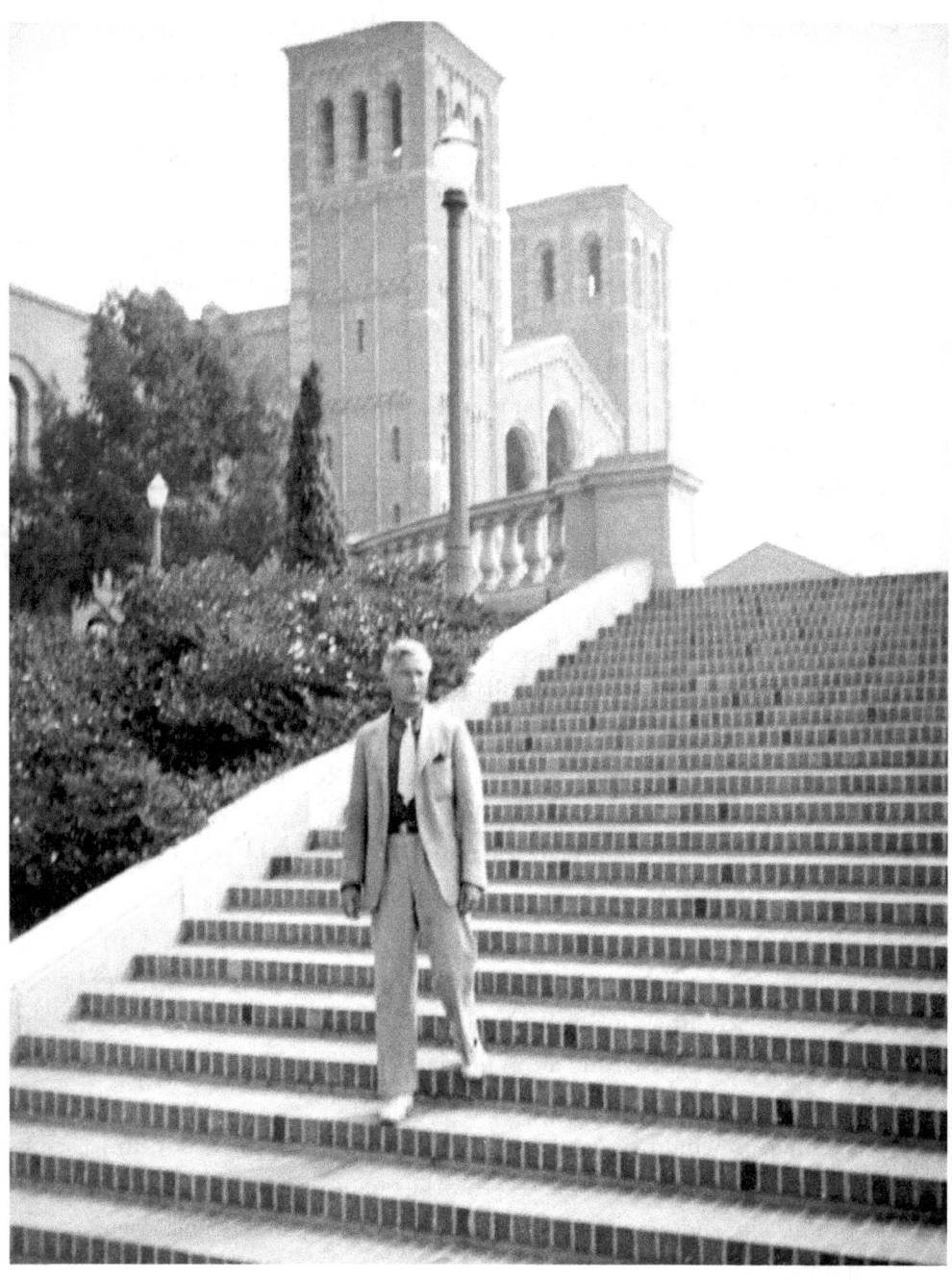

Herman Schultheis stands in front of Royce Hall at the
University of California Los Angeles (U.C.L.A.), ca. 1937. (Order #00096780)

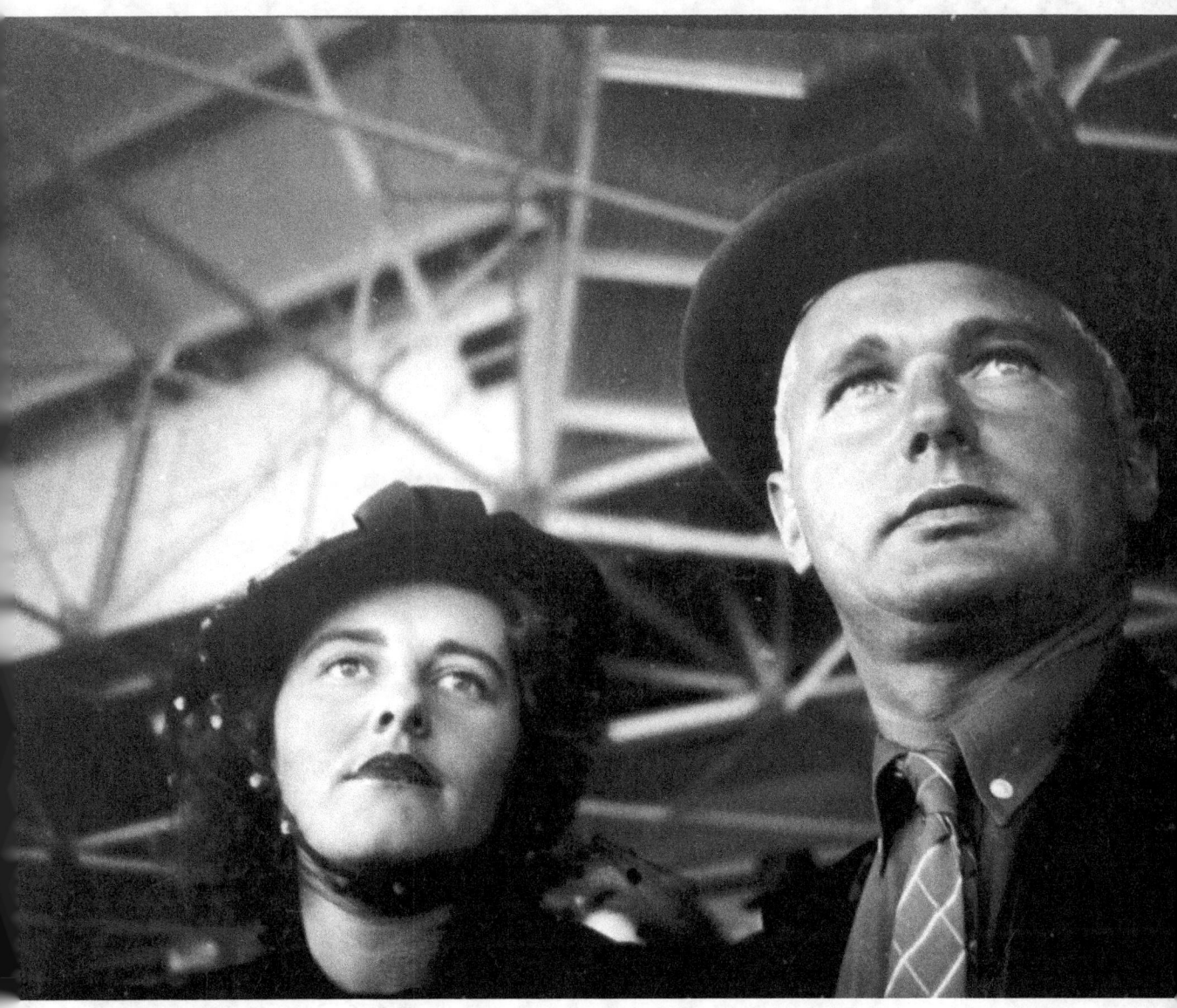

Herman and Ethel Schultheis at the Santa Anita Race Track, ca. 1938.
(Order #00099338)

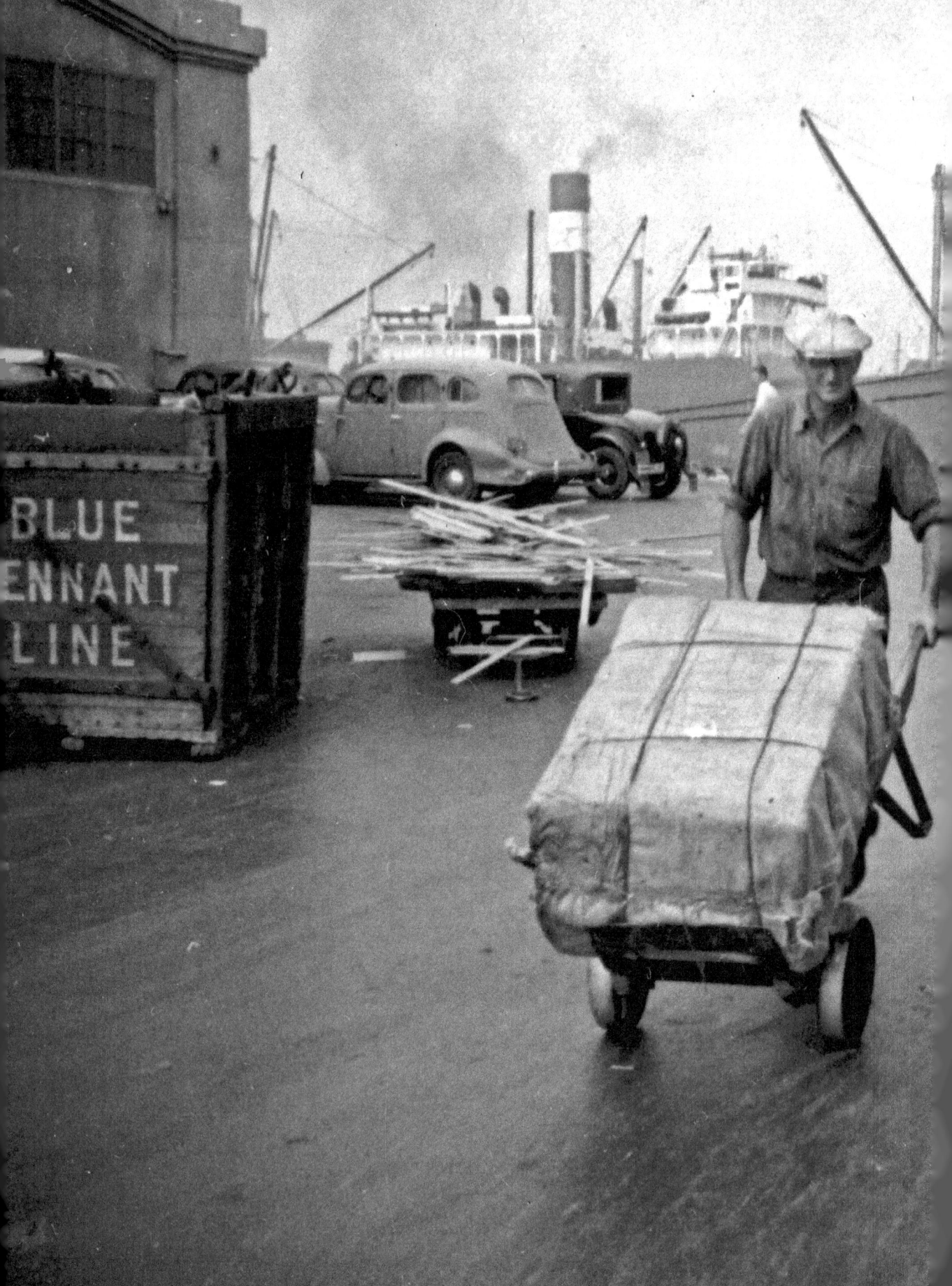

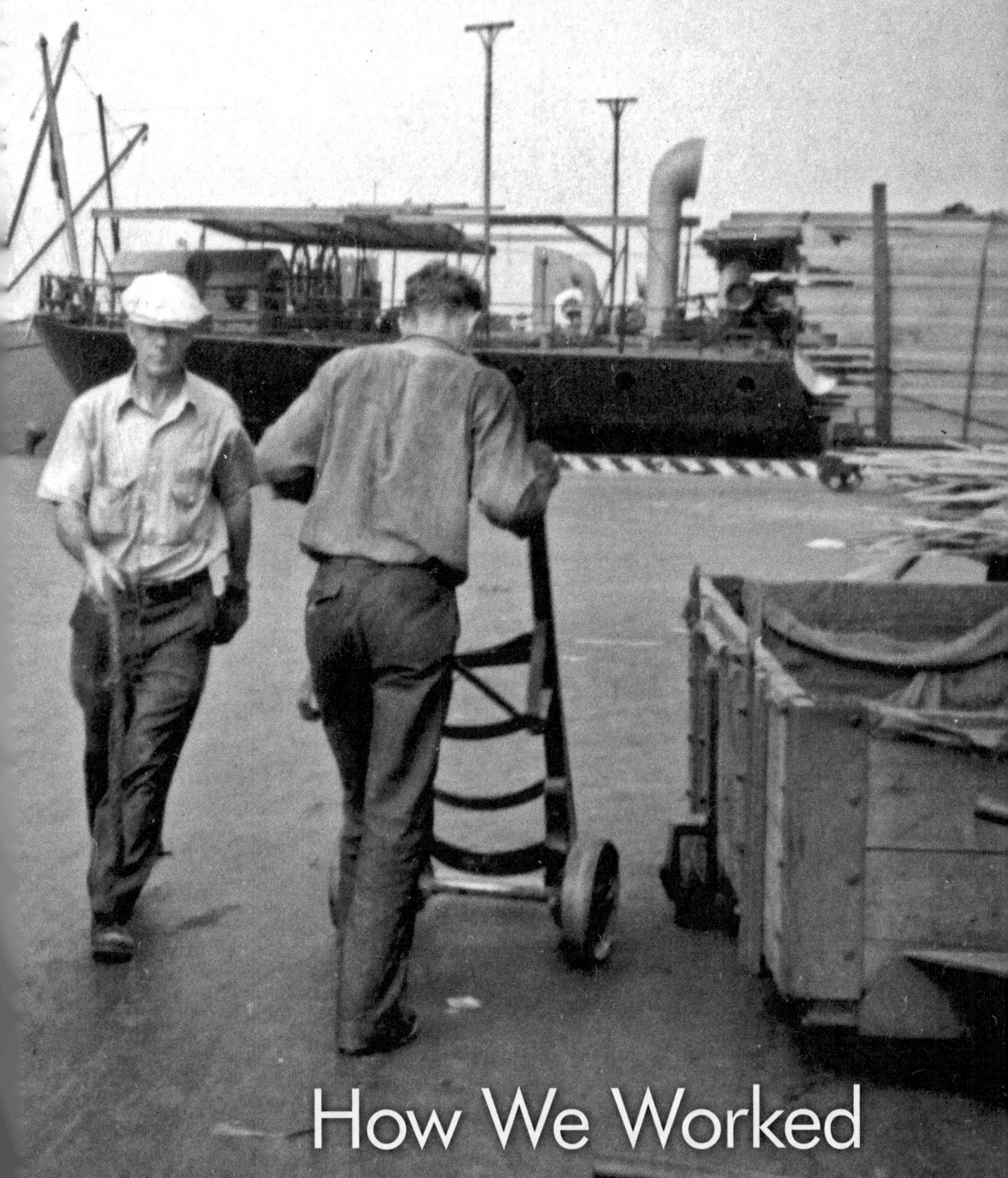

How We Worked

Overleaf:
Workers at the Port of Los Angeles, ca. 1938.
(Order #00100522)

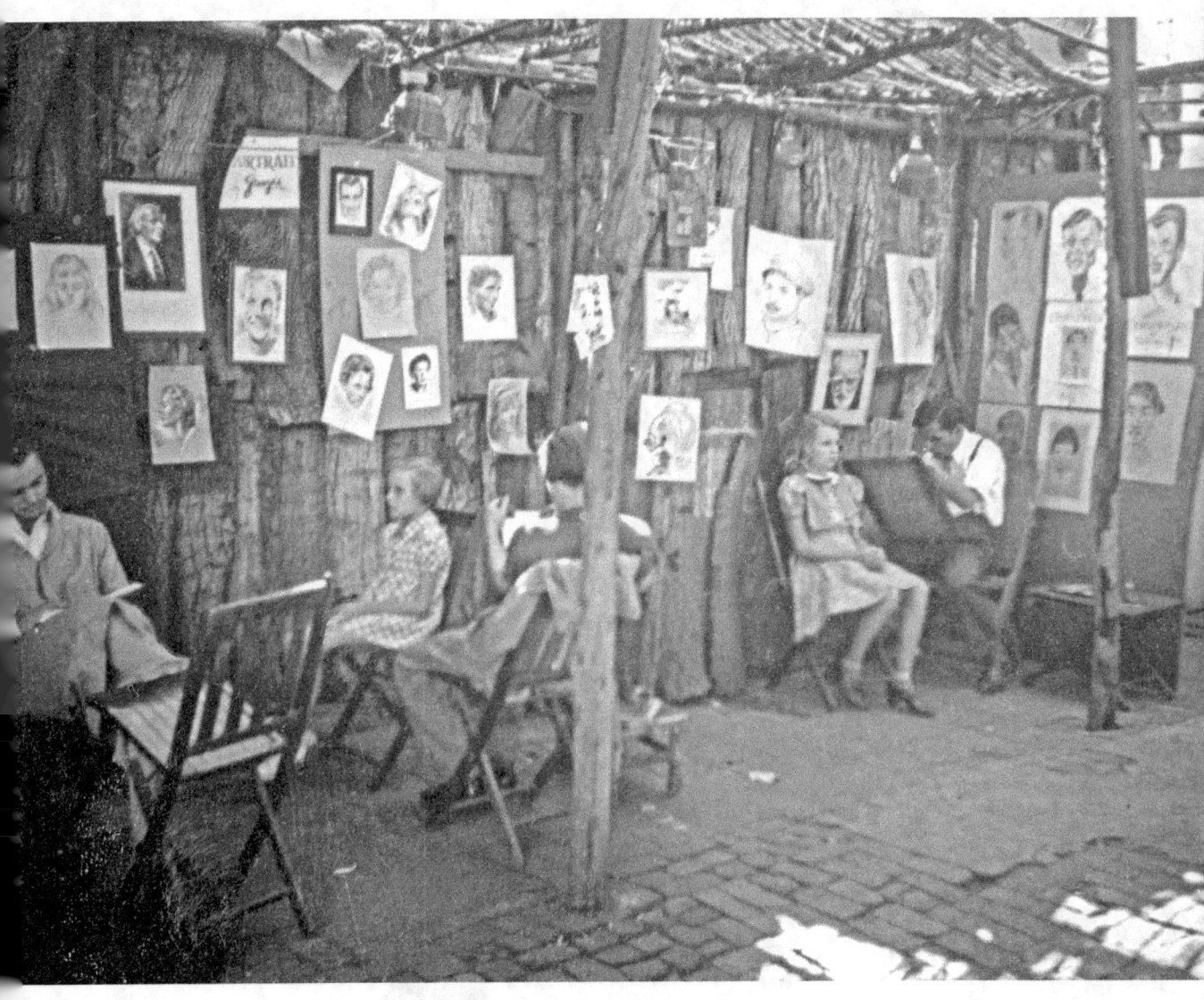

Customers get their portraits drawn at an Olvera Street stand, ca. 1938.
(Order #00008468)

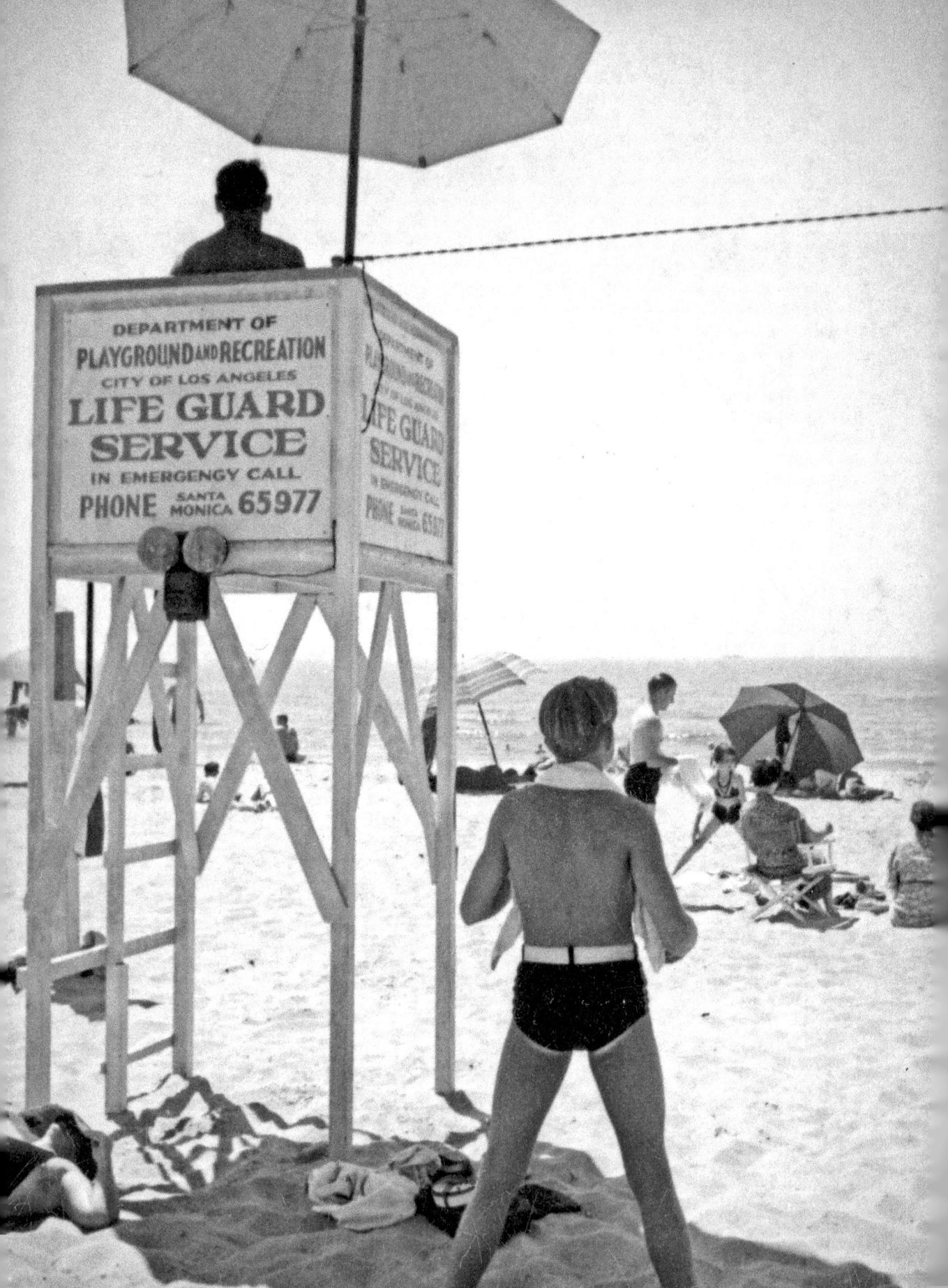

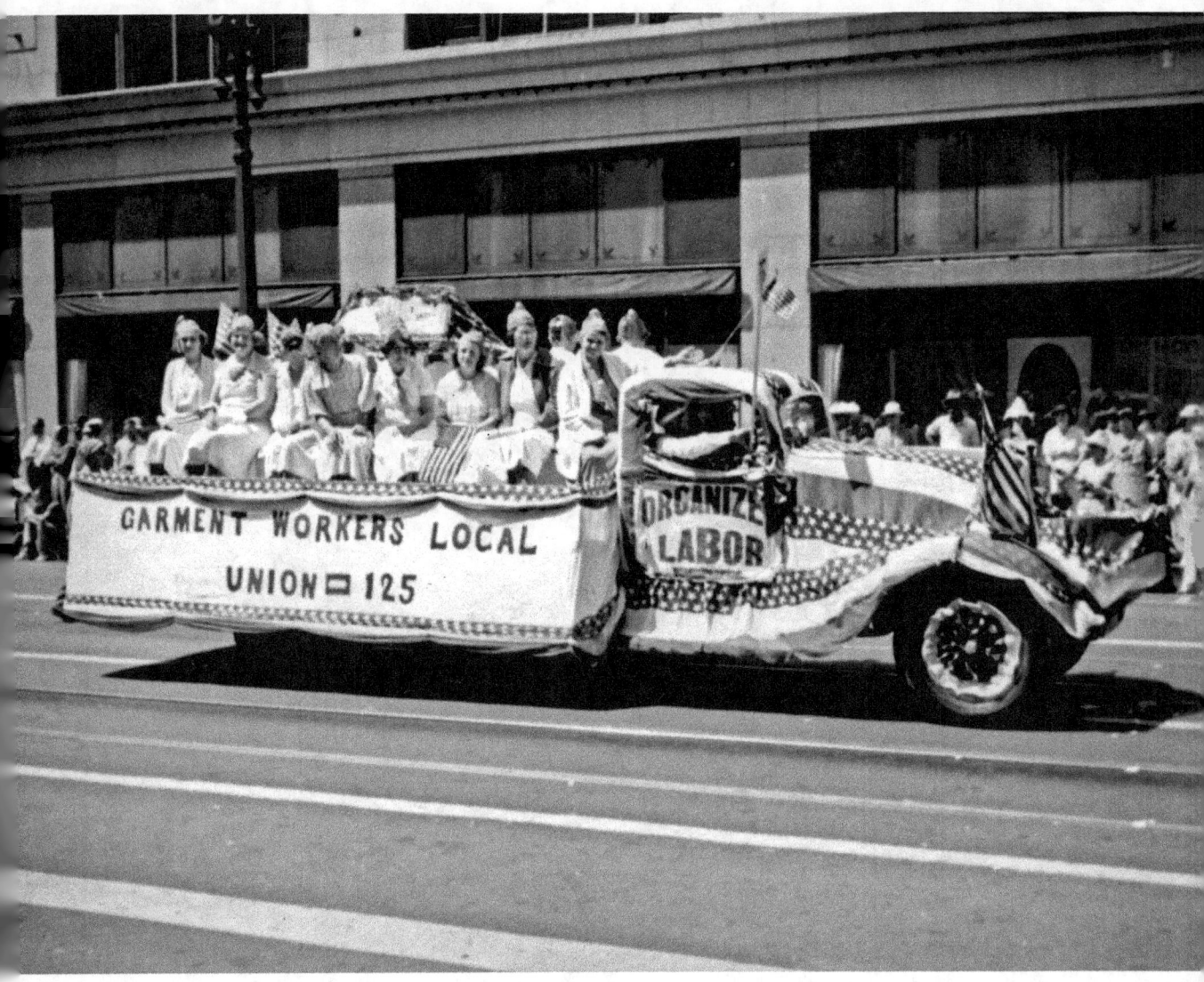

A parade float entered by Garment Workers Local Union 125 rides past the Broadway Department Store at 401 South Broadway, ca. 1937. (Order #00044174)

Opposite: A Santa Monica lifeguard on duty, ca. 1937.
(Order #00028372)

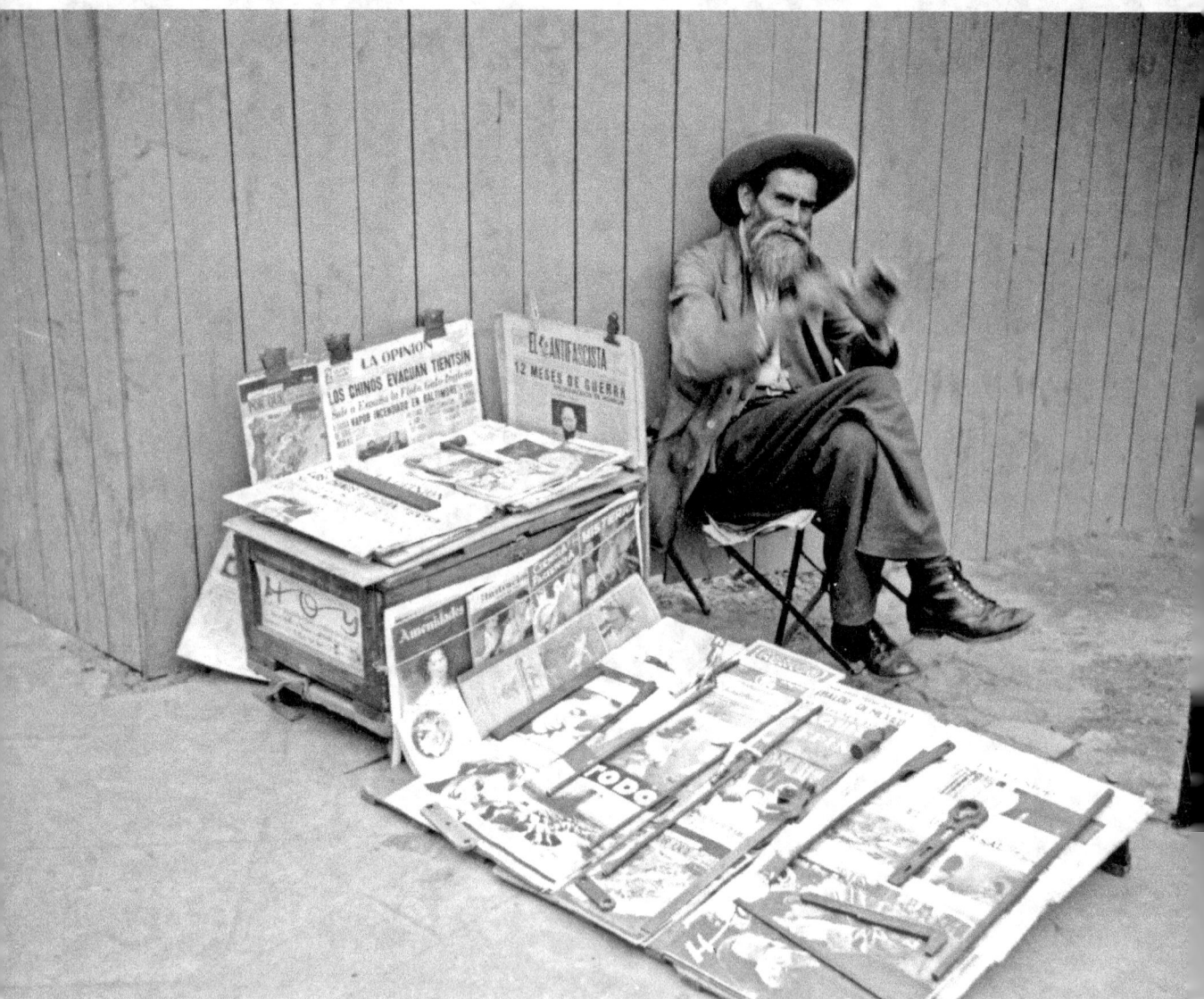

A sidewalk vendor near Olvera Street sells Spanish-language newspapers and magazines, ca. 1937. (Order #00064397)

Opposite: A man stocks an ice vending machine in Hollywood, ca. 1937. (Order #00072357)

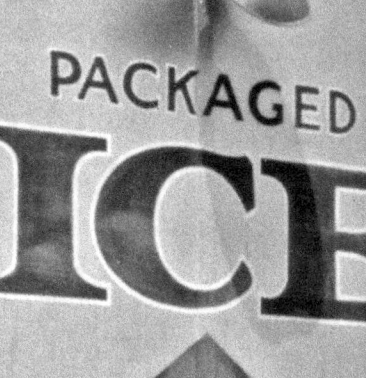

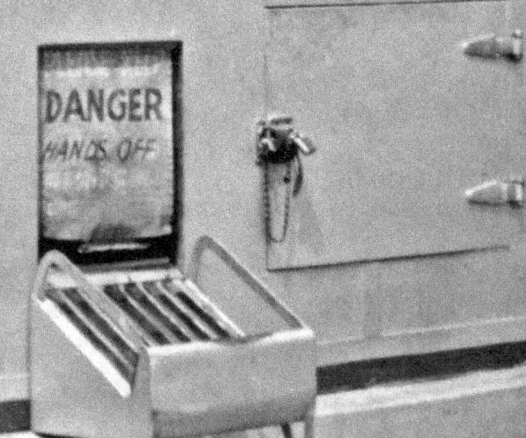

PACKAGED

ICE

DANGER

HANDS OFF

37

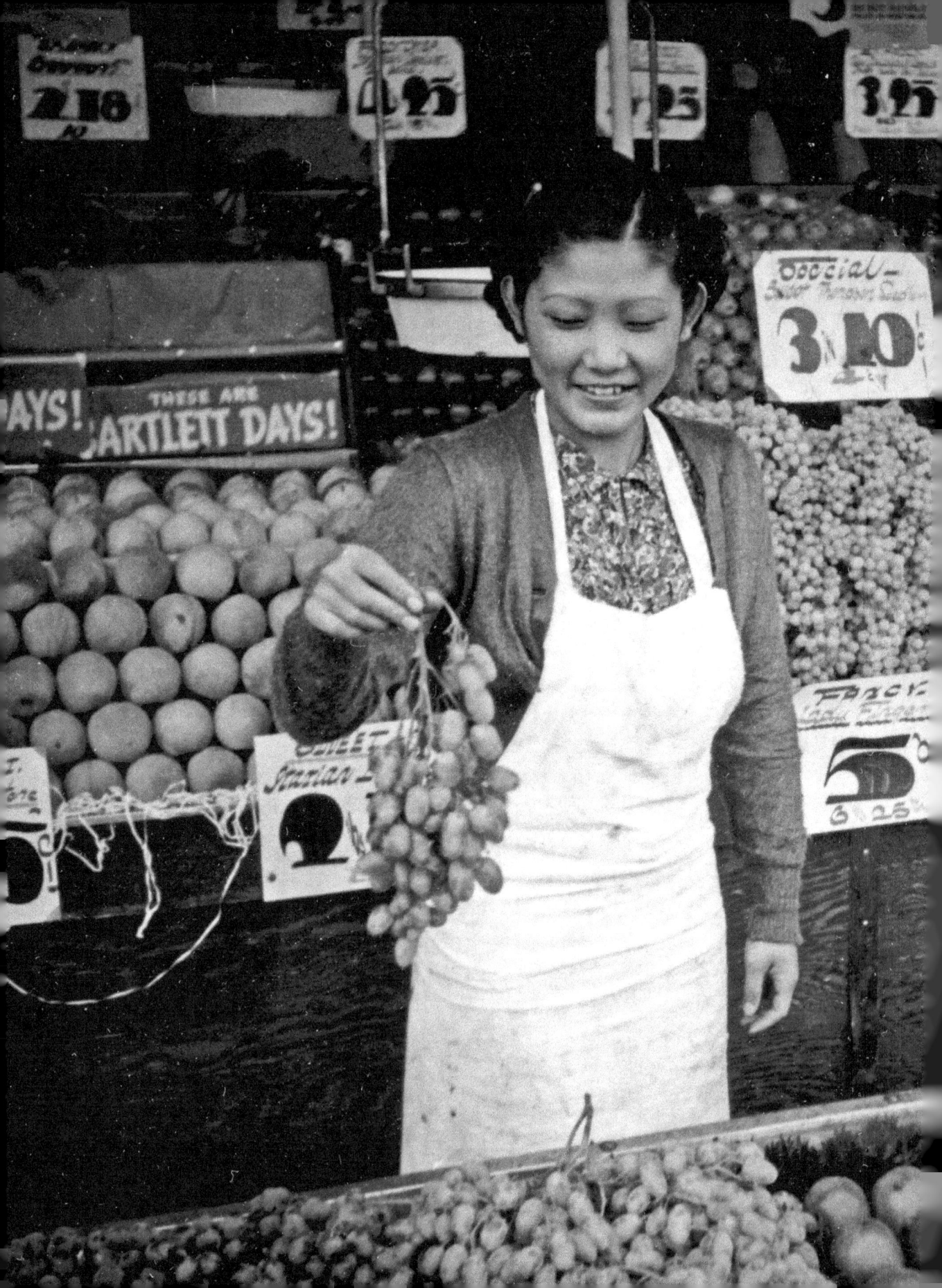

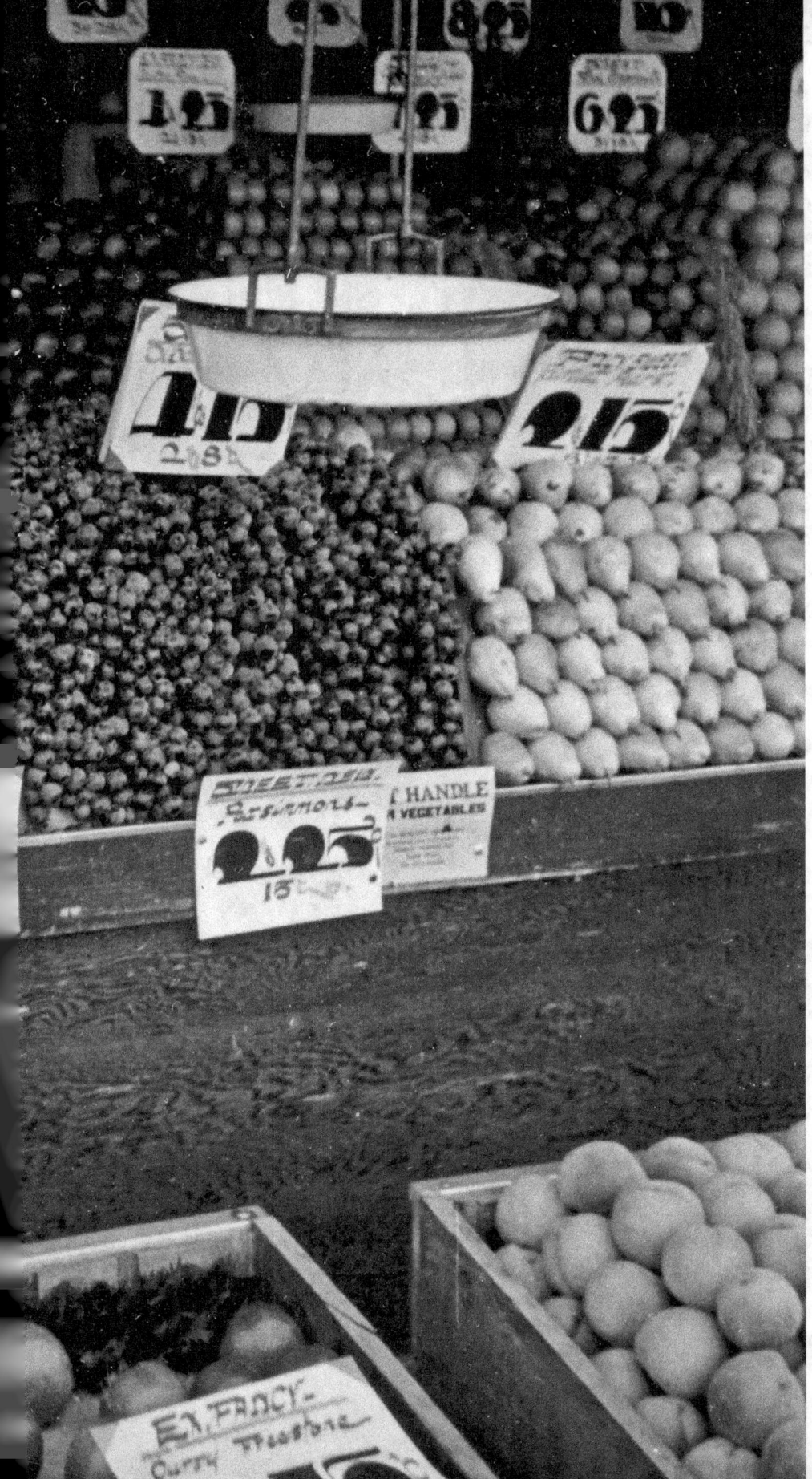

An employee of the Hollywood Market at 6565 Hollywood Boulevard inspects some grapes, ca. 1937. (Order #00071516)

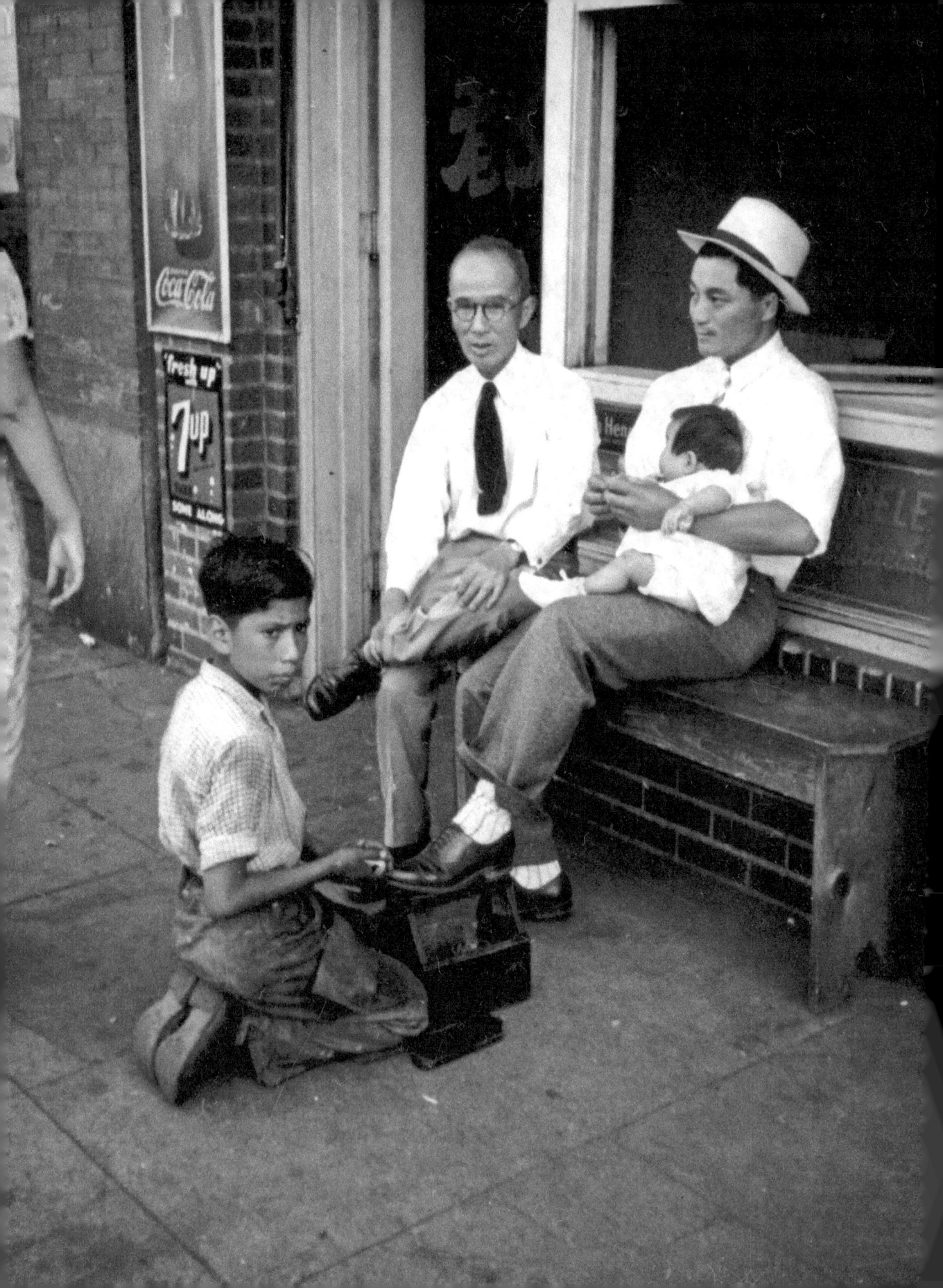

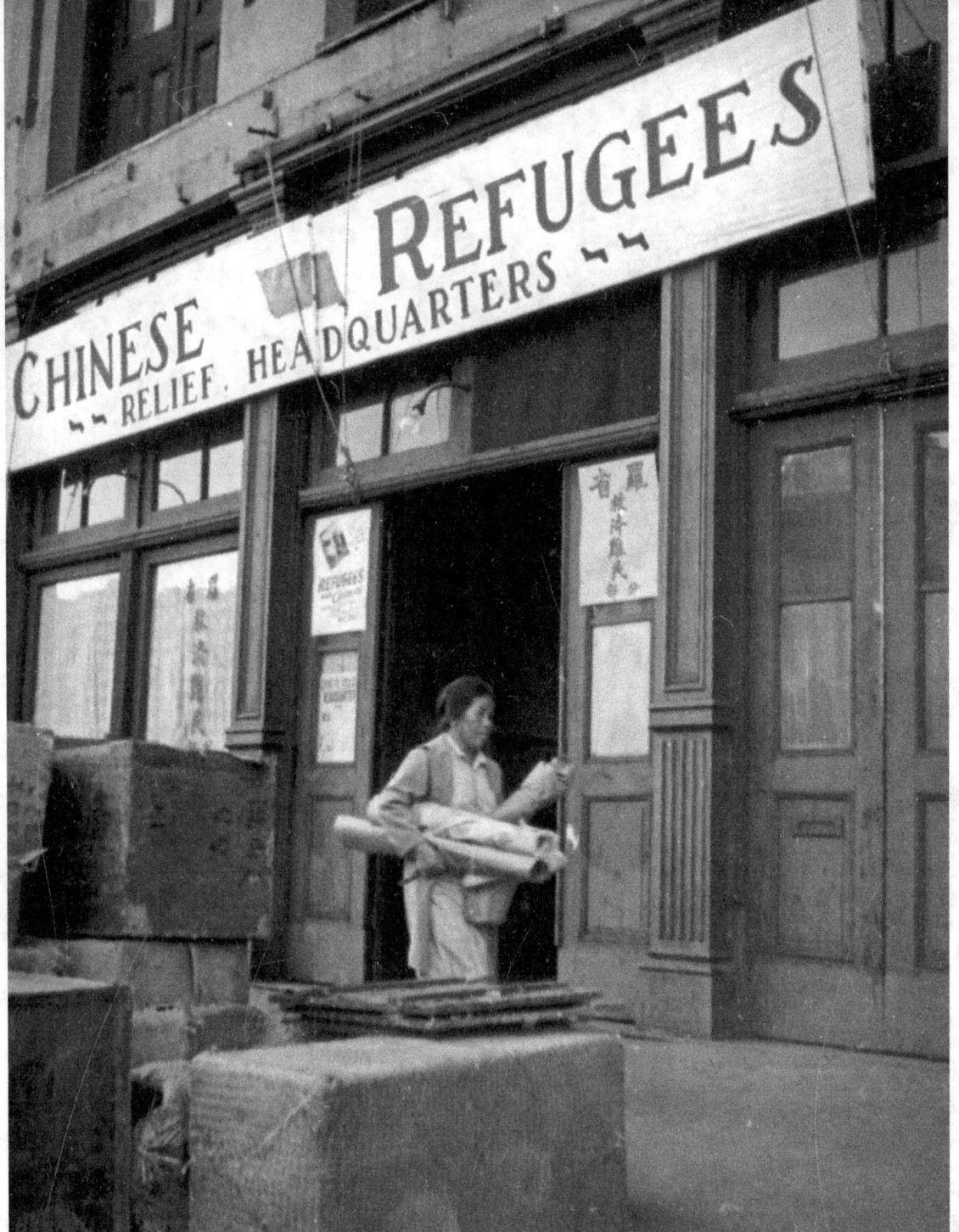

A woman walks past packages and crates of donations ready for shipping from the Chinese Refugees Relief Headquarters at 225 North Los Angeles Street, ca. 1937. (Order #00097184)

Opposite: Two men and a baby (and a shoe shiner) in Little Tokyo, ca. 1937.
(Order #00096733)

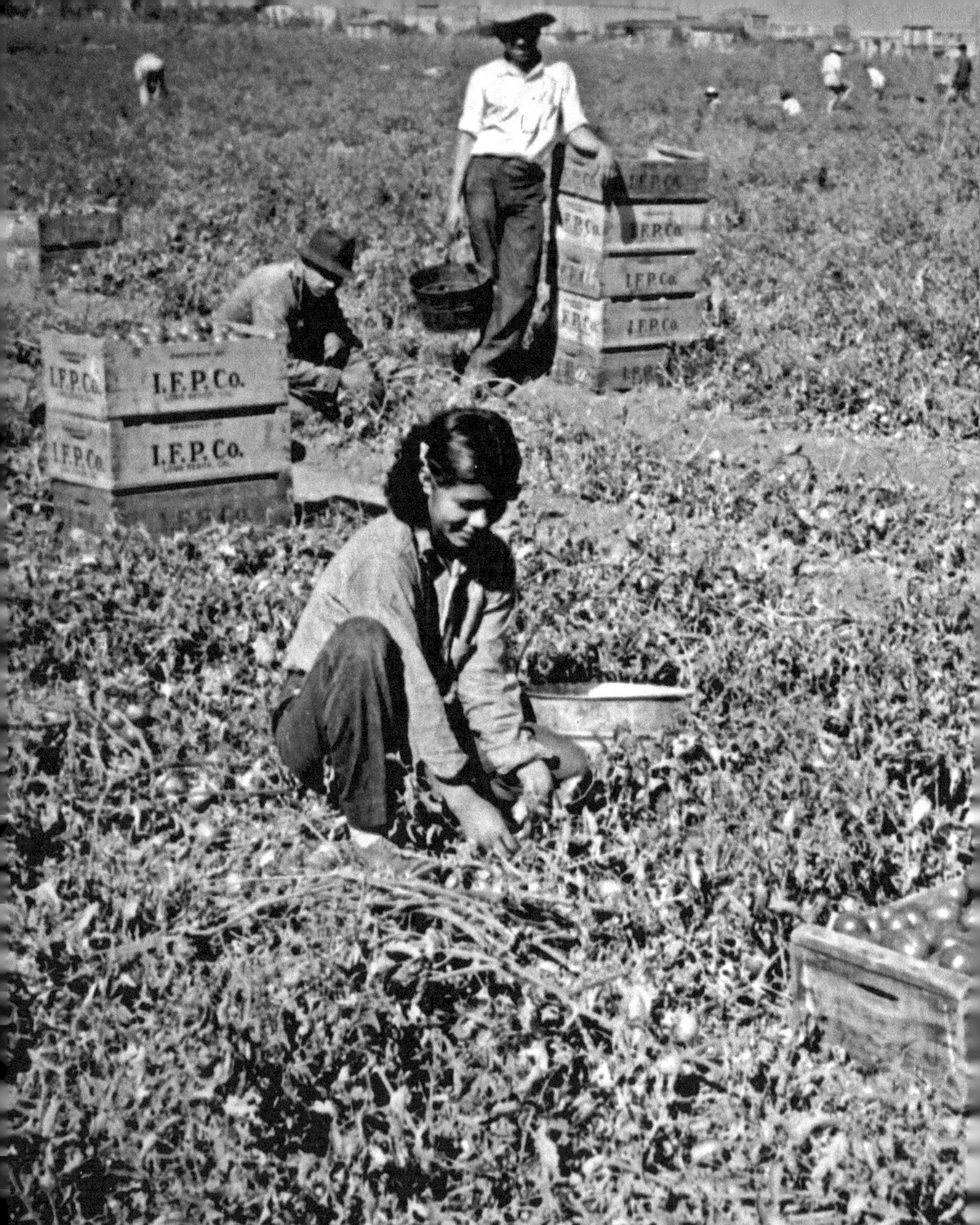

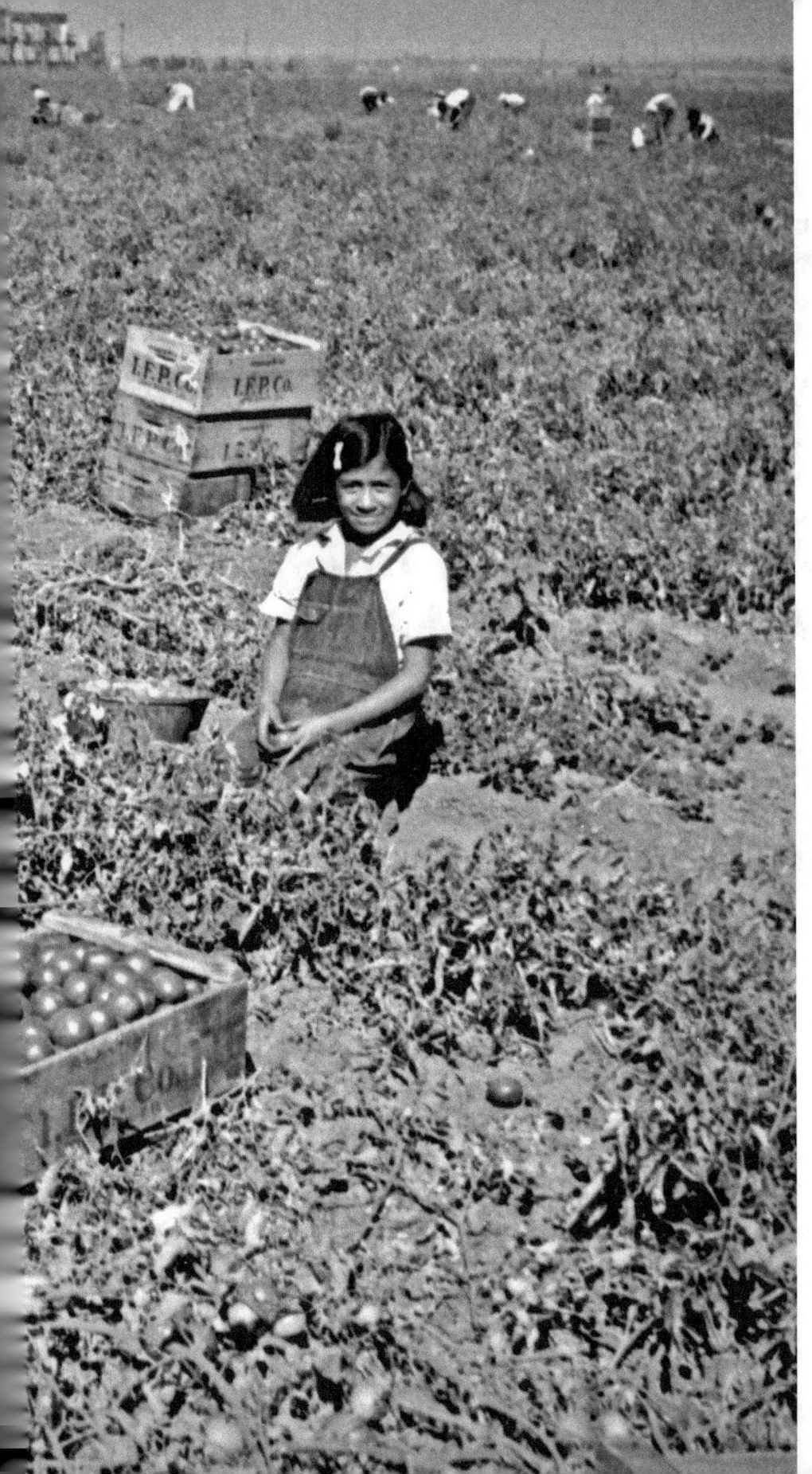

A family picks
tomatoes in the
fields of the San
Fernando Valley,
ca. 1937. (Order
#00097082)

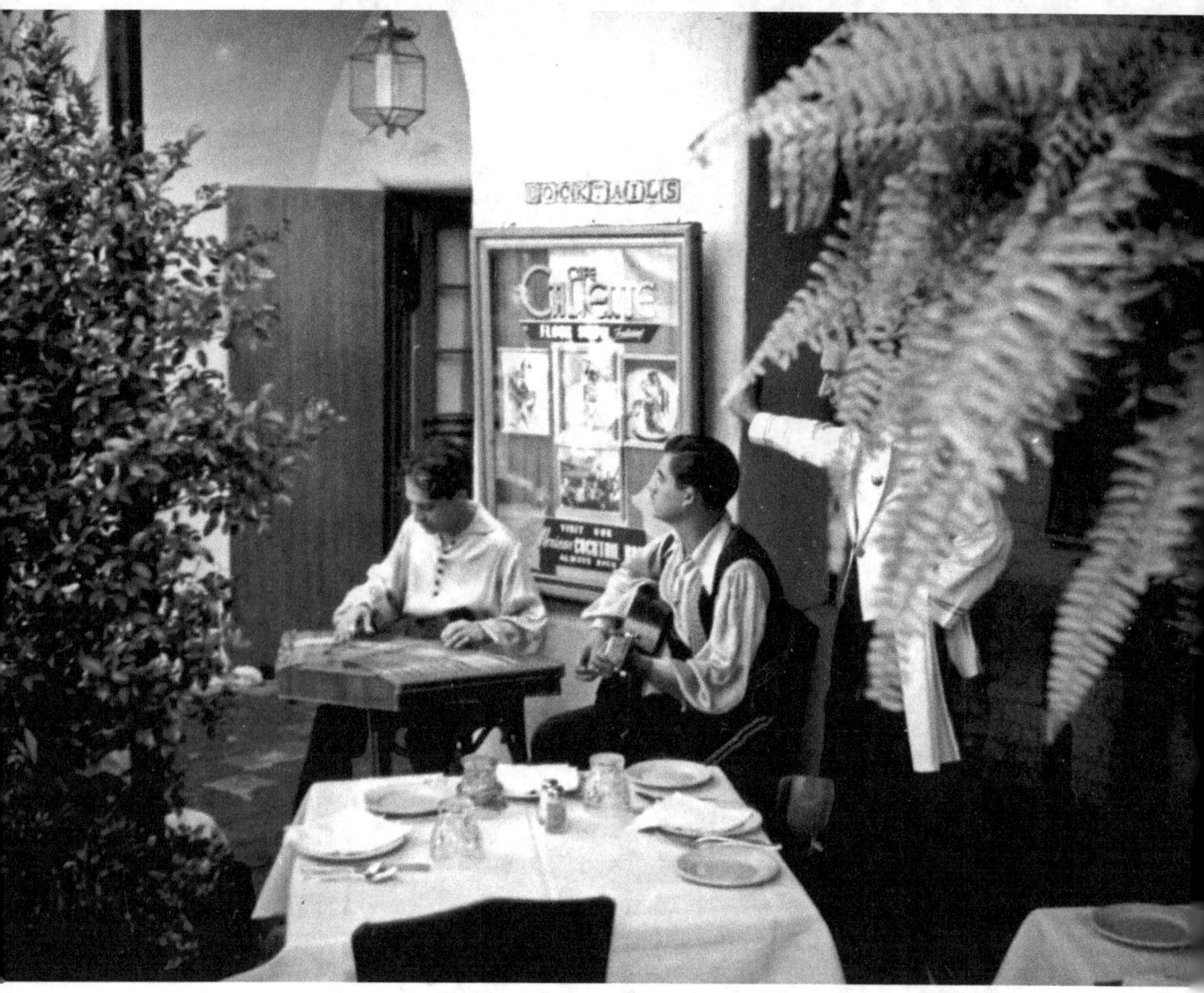

Musicians practice at the Cafe Caliente on Olvera Street, ca. 1937.
(Order #00097189)

Opposite: A worker builds fruit crates in the Del Monte packing house,
which was located just southwest of the Santa Ana train station on
First Street in Santa Ana, ca. 1937. (Order #00097217)

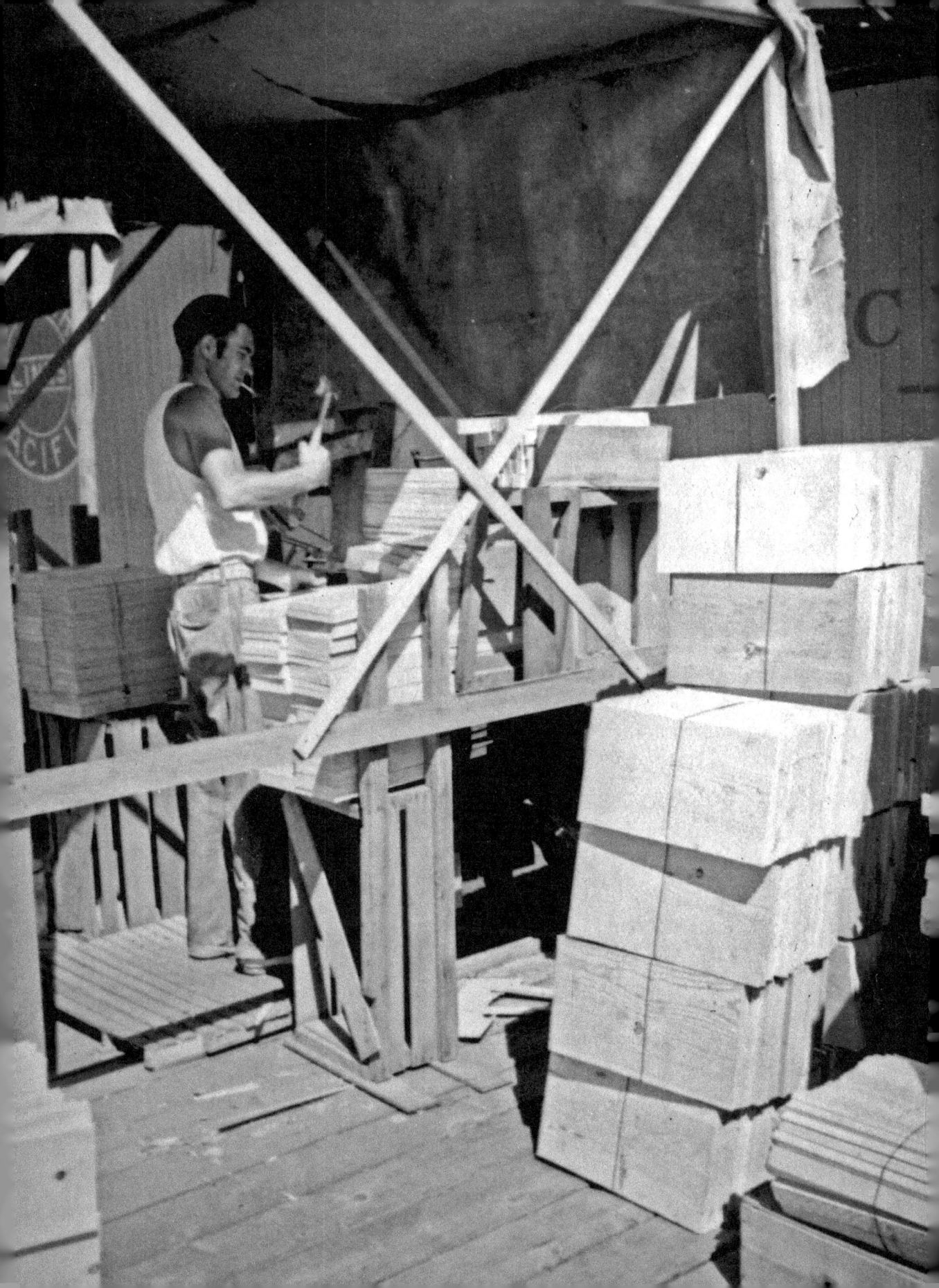

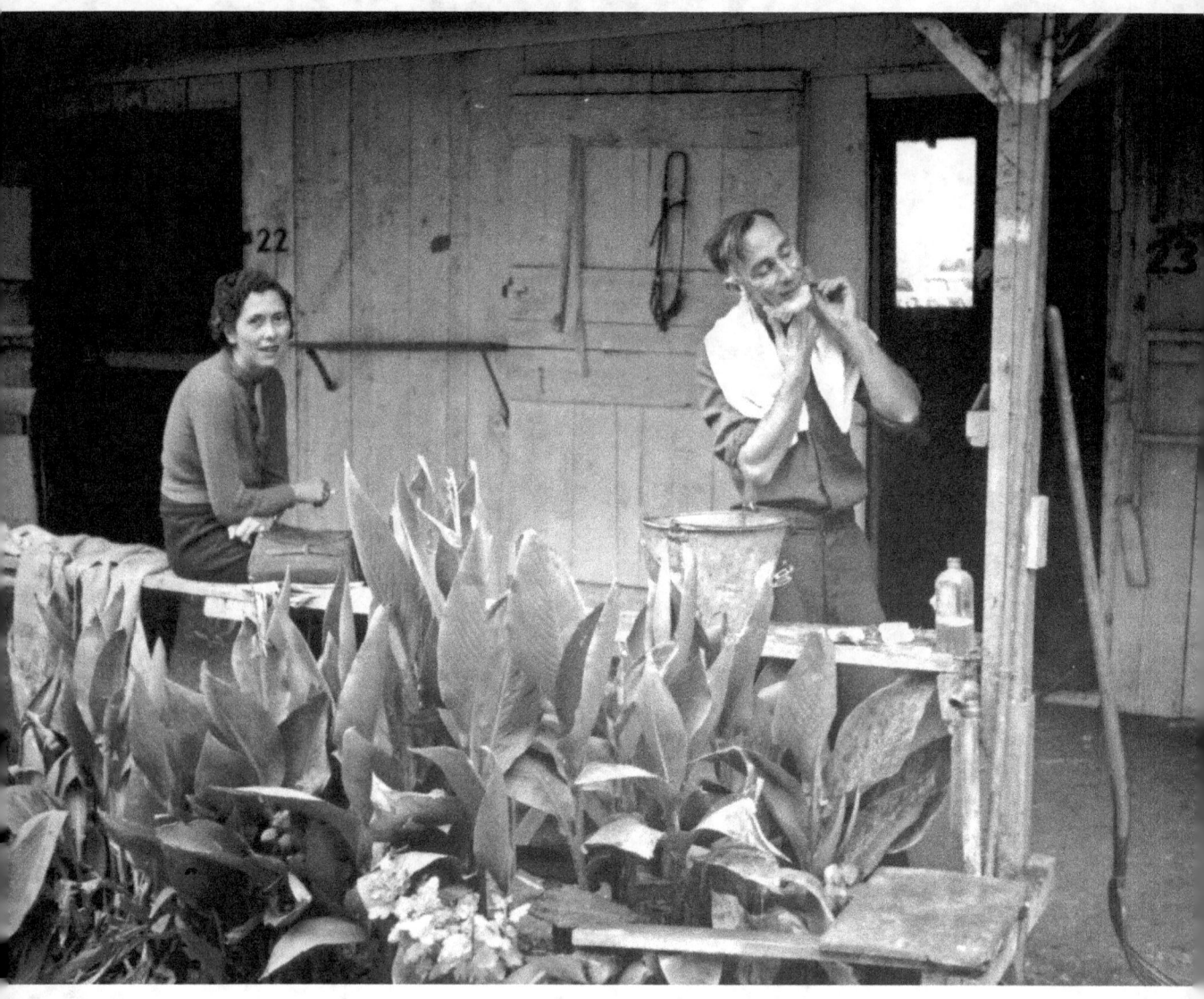

A man shaves at the Los Angeles County Fair, held in Pomona.
In 1937, the fair ran from September 17–October 3. (Order #00097277)

Opposite: An extremely bored employee stands in the entryway of the
New York Millinery at 551½ South Broadway, ca. 1937. (Order #00097555)

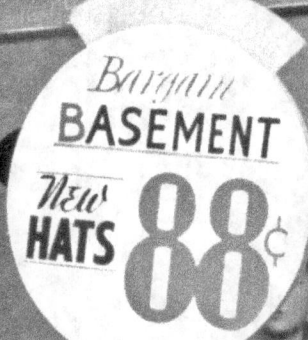

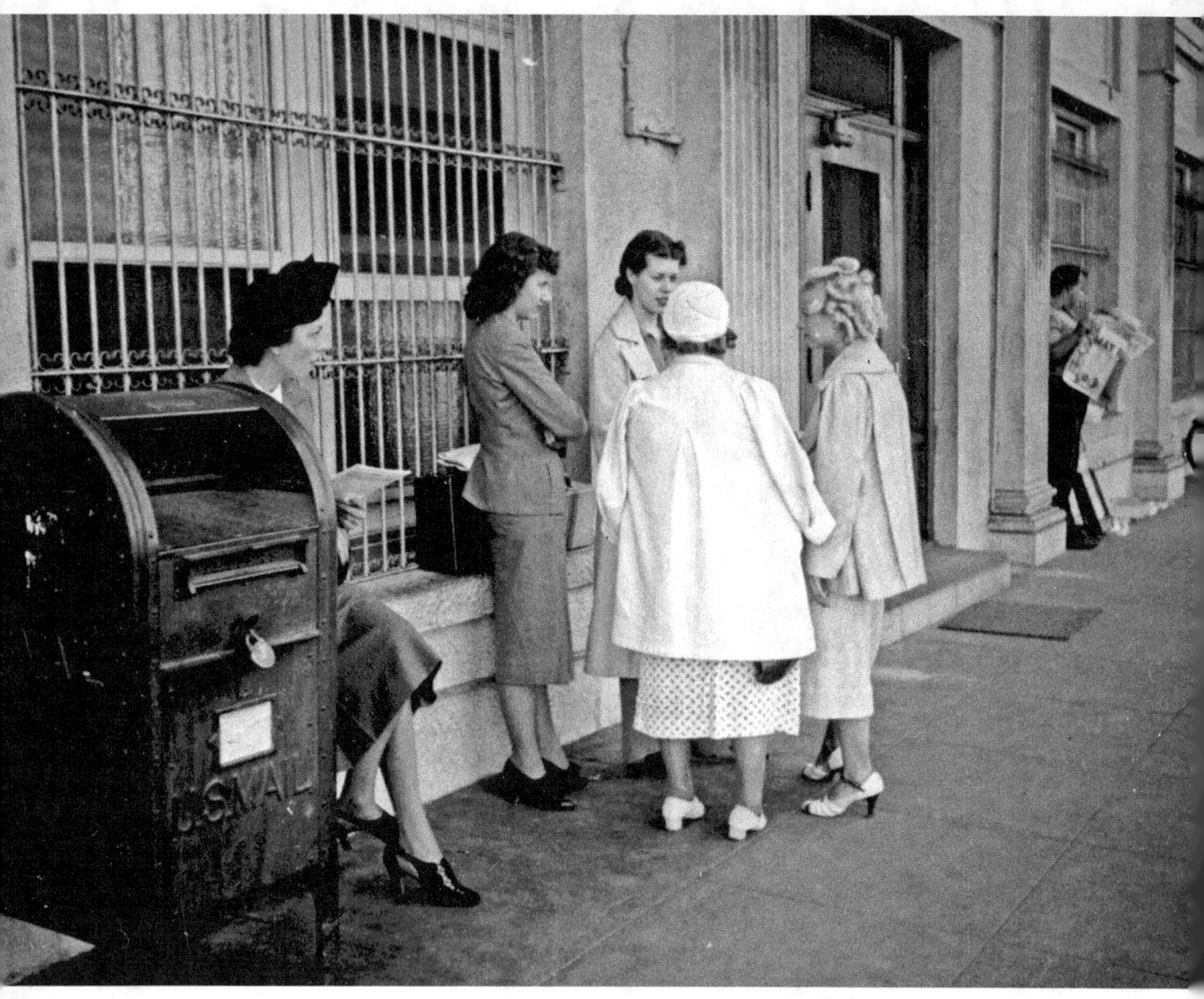

Hollywood hopefuls congregate outside the barred windows of
Metro-Goldwyn-Mayer Studios in Culver City, ca. 1937. (Order #00097563)

Opposite: Streetcar traffic is navigated from an elevated kiosk at the
busy corner of 9th and Main Streets, ca. 1937. (Order #00097709)

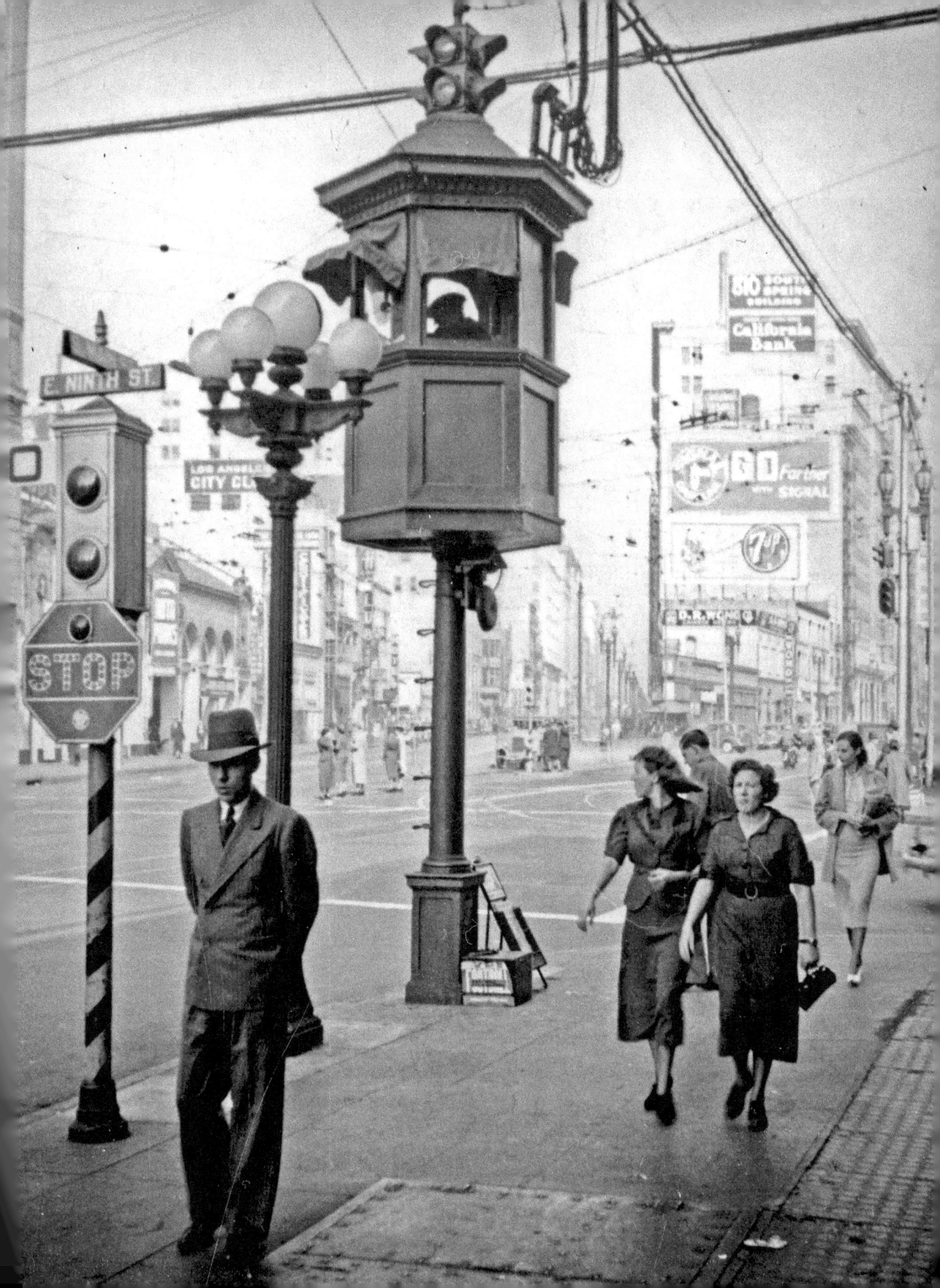

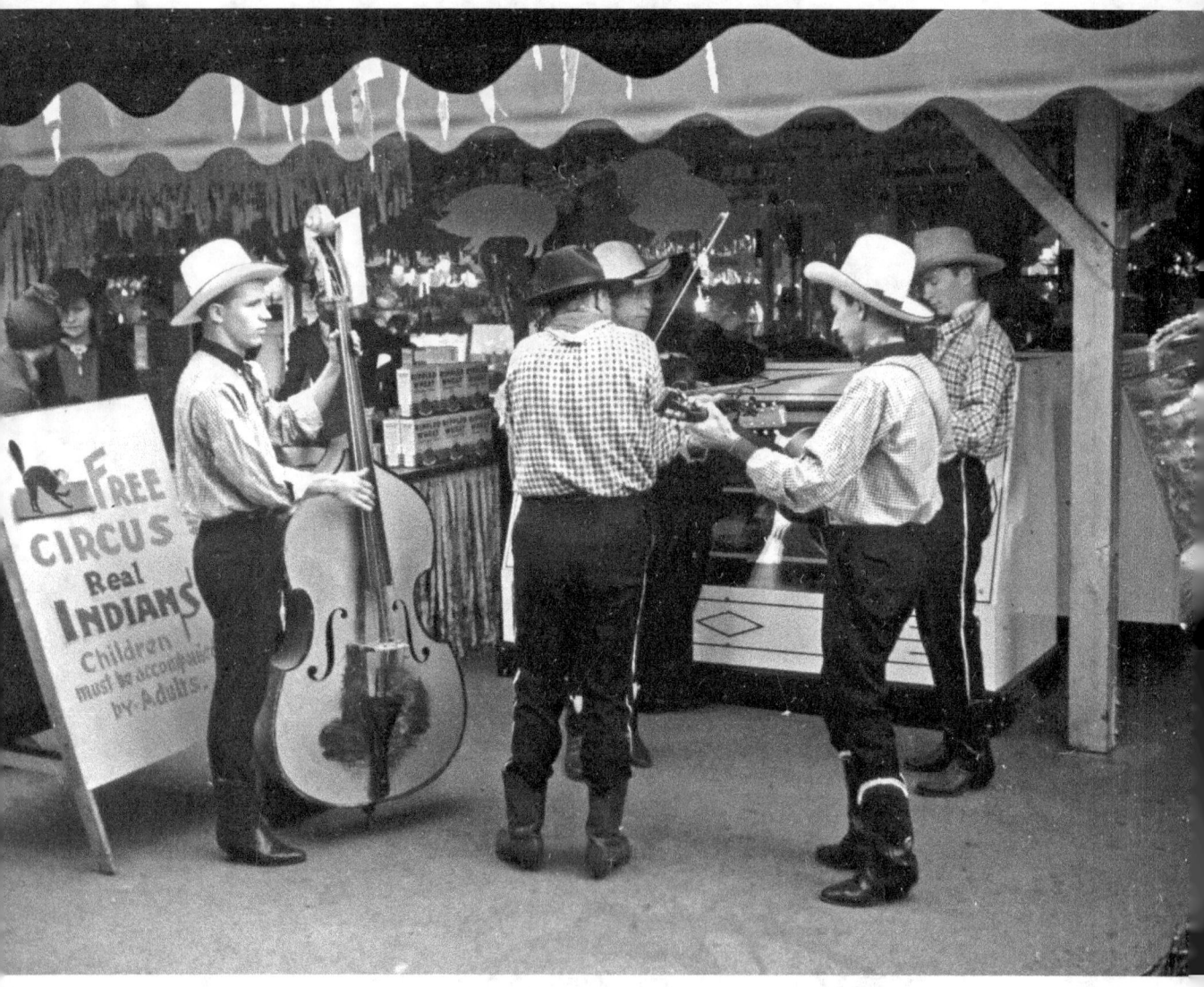

A country and western band performs at the Farmers Market Fall Festival,
which ran October 27–30, 1937. (Order #00097735)

Opposite: A "newsie" for the *Los Angeles Evening Herald & Express* stands in front
of the Thriftimart, located at 9690 Santa Monica Boulevard in Beverly Hills,
ca. 1937. (Order #00097814)

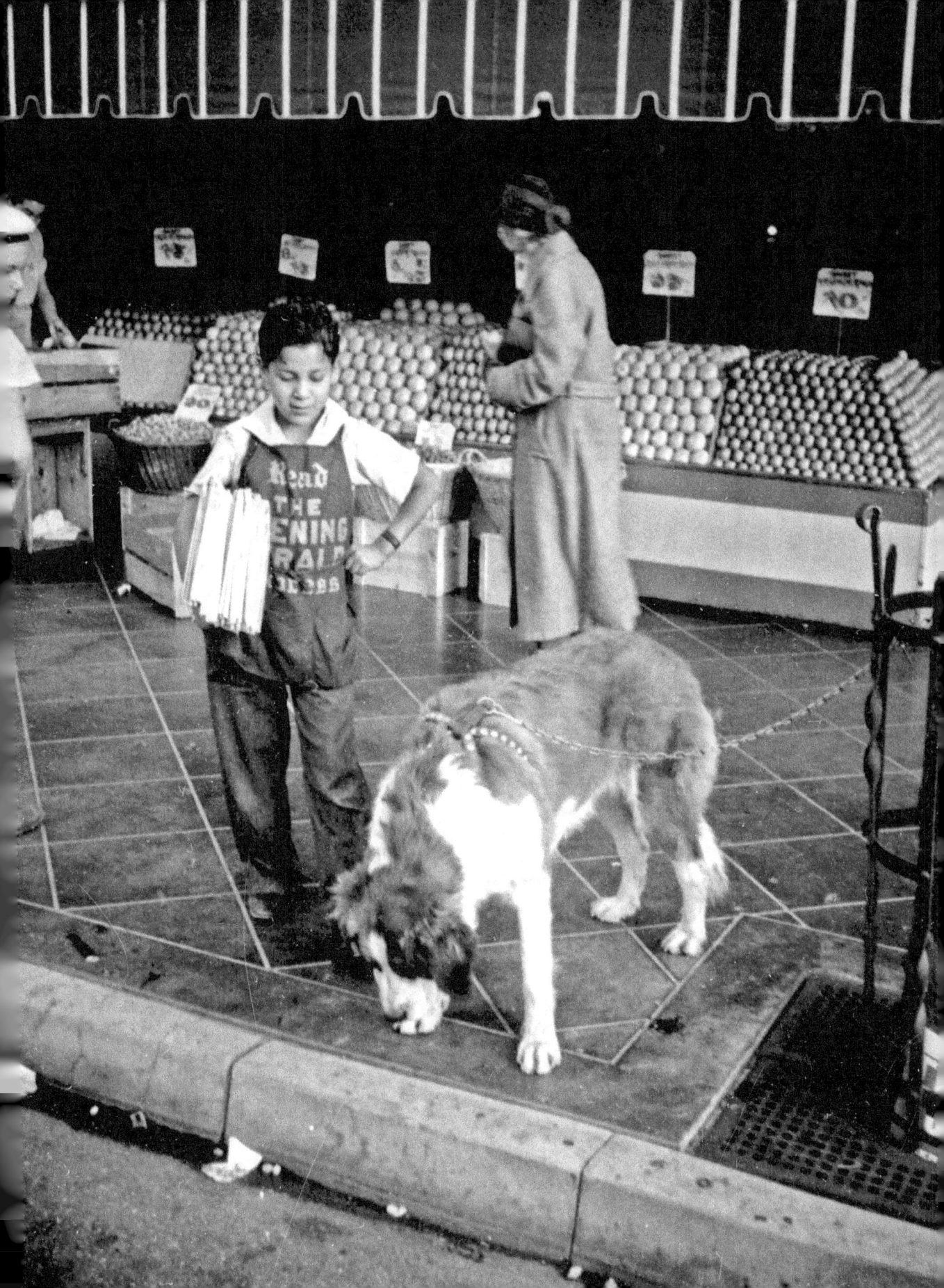

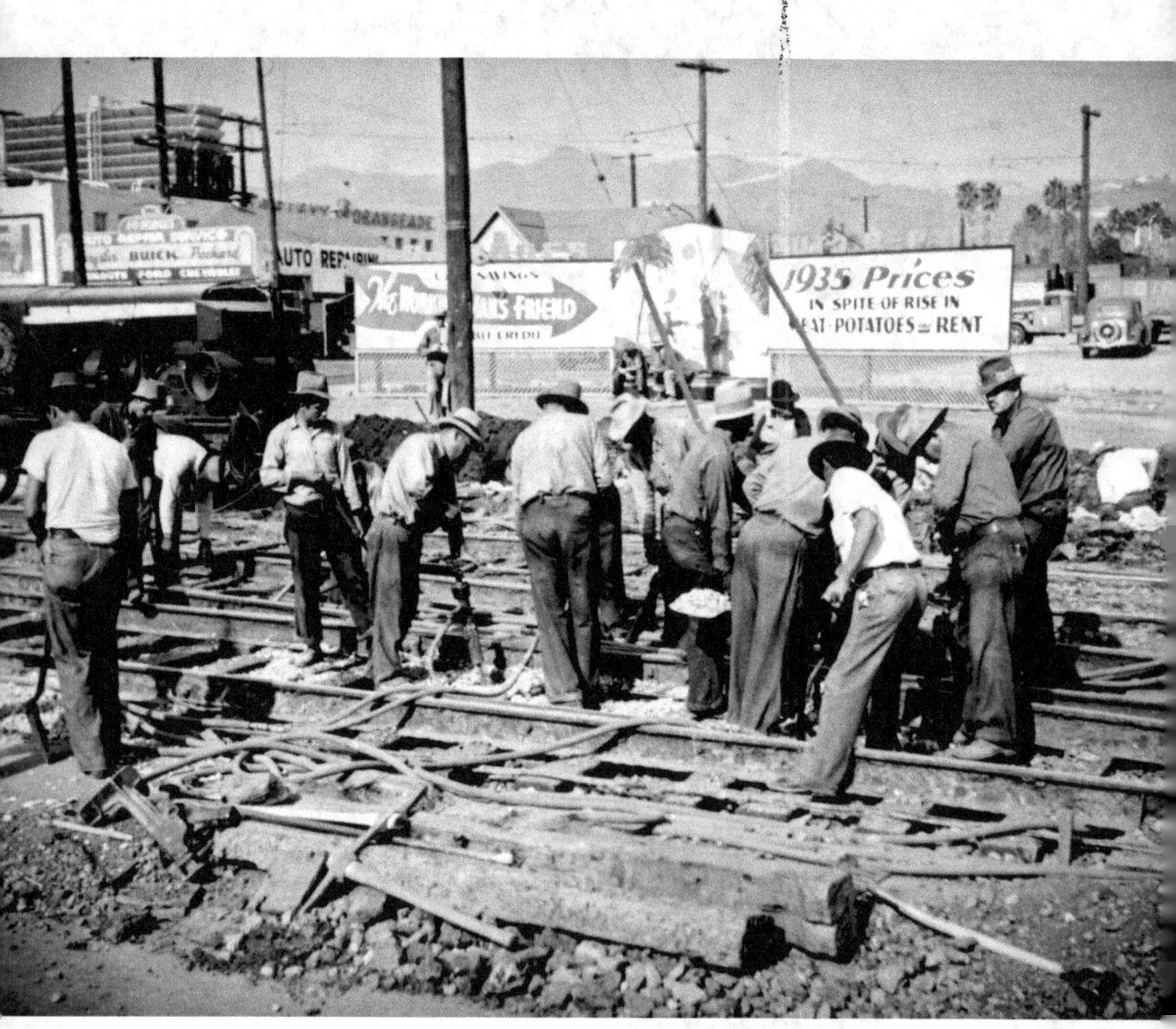

Pacific Electric construction workers on Santa Monica Boulevard
near Highland Avenue, ca. 1937. (Order #00097997)

Opposite: A surveyor works near the intersection of Santa Monica Boulevard
and Highland Avenue, where some Pacific Electric construction
is taking place, ca. 1937. (Order #00098001)

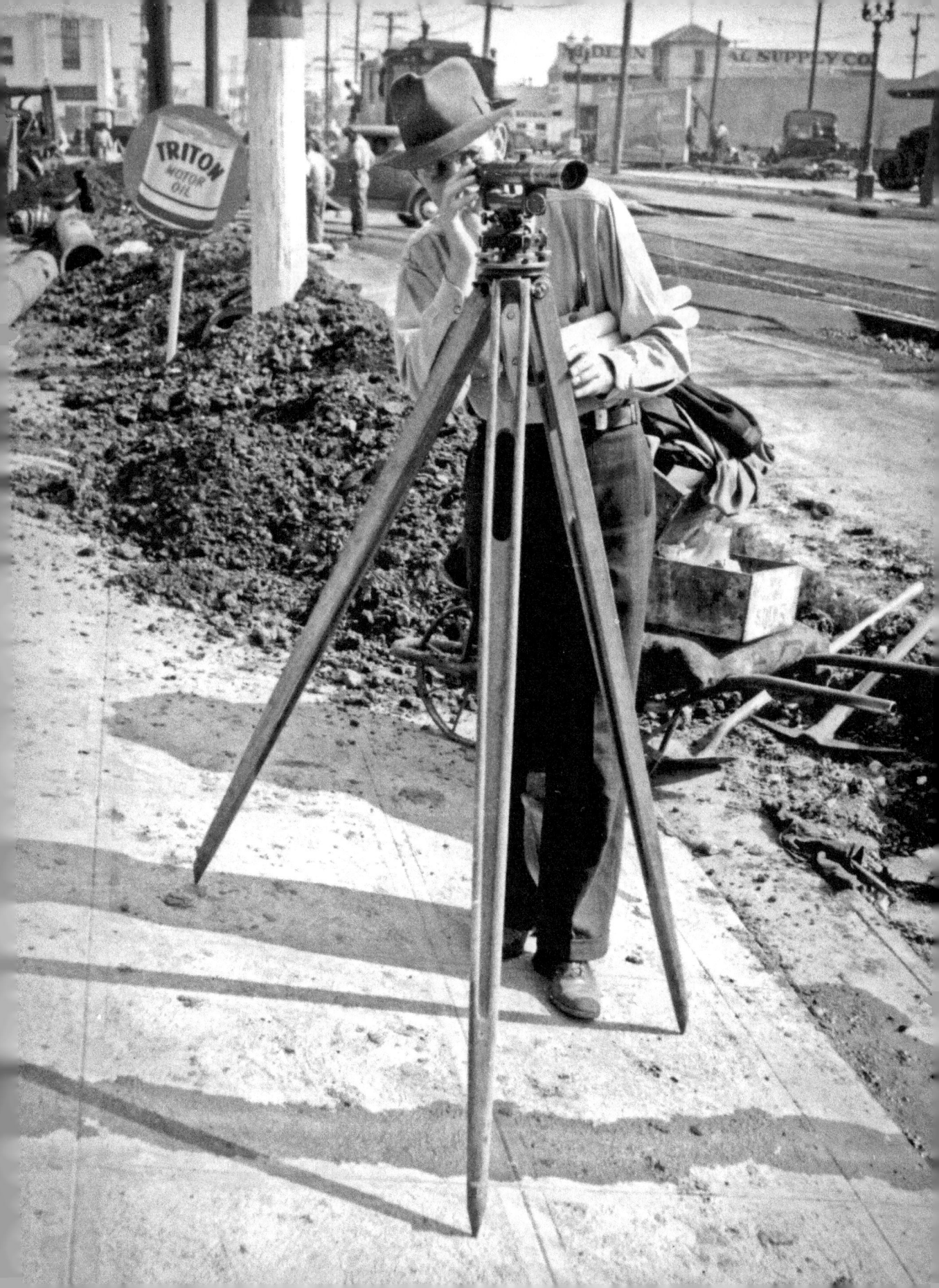

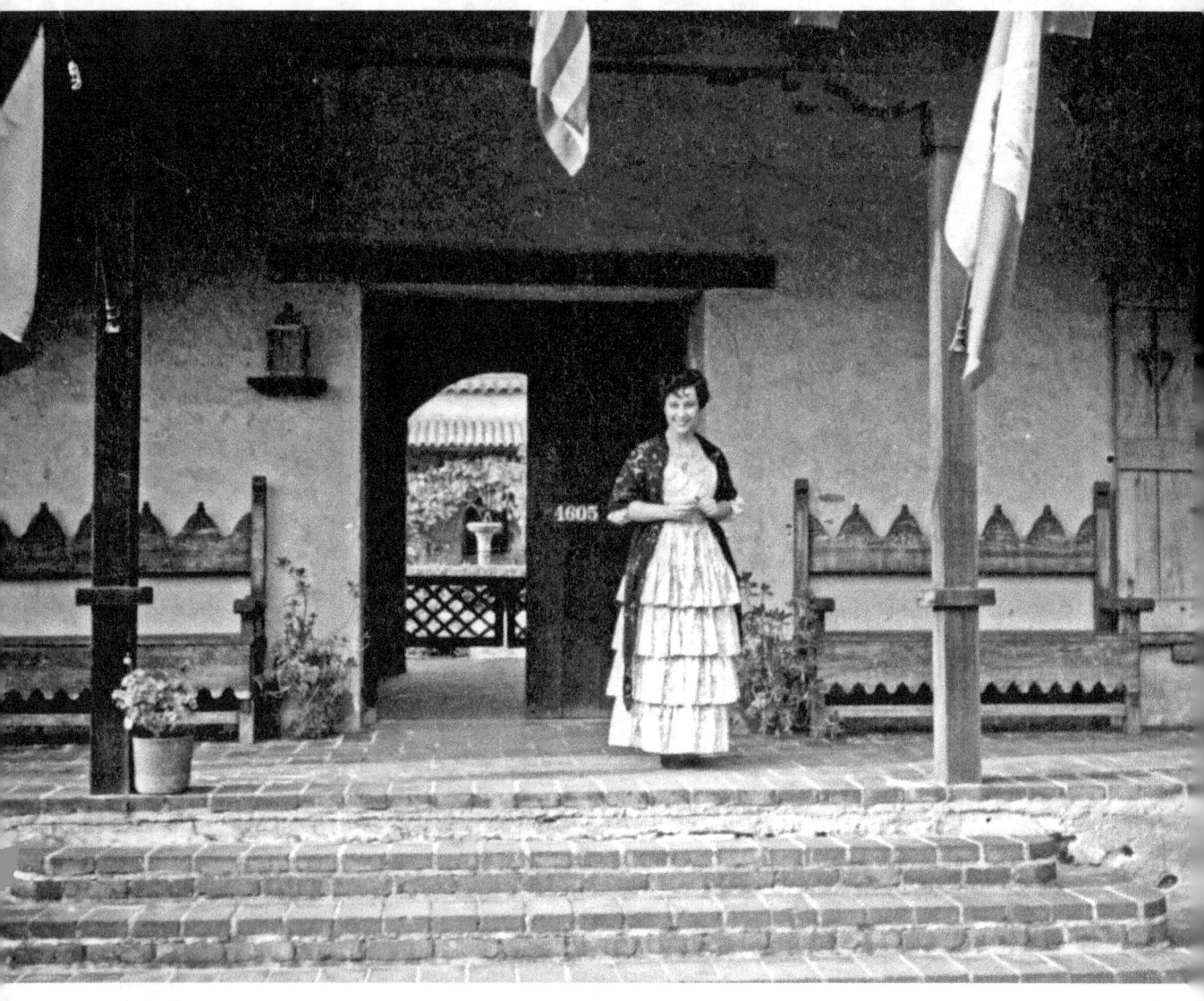

An employee of Casa De Adobe poses at the entrance of the structure located at 4605 North Figueroa Street in Highland Park, ca. 1937. (Order #00098262)

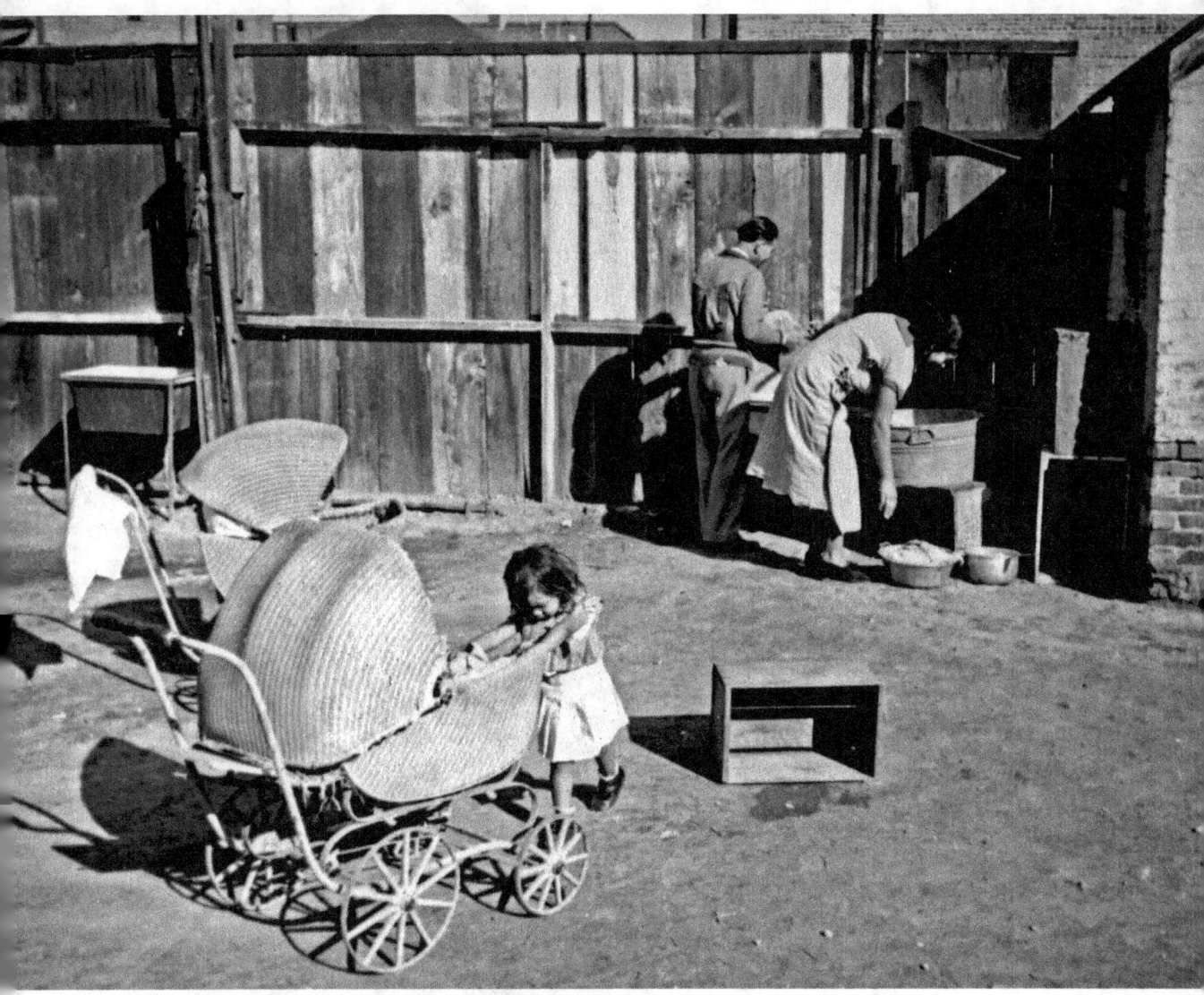

Laundry day for a family at the Santa Cruz Adobe, located at
641-643 North Broadway, ca. 1937. Isabel Santa Cruz purchased this adobe
from José Mascarel in the early 1860s, and it was demolished in 1957.
(Order #00098728)

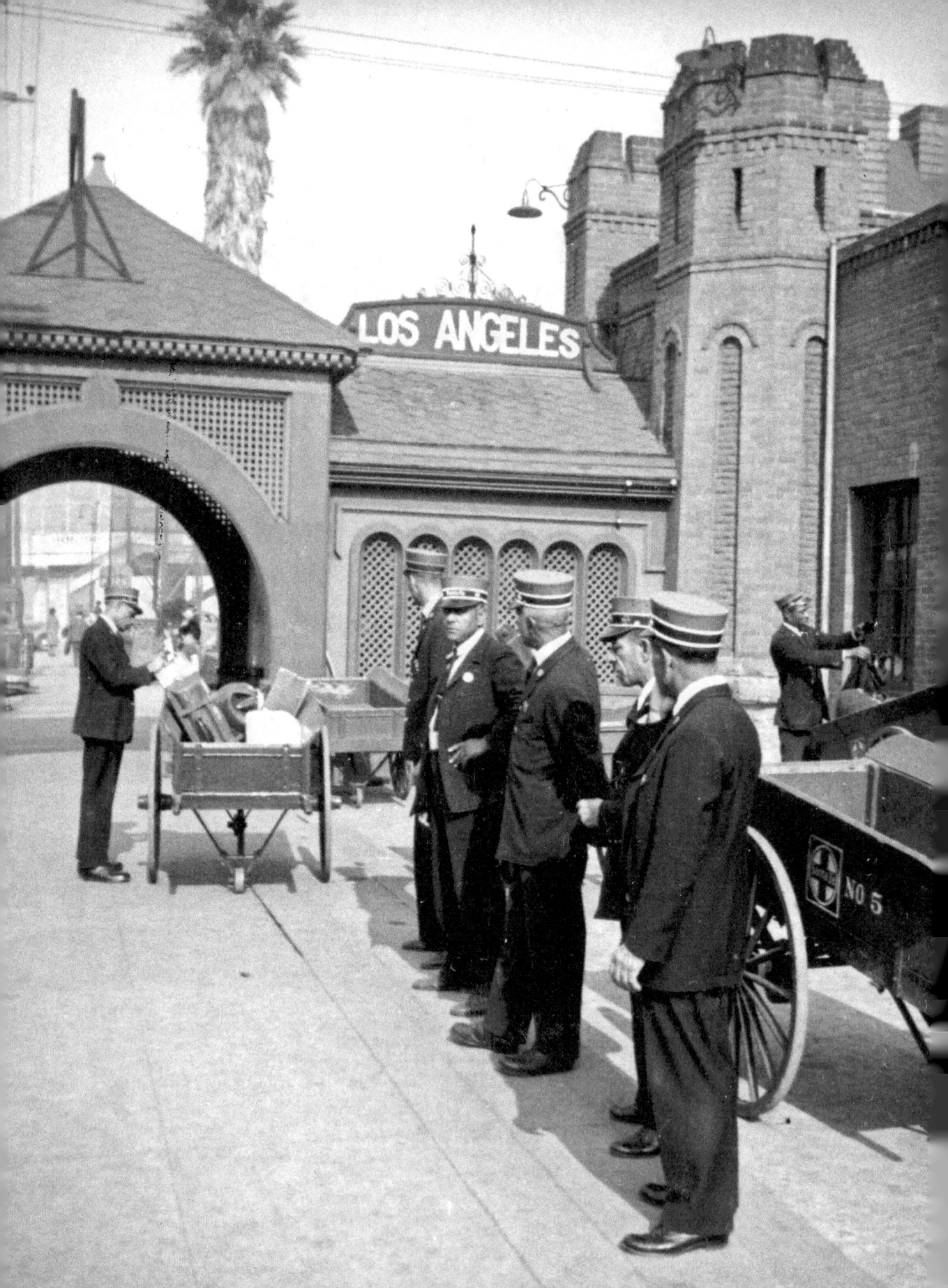

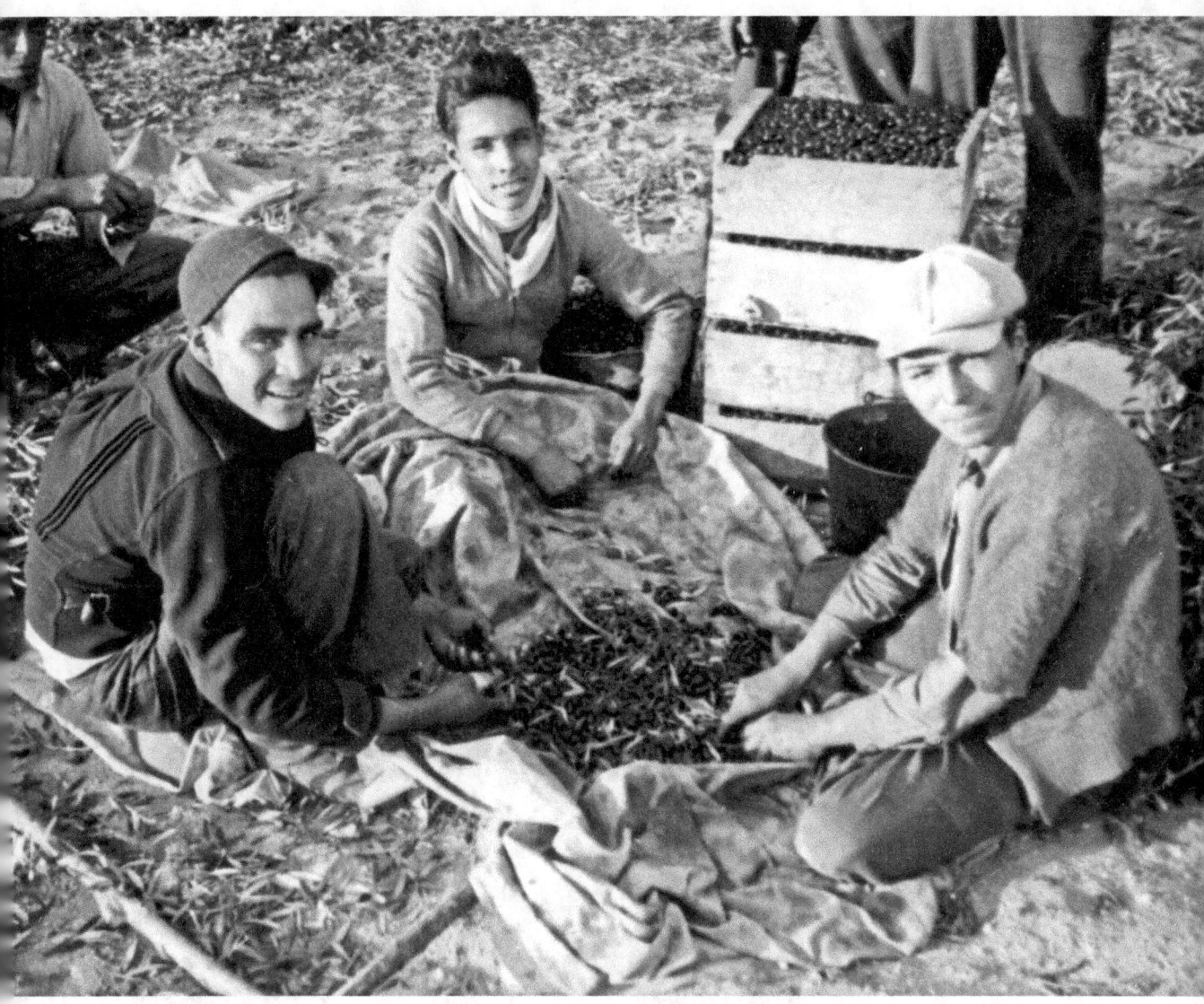

Olive pickers at a farm near Piru, ca. 1937.
(Order #00098819)

Opposite: Employees line up in the courtyard of the La Grande railroad station, ca. 1937.
Santa Fe opened the Moorish-inspired railroad station, located on the corner of
2nd and Santa Fe, on July 29, 1893. It was used as a passenger terminal for Atchison,
Topeka and Santa Fe railway. The station was damaged in the 1933 Long Beach
earthquake, and was replaced by Union Station in 1939. (Order #00098732)

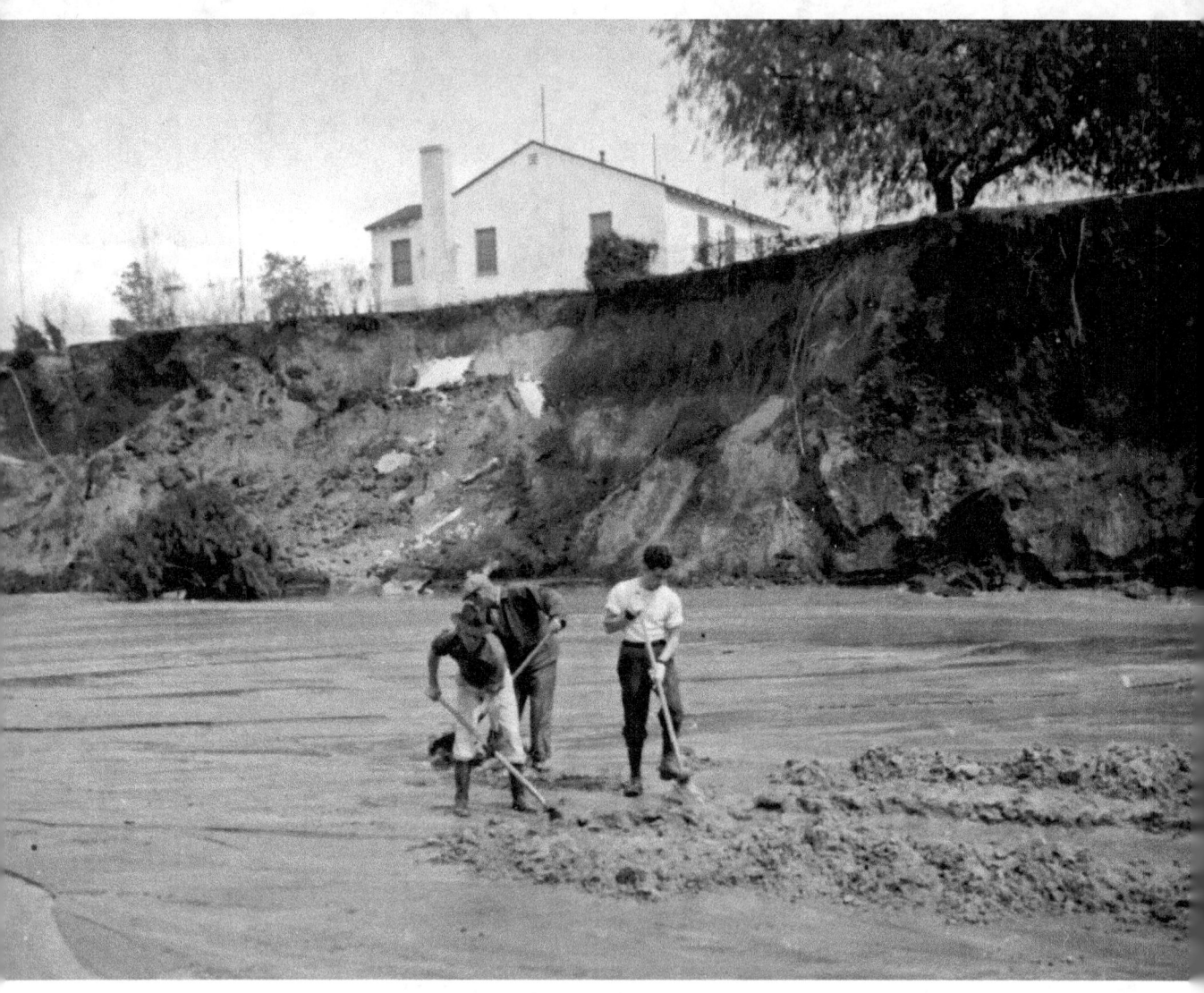

Three men dig in the almost dry riverbed of the Los Angeles River
in North Hollywood in 1938, as part of an Army Corps of Engineers project
to transform the Los Angeles River into a concrete channel,
which still contains most of the of riverbed today. (Order #00099556)

Opposite: Two uniformed women work at the National Orange Show,
which was held March 17–27, 1938 in San Bernardino. (Order #00099789)

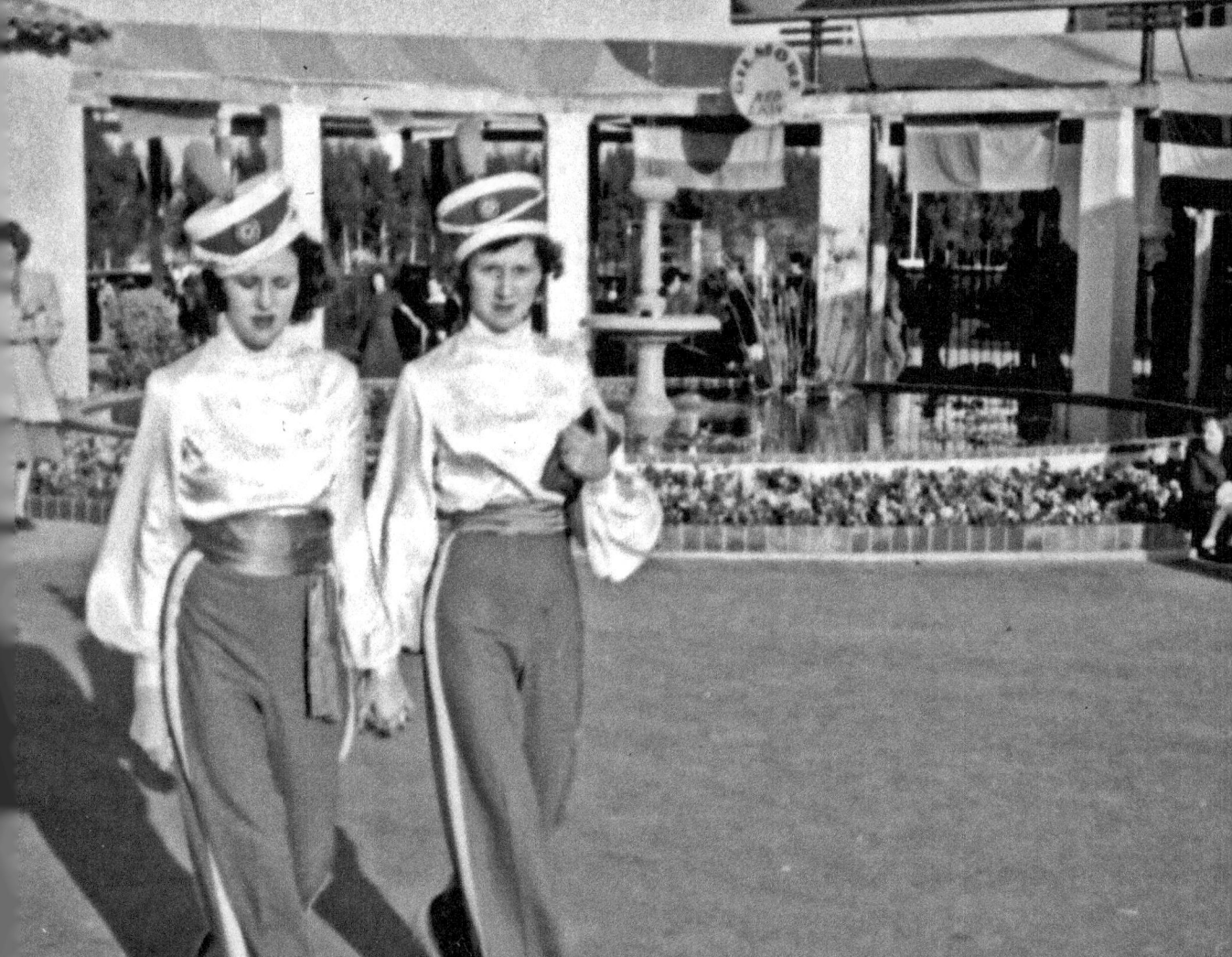

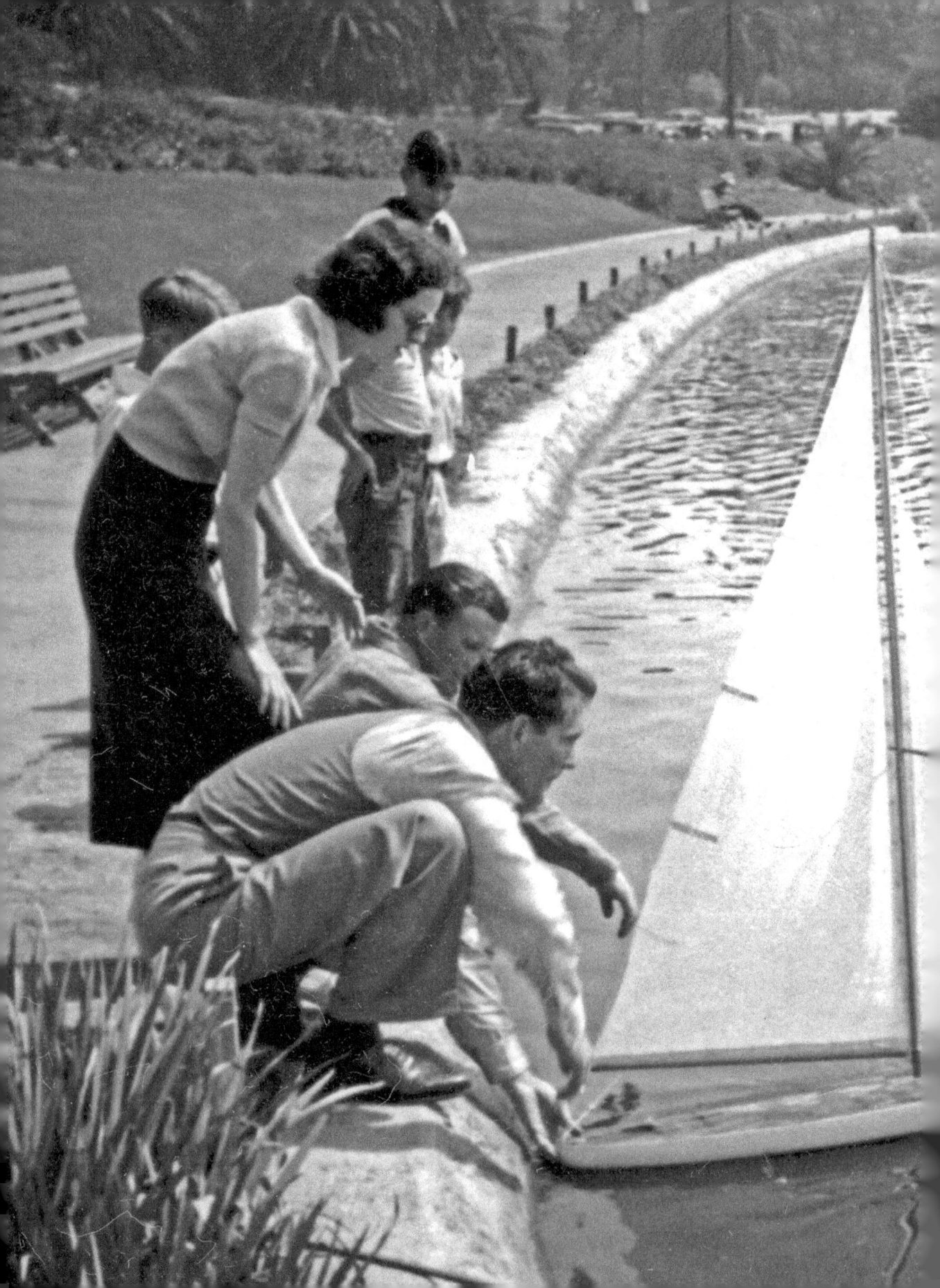

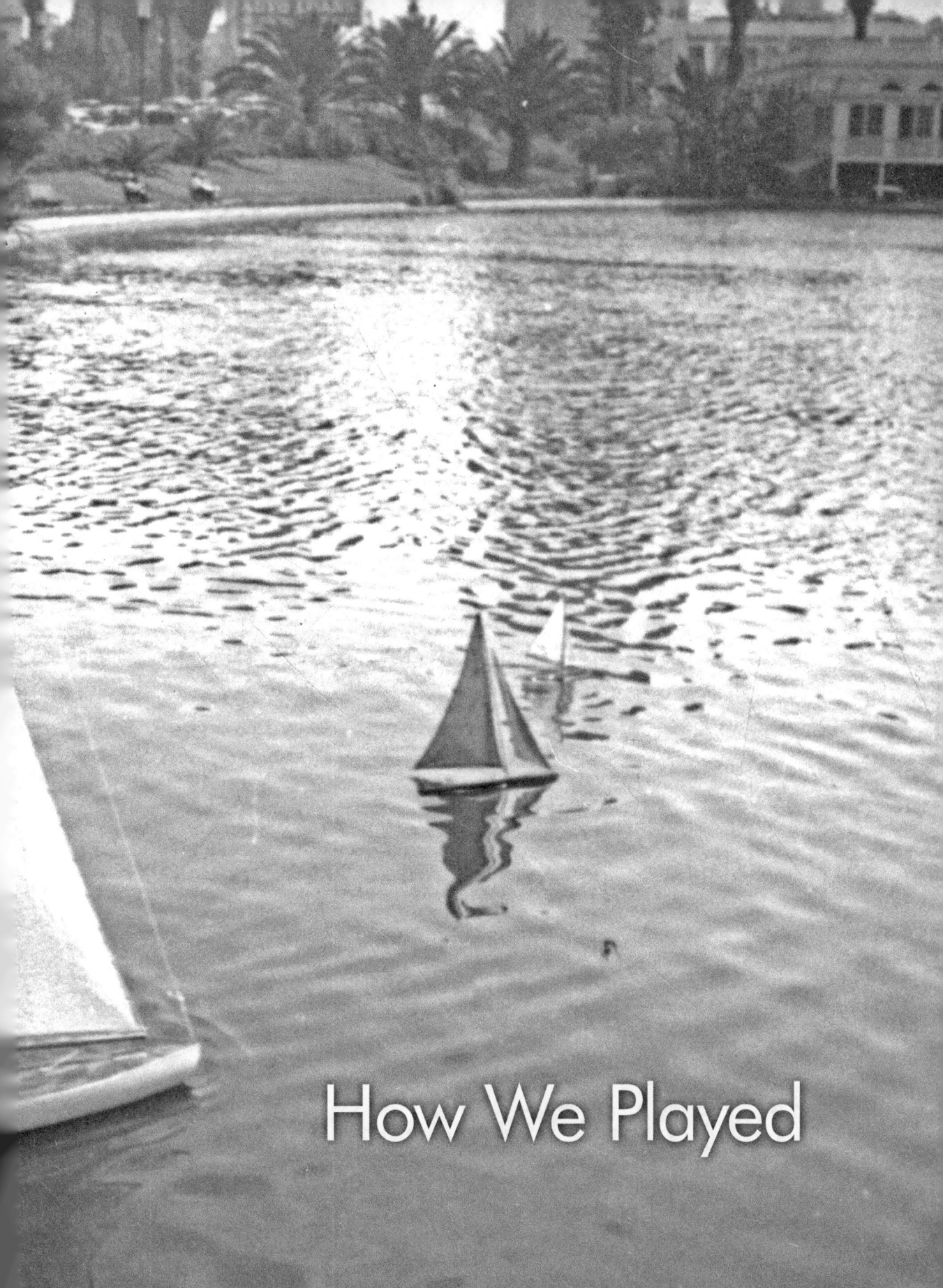

How We Played

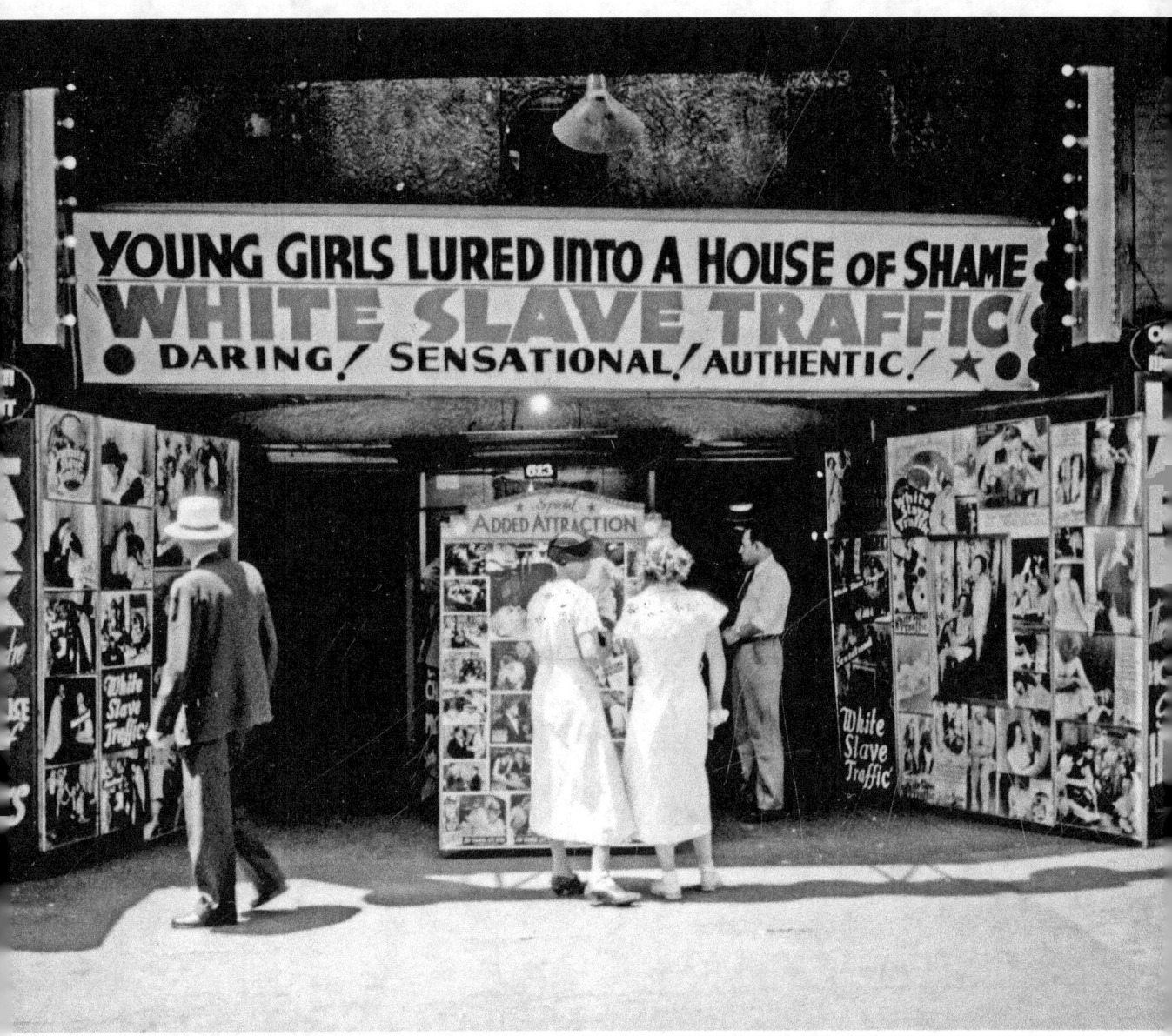

Movie-goers check out the offerings at the Lark Theater,
located at 613 S. Main Street, ca. 1937. (Order #00015349)

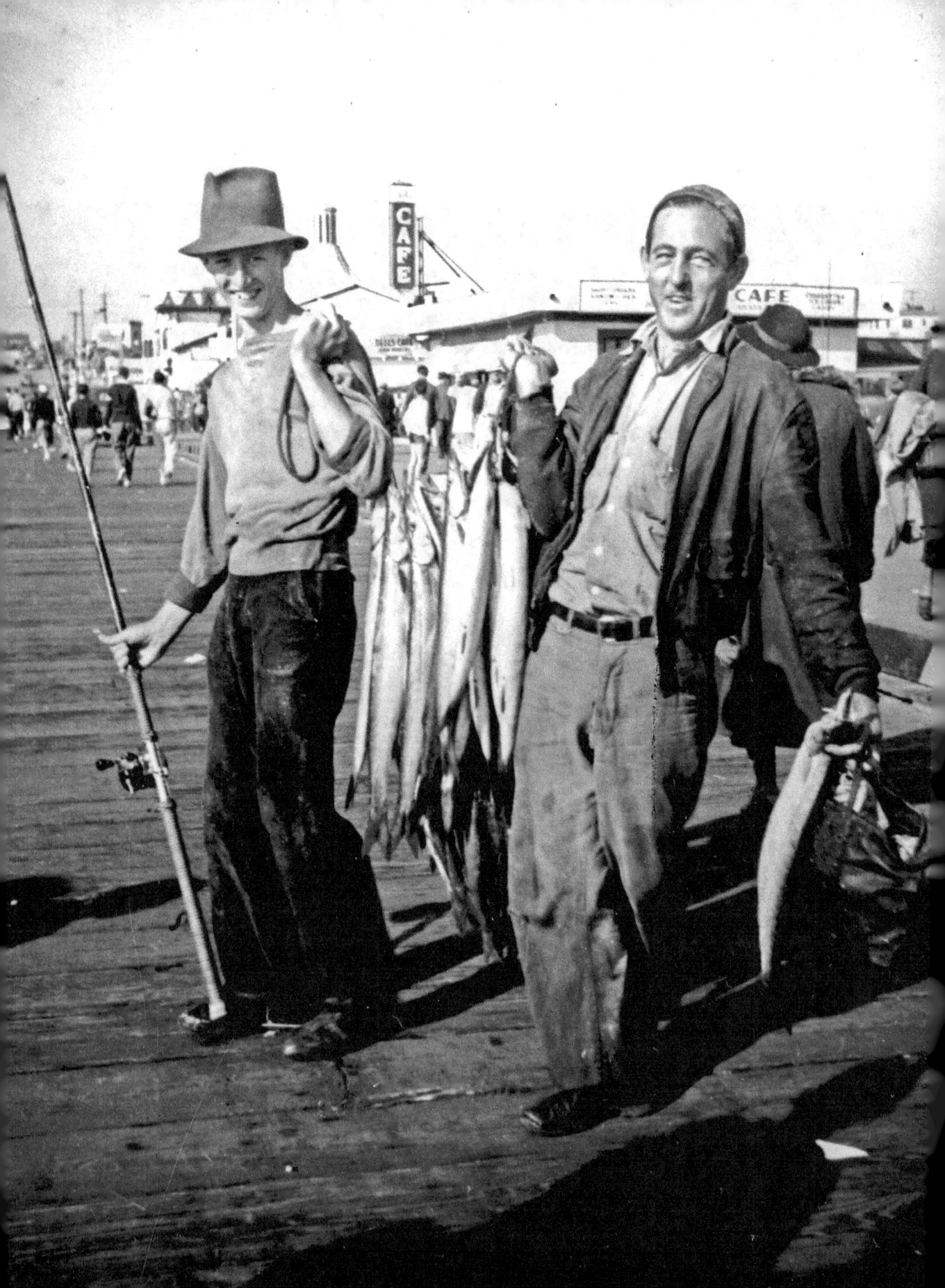

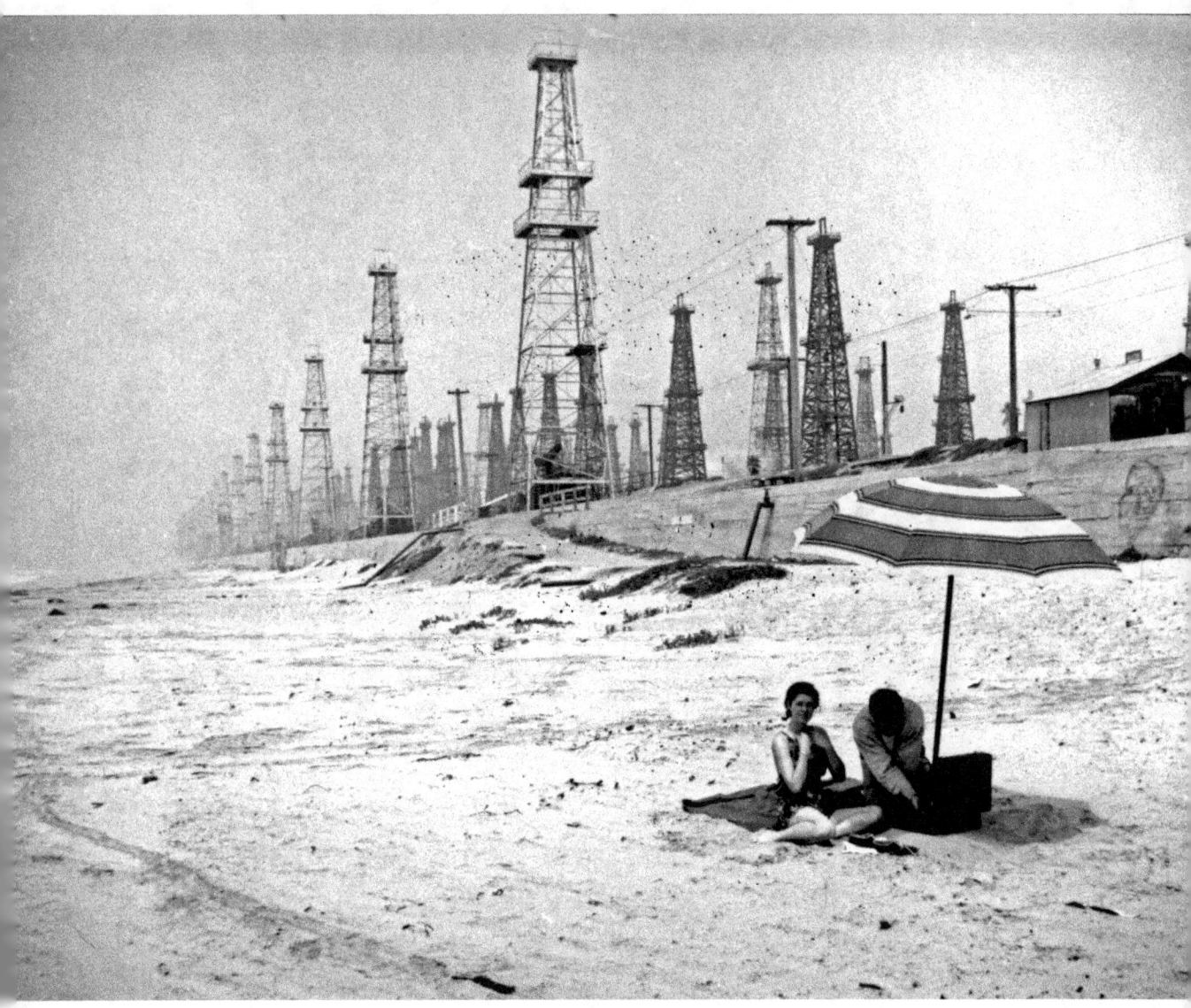

A couple spreads out a picnic in the shadows of
Huntington Beach oil derricks, ca. 1937. (Order #00042228)

Opposite: Two men hold up their daily catch on a pier in Santa Monica, ca. 1937.
(Order #00096640)

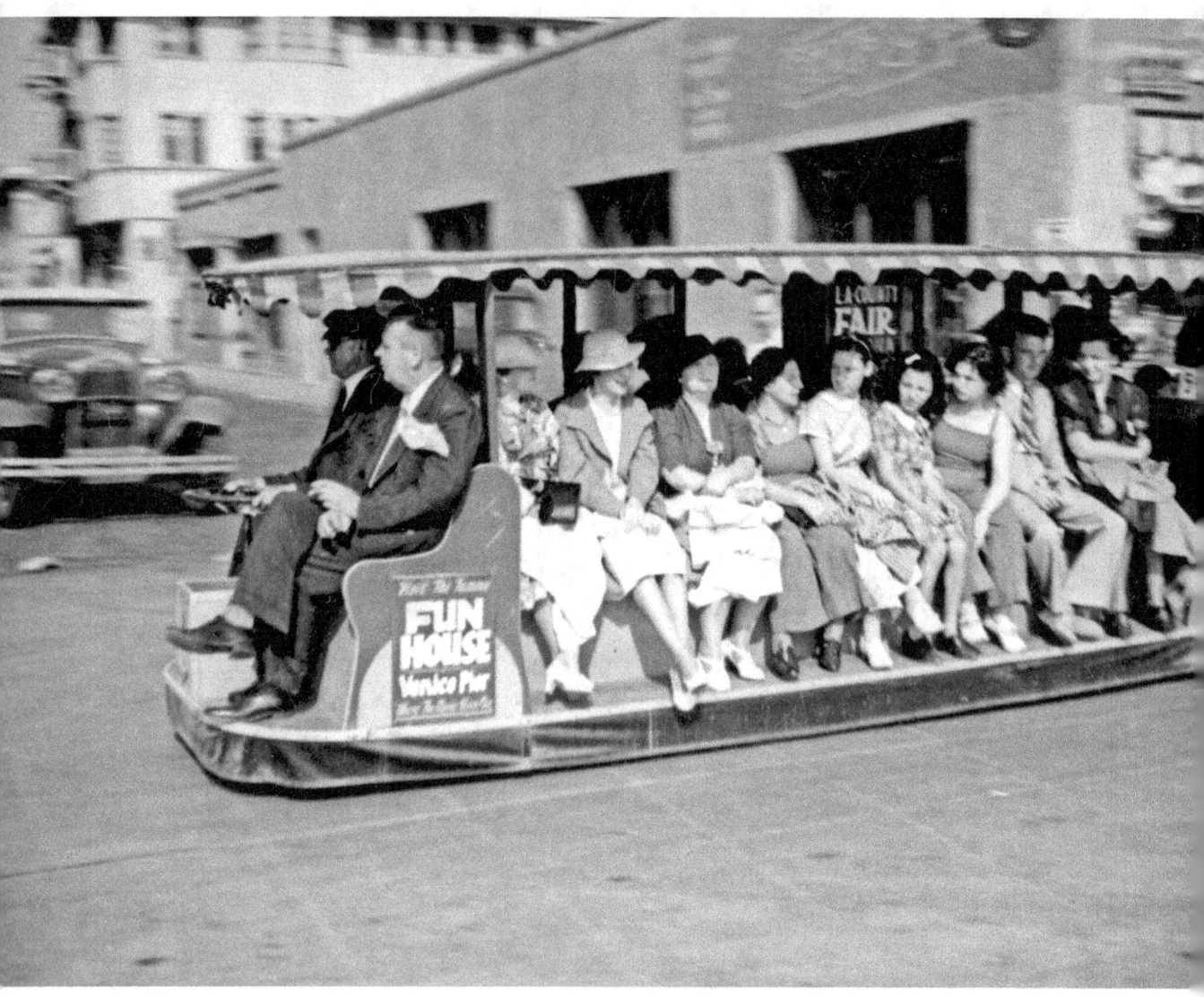

Venice beach-goers enjoy a ride in an electric tram, ca. 1937.
(Order #00047470)

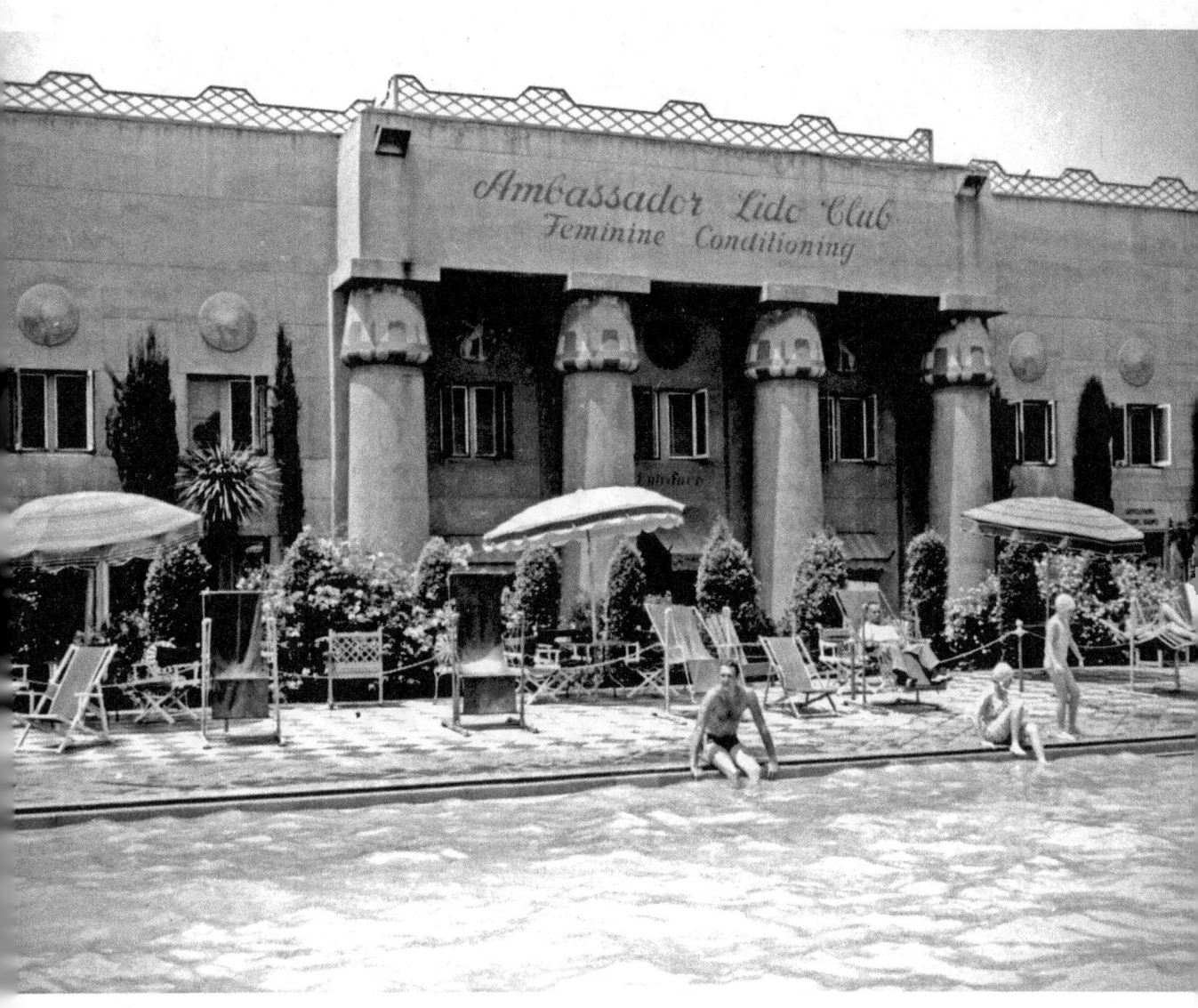

Sun bathers relax by the pool of the Ambassador Lido Club at the
fabled Ambassador Hotel on Wilshire Boulevard, ca. 1937. (Order #00072122)

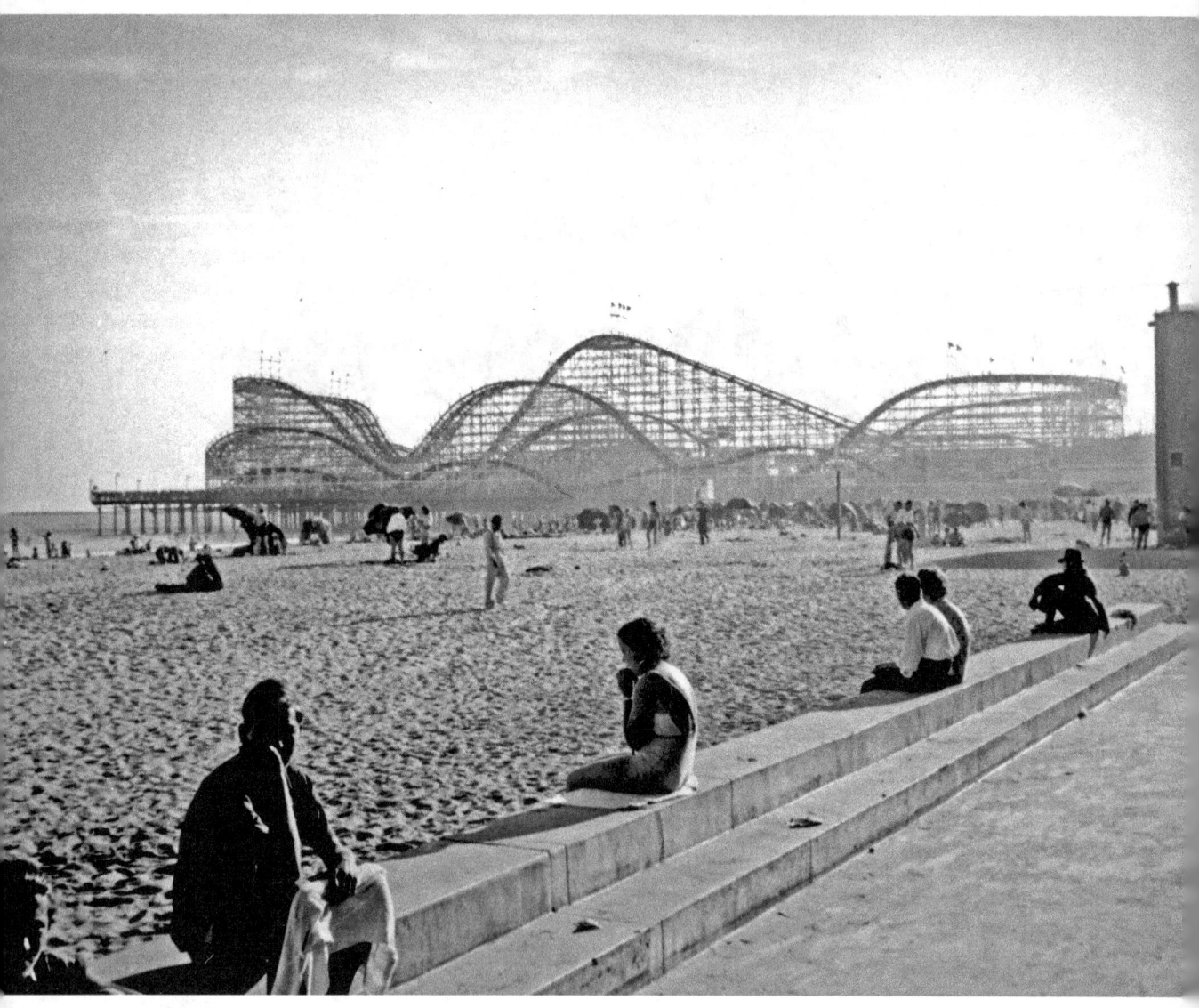

Beach goers lounge near the Cyclone roller coaster at the
Pike in Long Beach, ca.1937. (Order #00074684)

Opposite: Customers visit the "Mouse Circus" at the
L.A. County Fair in 1937. (Order #00081988)

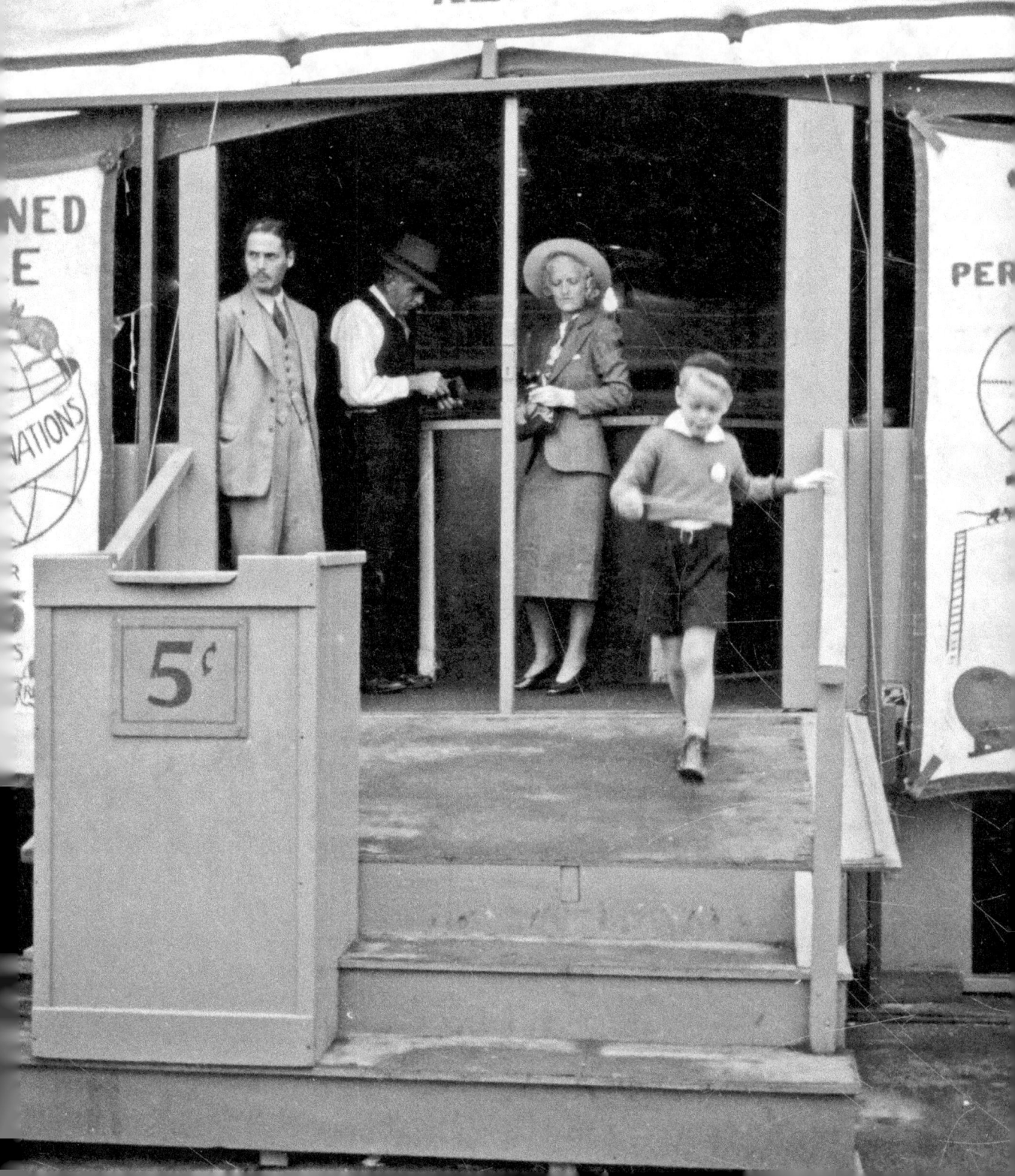

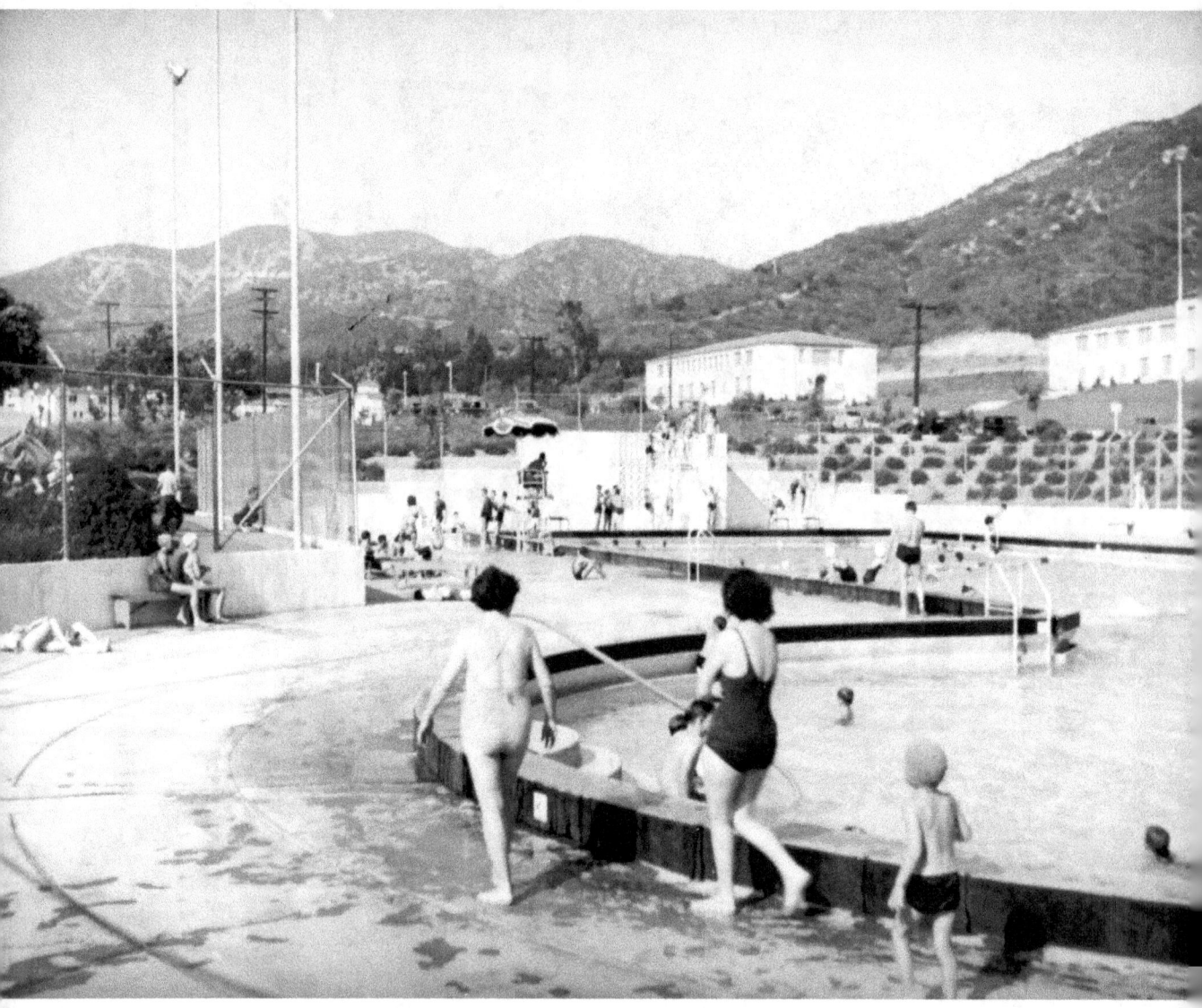

Residents enjoy the community pool in Glendale located across the street from the new Glendale Community College buildings on Verdugo Road, ca. 1938. (Order #00082288)

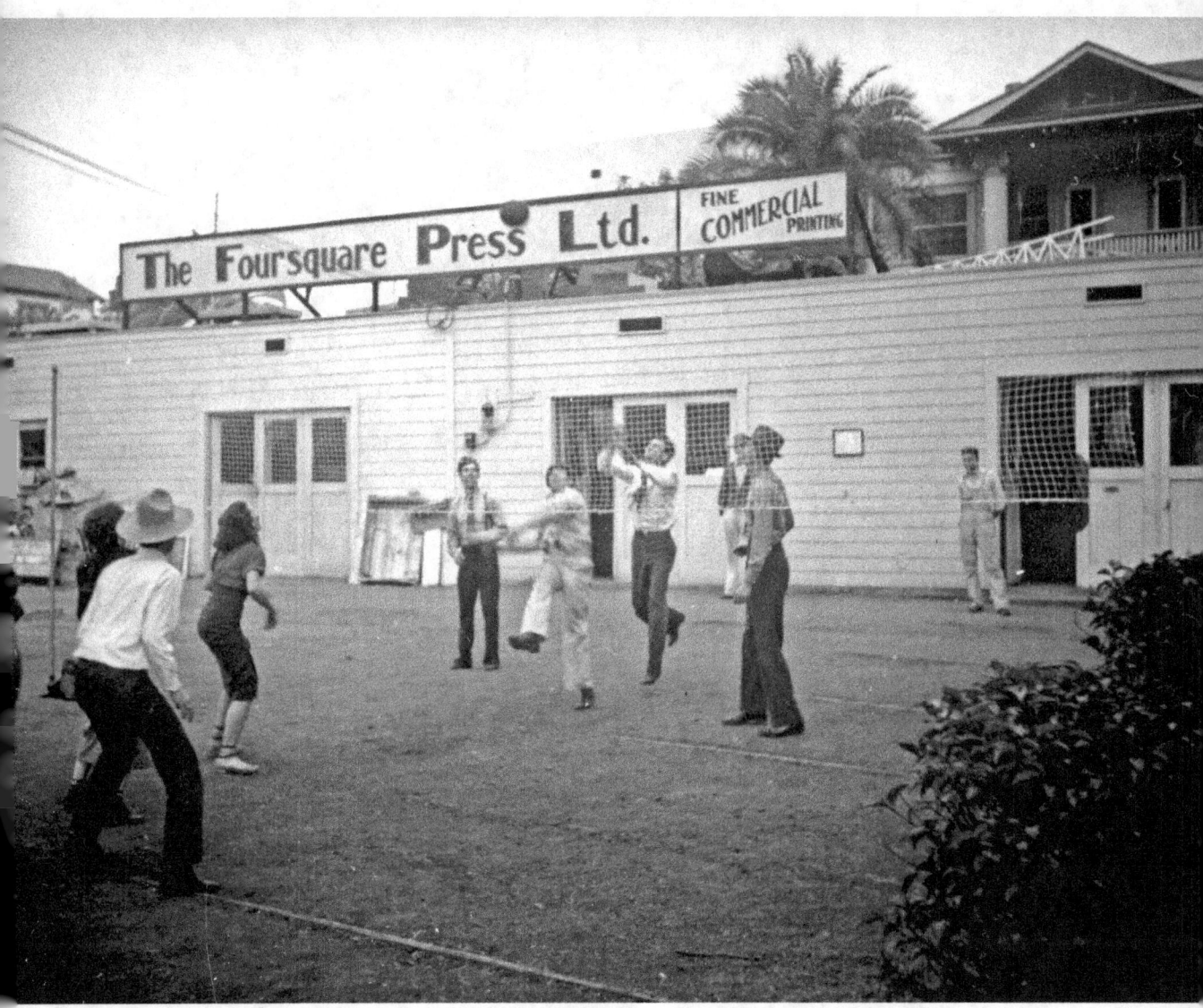

A group plays volleyball in front of the Foursquare Press, Ltd. building
at 1120 Glendale Boulevard, ca. 1937. Aimee Semple McPherson founded
the Pentecostal Foursquare Church in 1927. (Order #0097839)

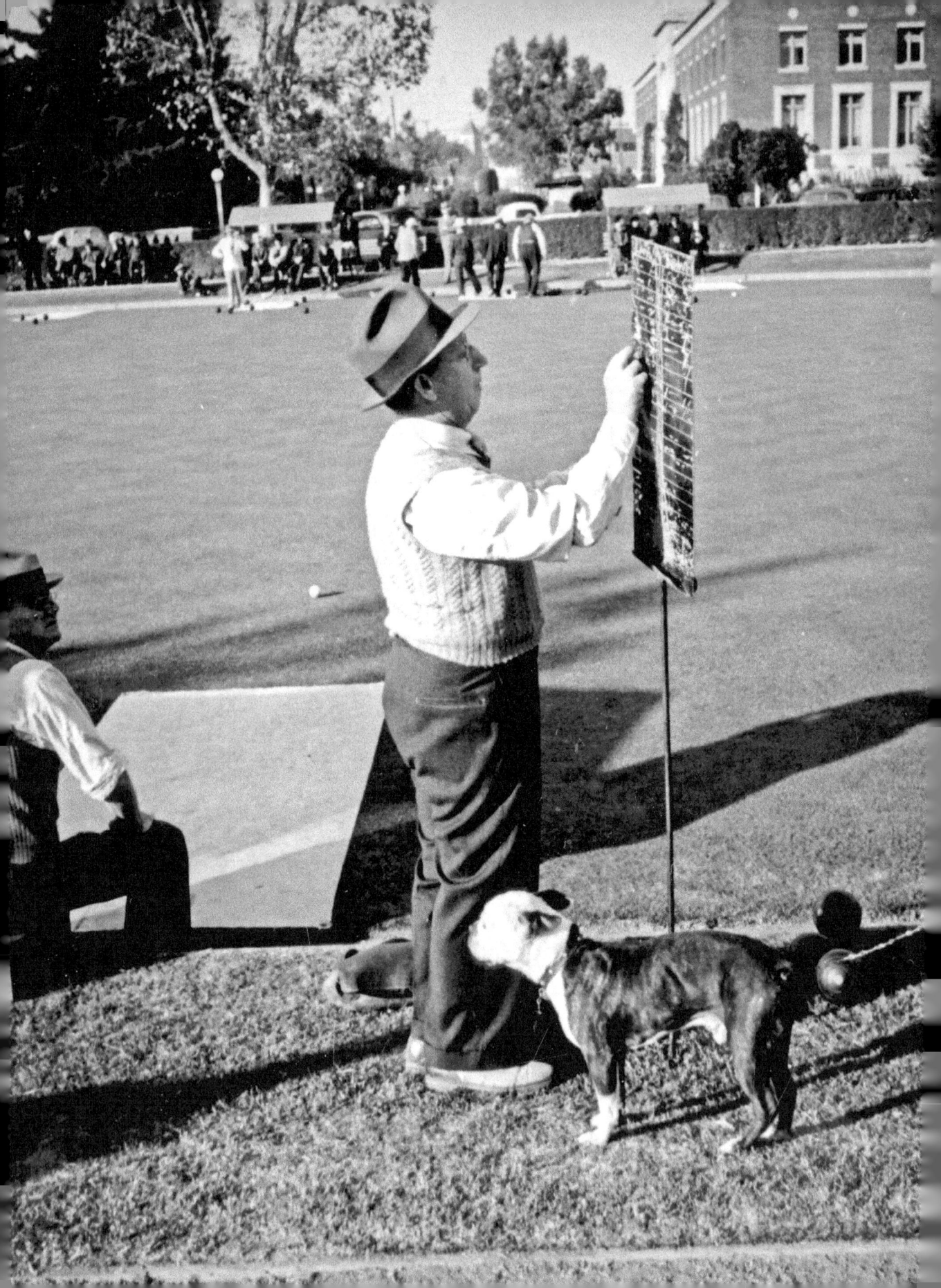

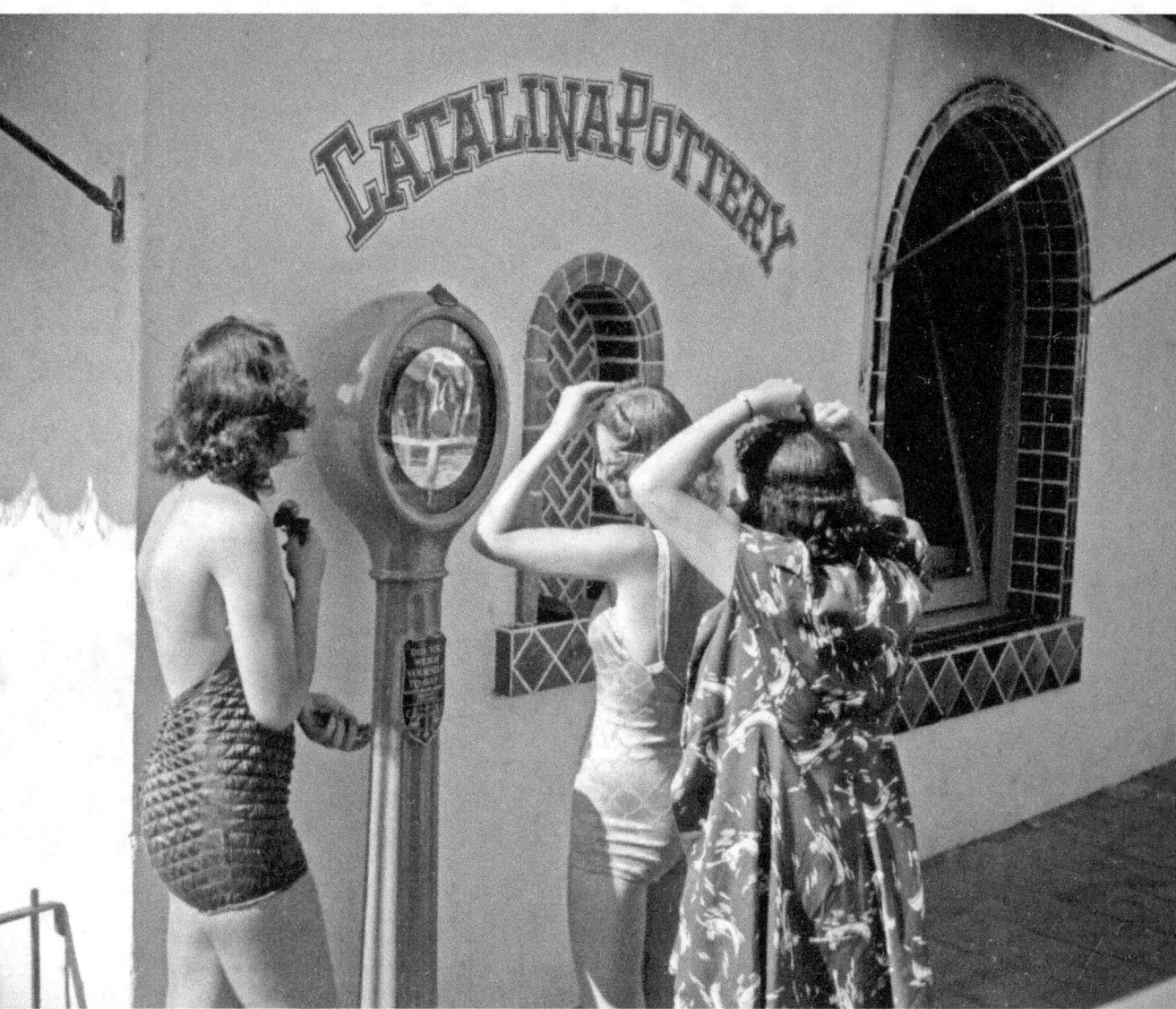

Three women check their hairstyles in front of
Catalina Pottery in Avalon, ca. 1938. (Order #00100603)

Opposite: Man and dog keep score during a lawn bowling game near the
Armory Building in Exposition Park, ca. 1937. (Order #00098130)

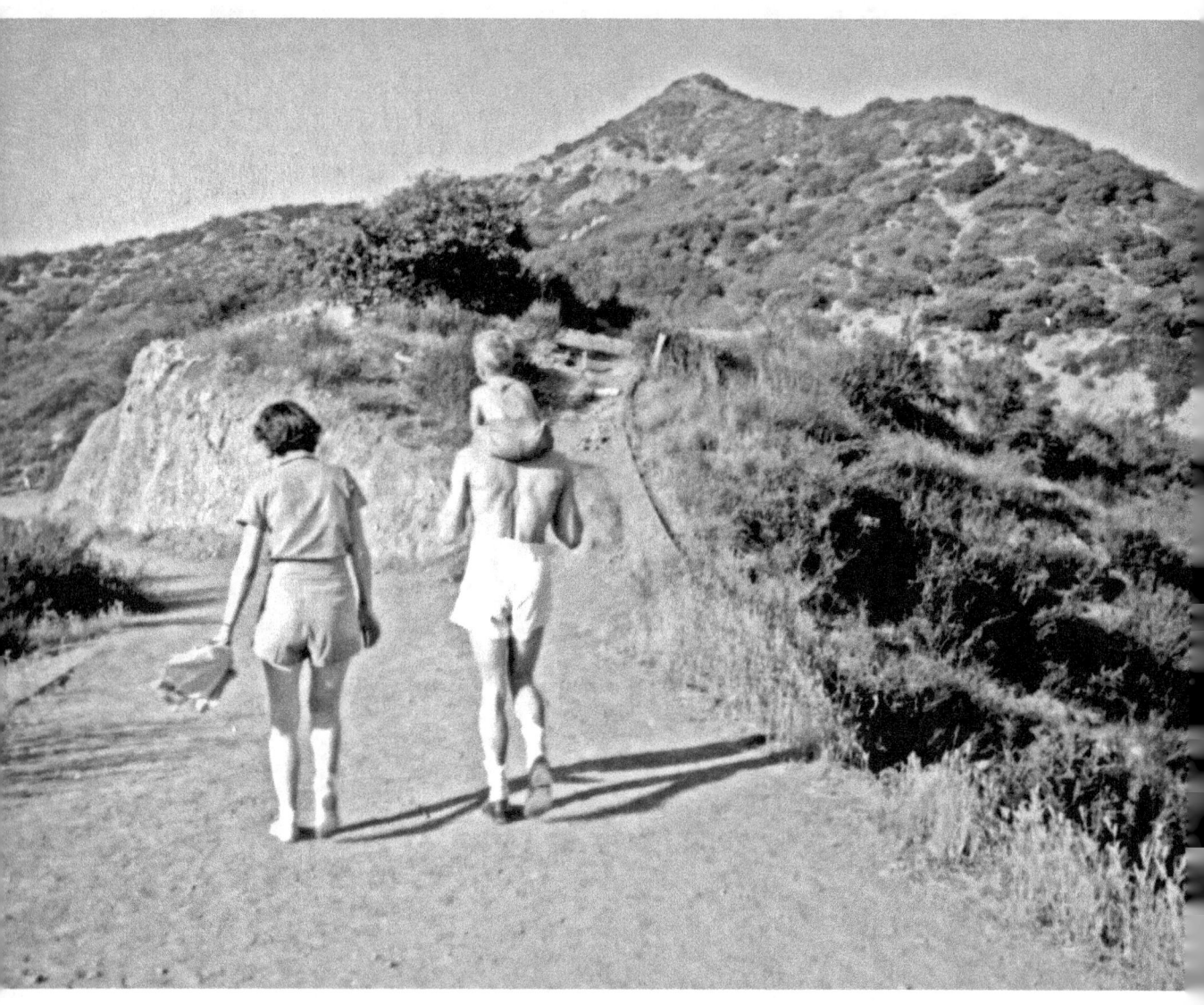

A family walks up a wide path towards the peak of
Mount Hollywood, ca. 1937. (Order #00098468)

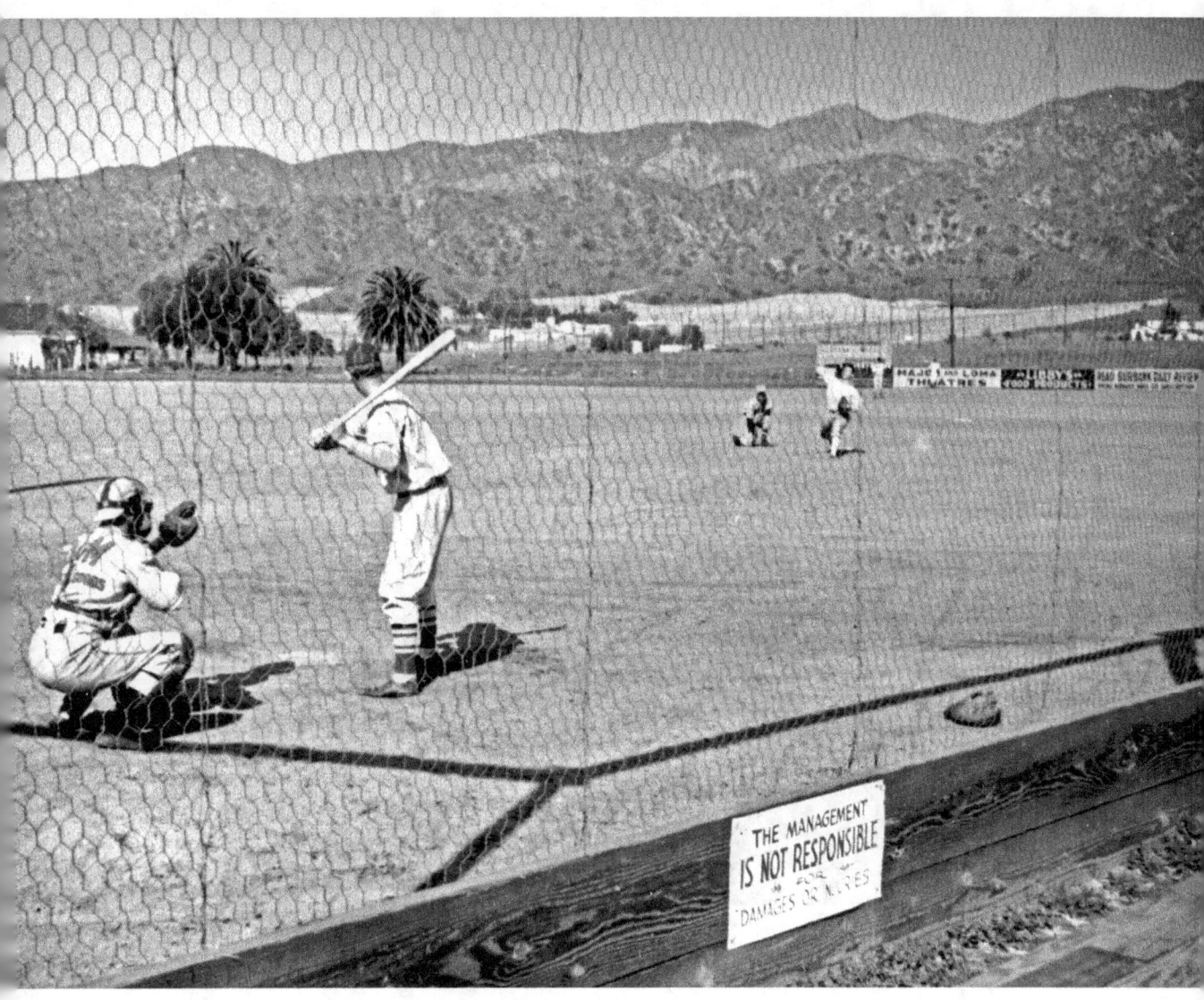

A Burbank baseball team practice, ca. 1938.
(Order #00099042)

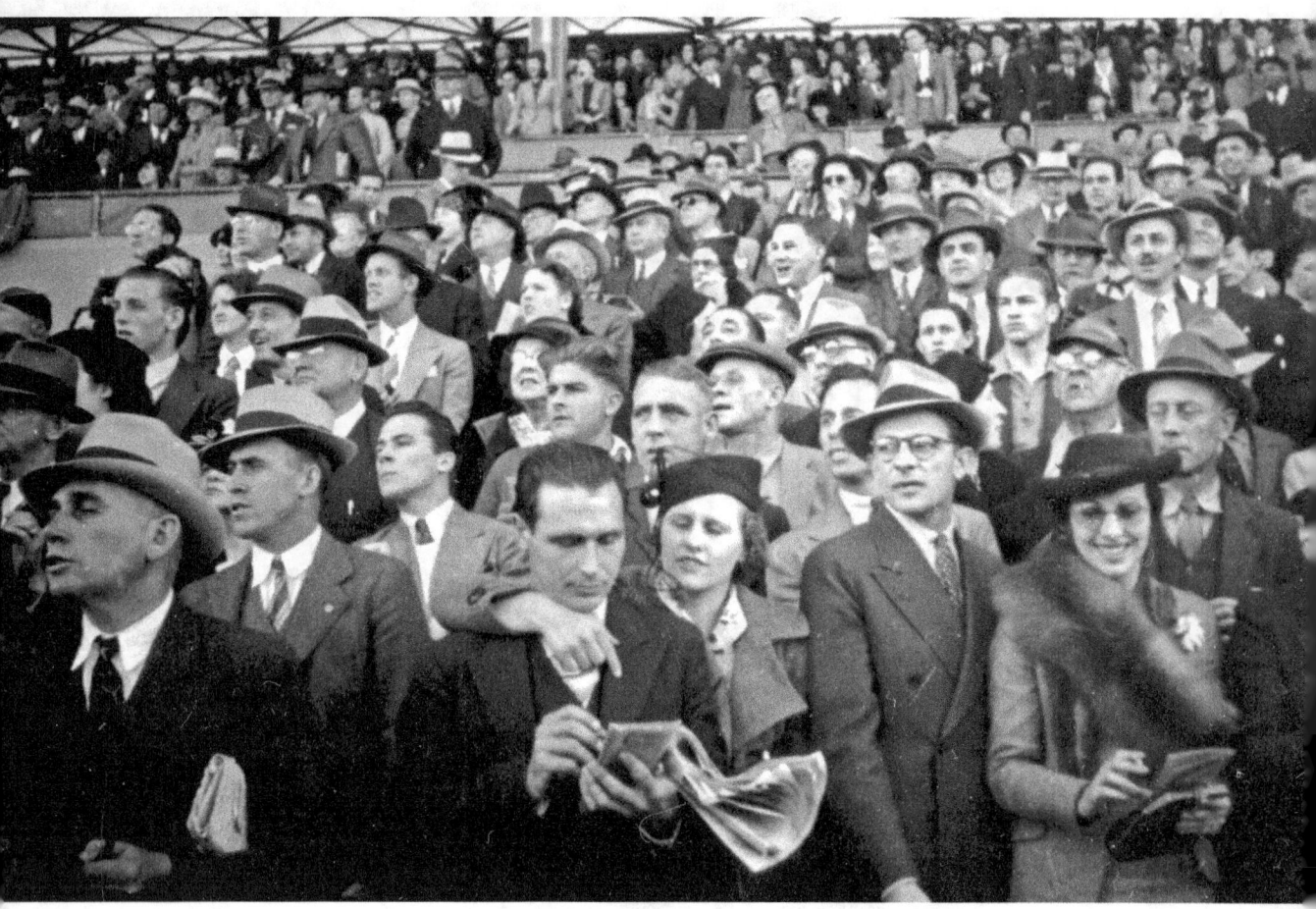

Crowds gather in the grandstand at the Santa Anita Race Track, ca. 1938.
(Order #00099315)

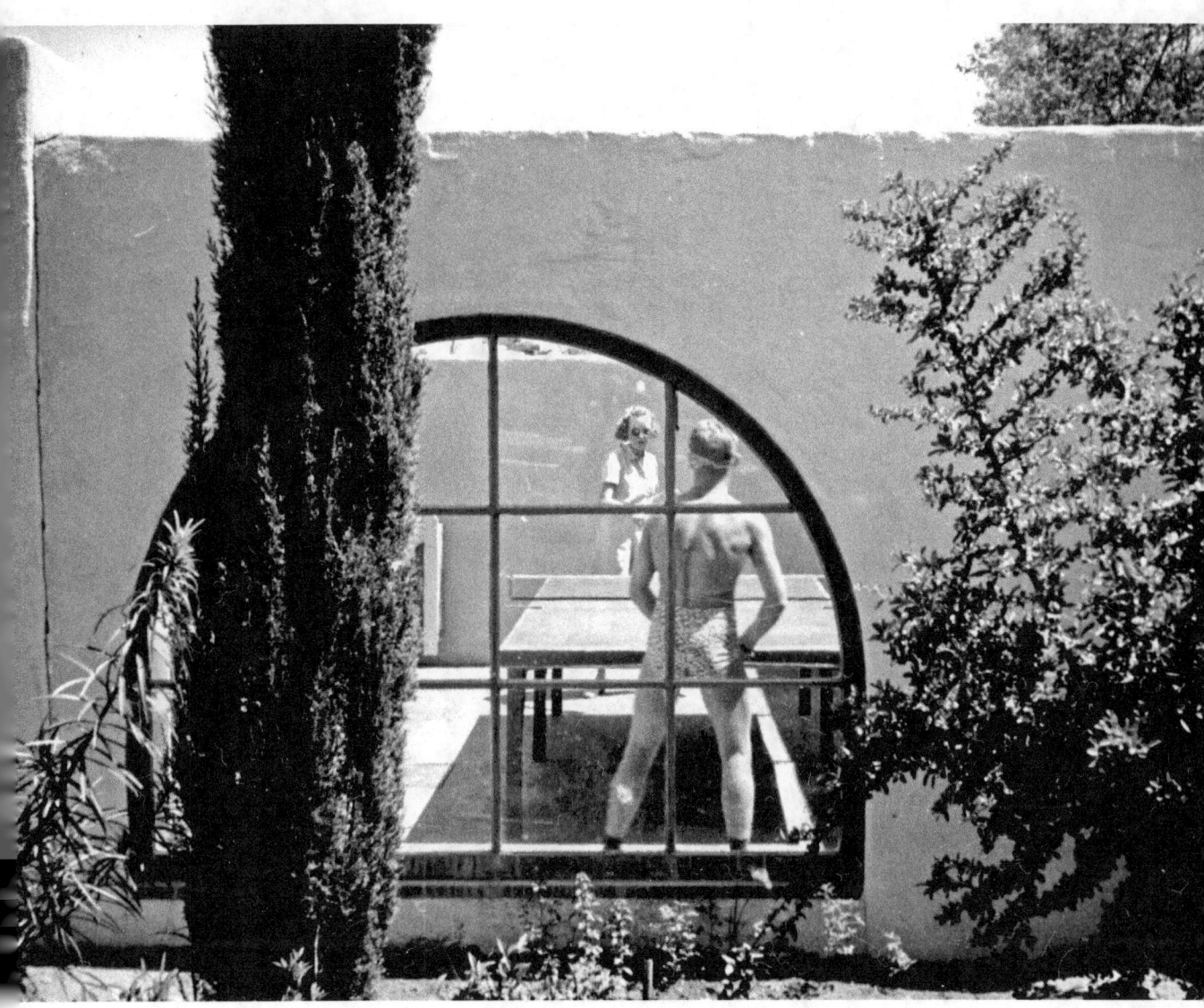

A couple engages in a game of ping-pong at the El Mirador Hotel
in Palm Springs, ca. 1938. (Order #00099846)

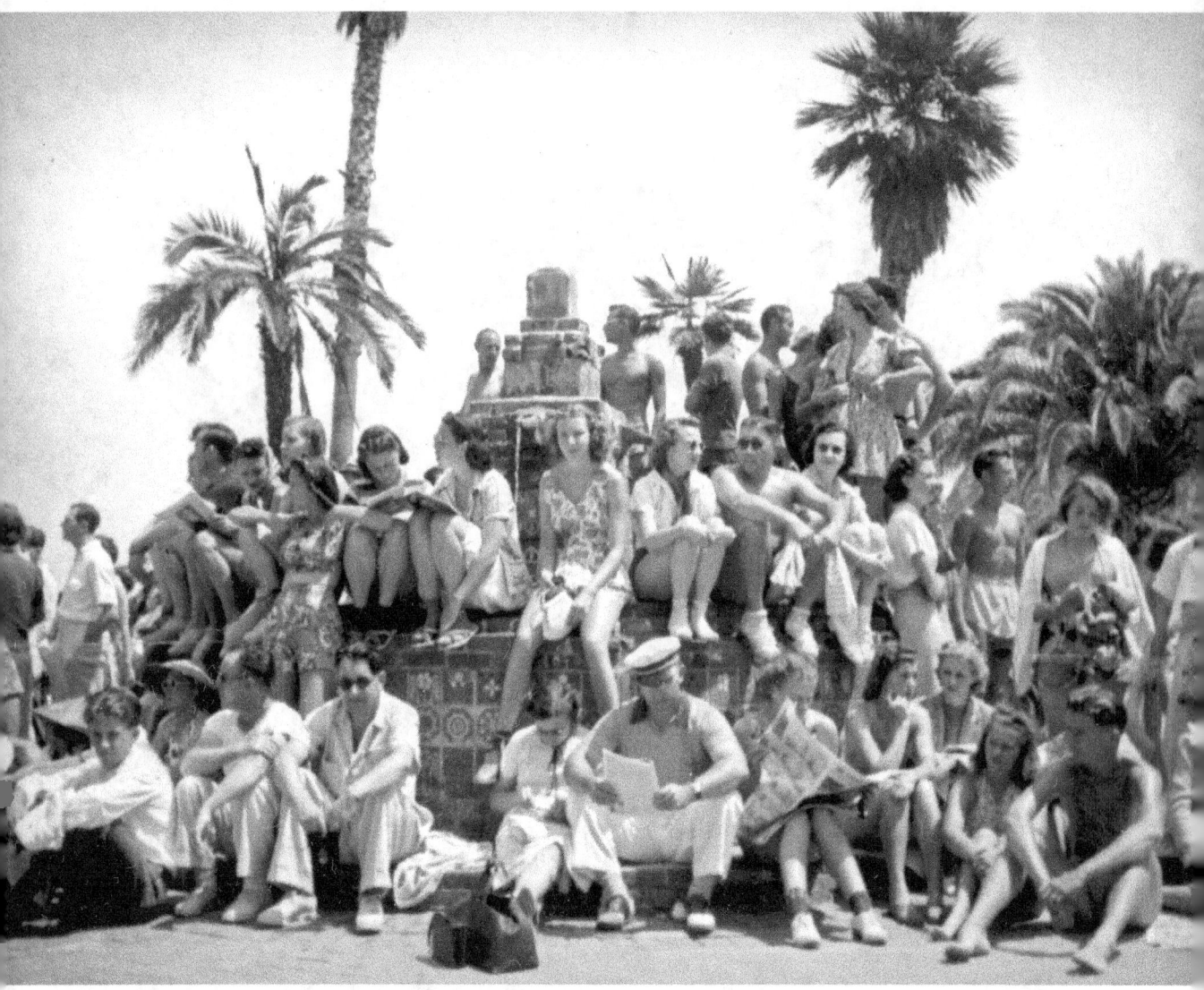

A group readies for the return trip to Los Angeles Harbor from Catalina, ca. 1938.
(Order #00100636)

Opposite: Three men gather around a telescope pointed toward the Elysian Park landslide.
This started near the top of Point Grand View (Buena Vista Peak) as a small crack in the earth
and grew to become a 500-foot fissure over three weeks. On November 26, 1937,
a million and a half tons of loose rock and dirt created a "moving mountain"
that destroyed a 600-foot stretch of Riverside Drive, 1937. (Order #00098281)

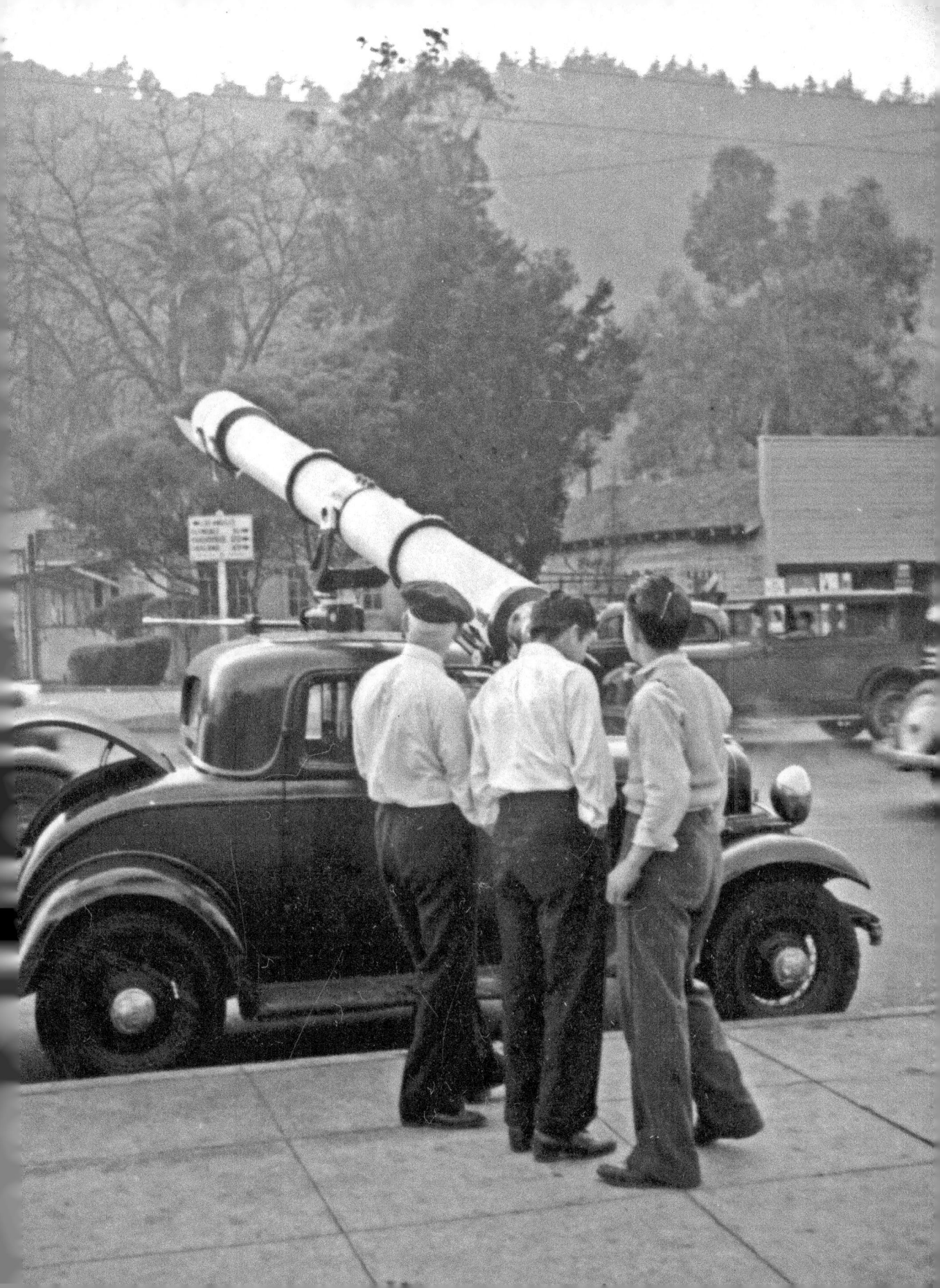

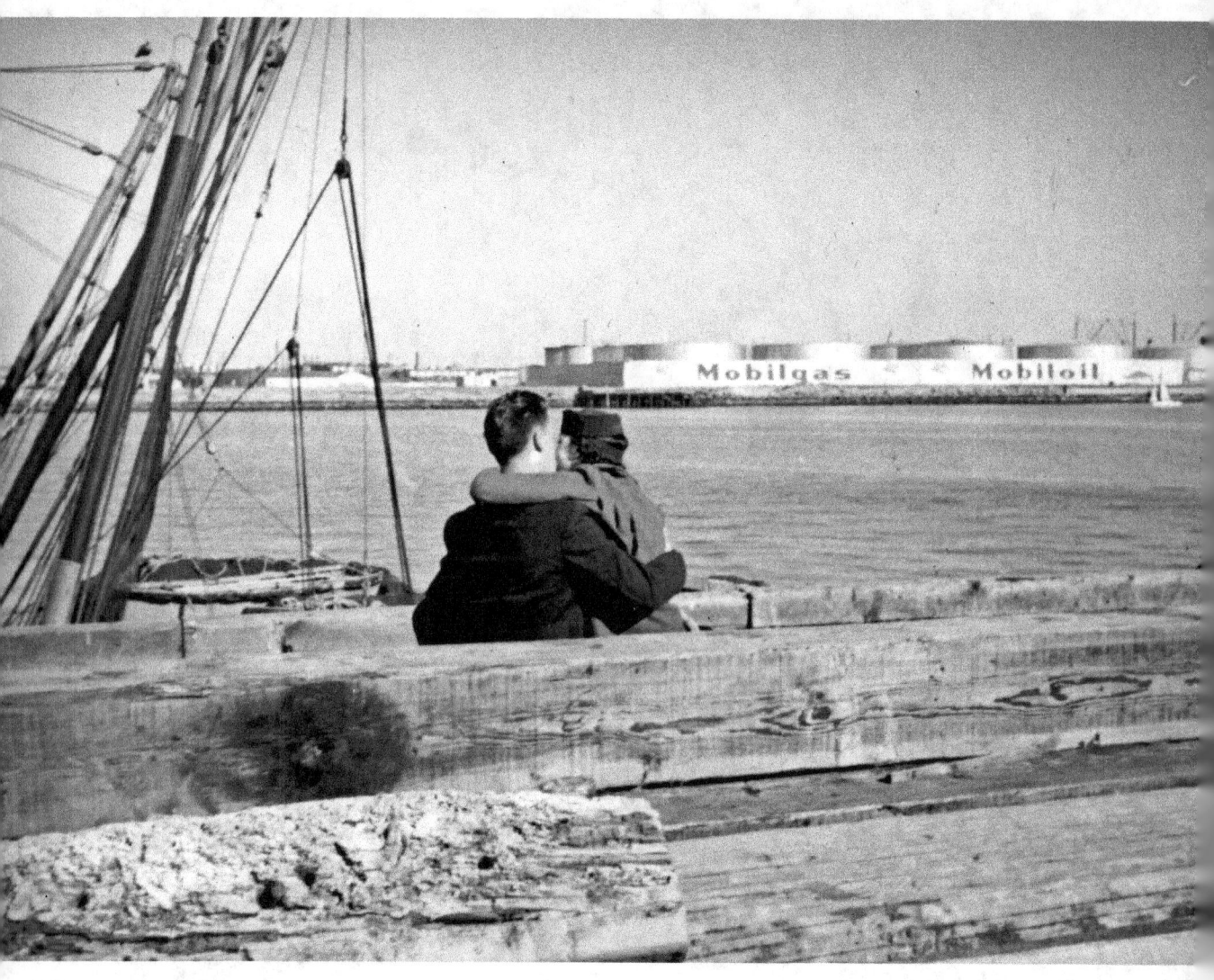

A couple share an intimate moment on Terminal Island, ca. 1938.
(Order #00100889)

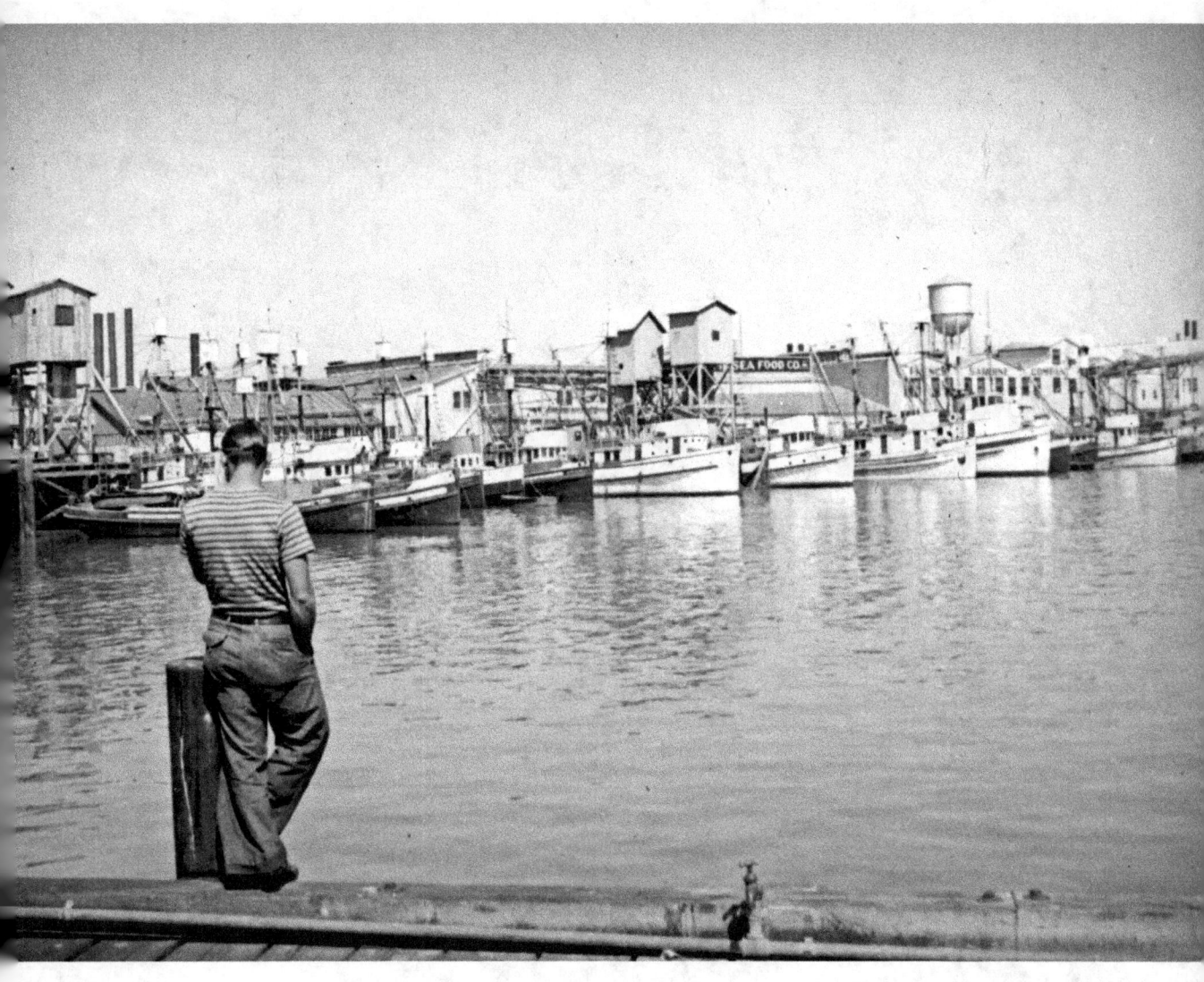

A man looks across the water at Terminal Island, ca. 1938.
(Order #00100895)

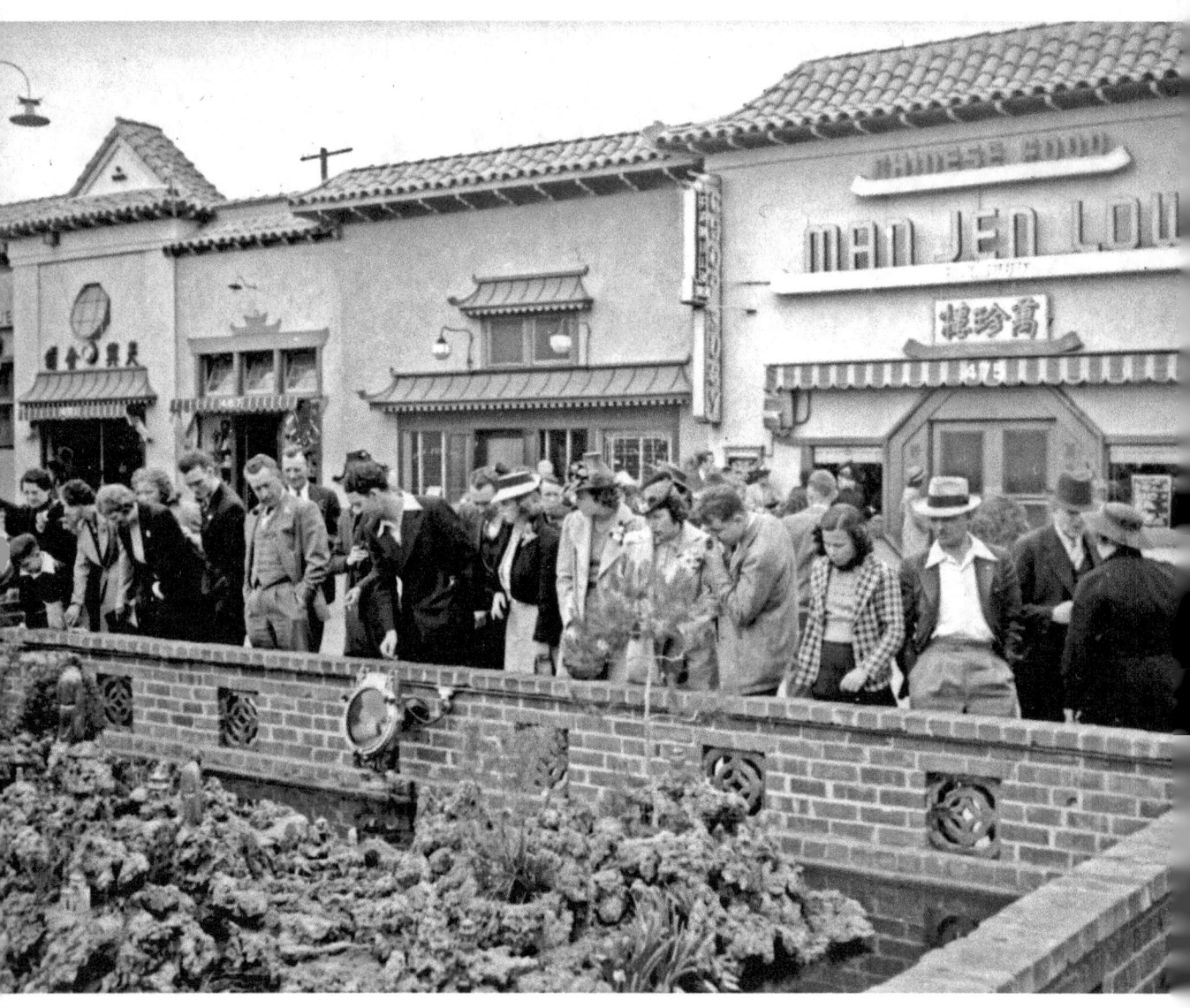

Visitors are gathered at the wishing pool in New Chinatown, ca. 1939.
(Order #00101108)

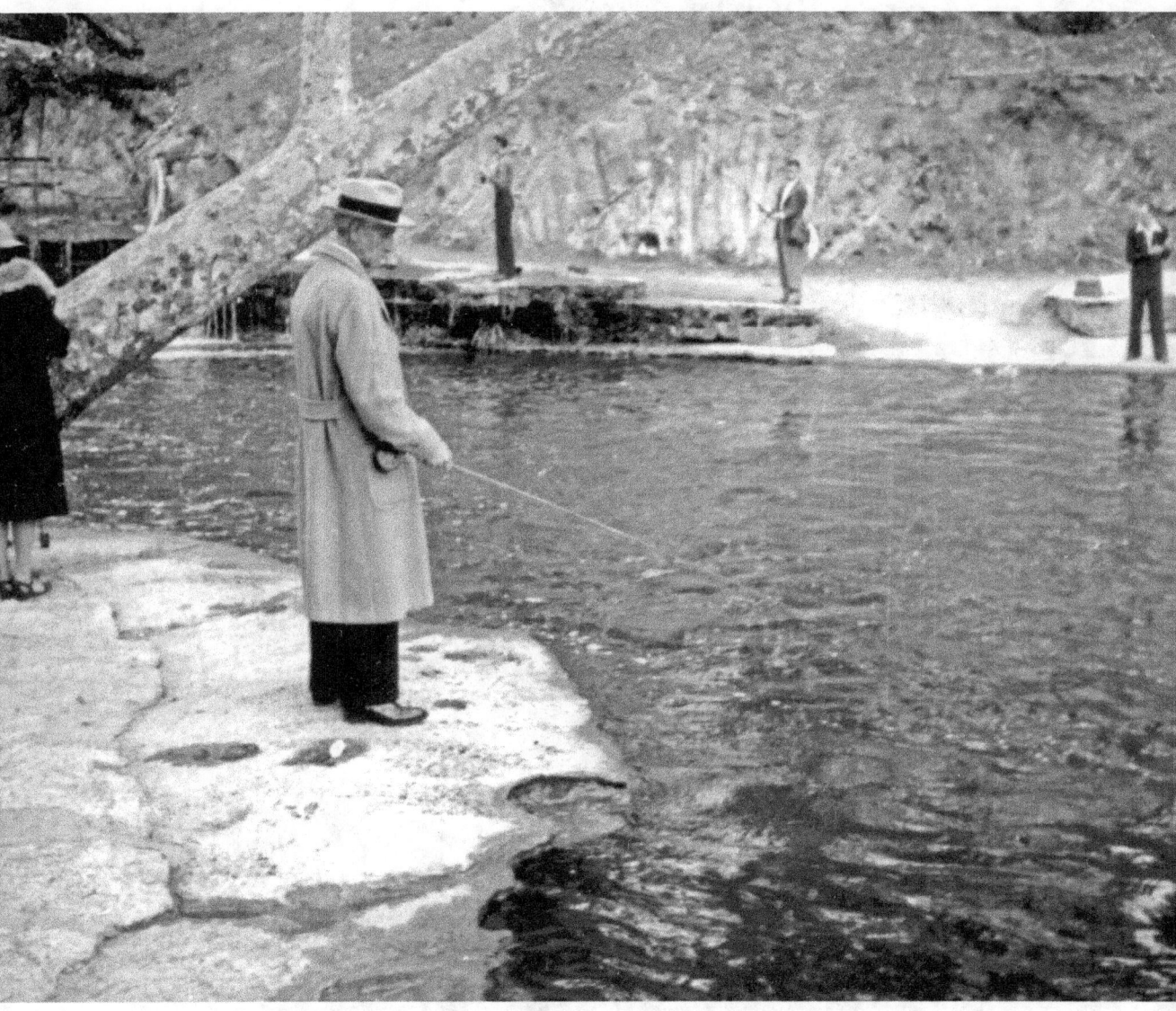

Guests fish along the banks of the Rainbow Angling Club in Azusa, ca. 1938.
(Order #00101352)

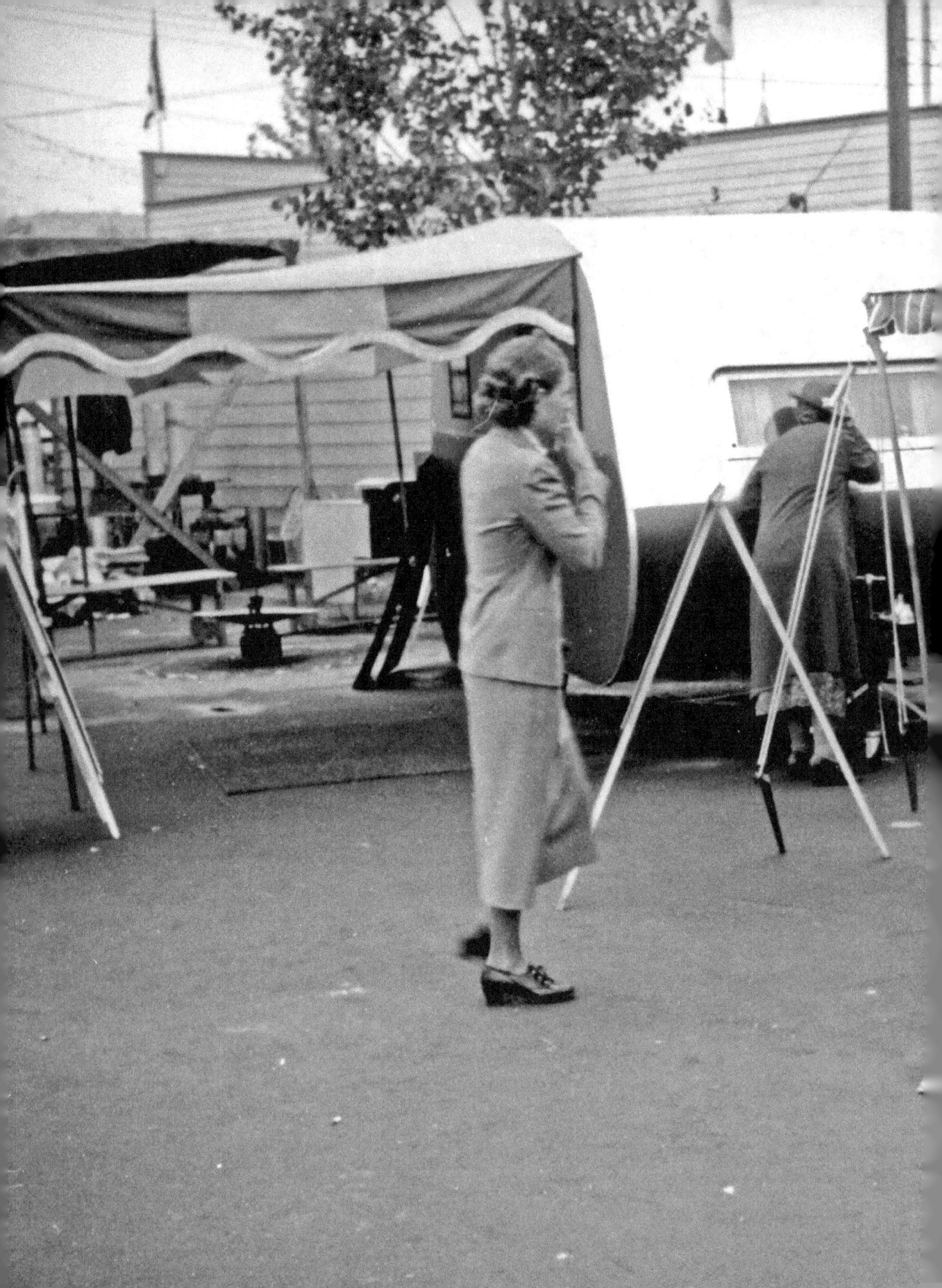

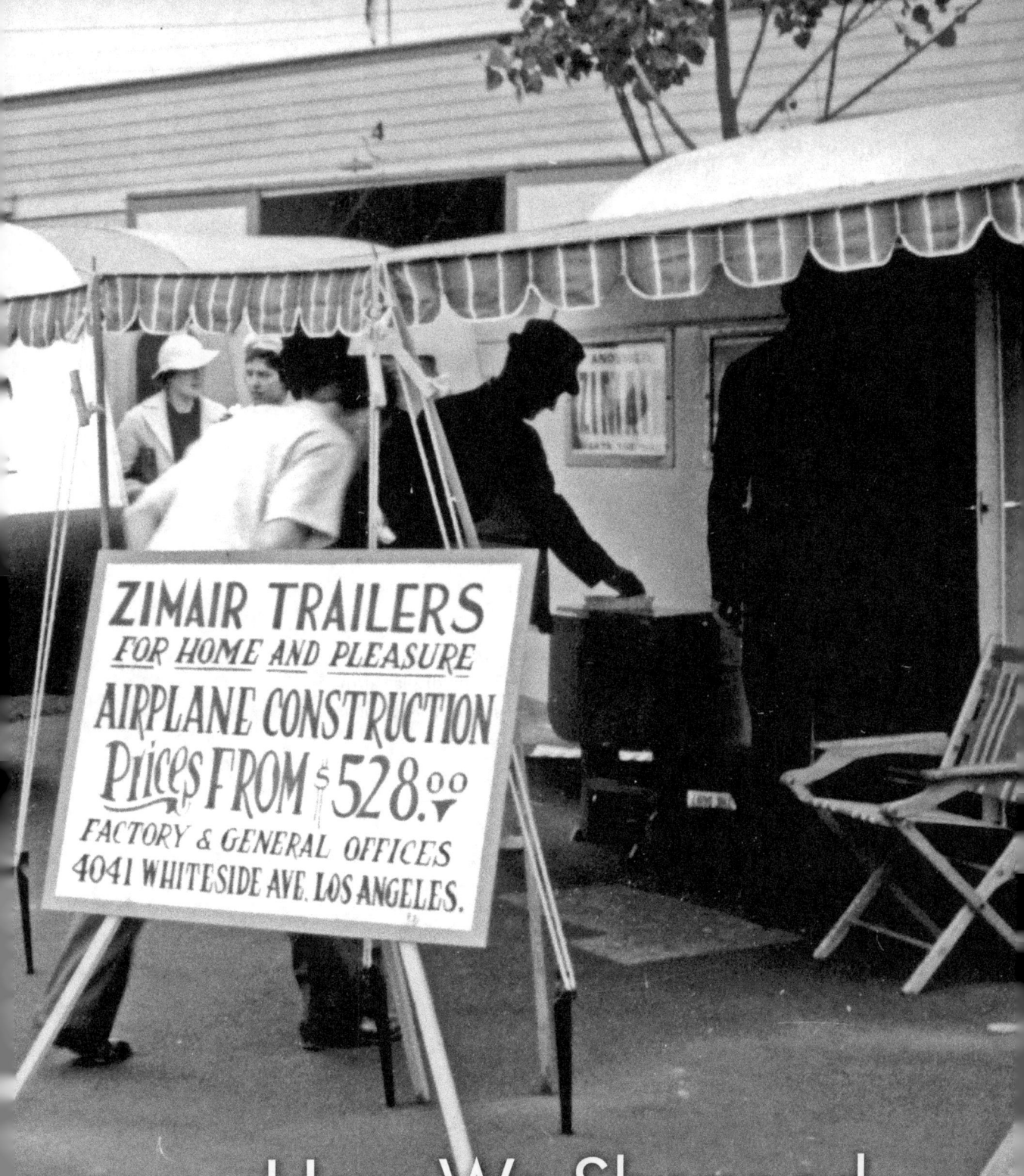

ZIMAIR TRAILERS
FOR HOME AND PLEASURE
AIRPLANE CONSTRUCTION
Prices FROM $528.00
FACTORY & GENERAL OFFICES
4041 WHITESIDE AVE. LOS ANGELES.

How We Shopped

Overleaf:
House trailers for sale are on display at the
Los Angeles County Fair in 1937. (Order #00082009)

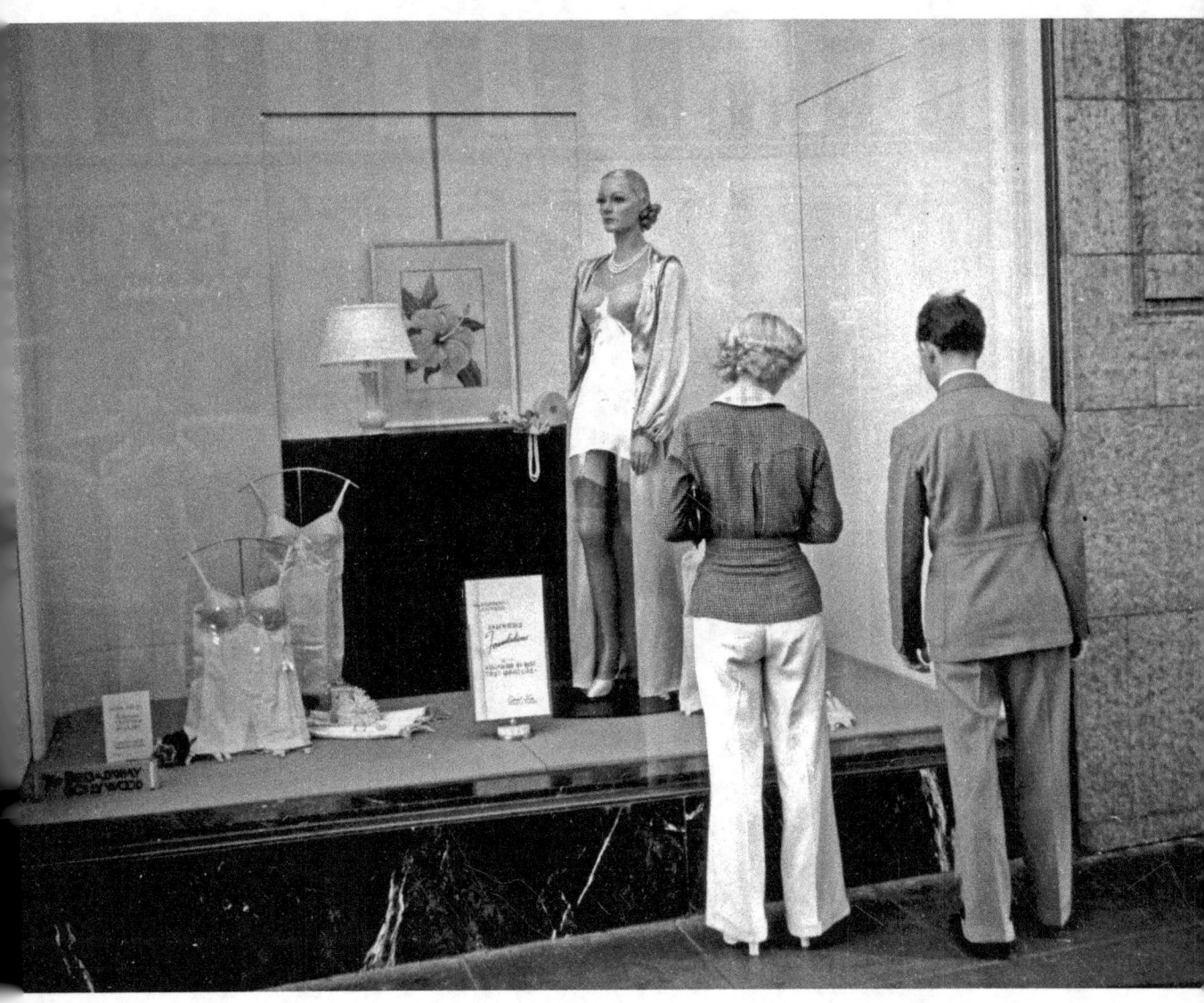

Window-shoppers at the Broadway Department Store on
Hollywood Boulevard, ca. 1938. (Order #00011291)

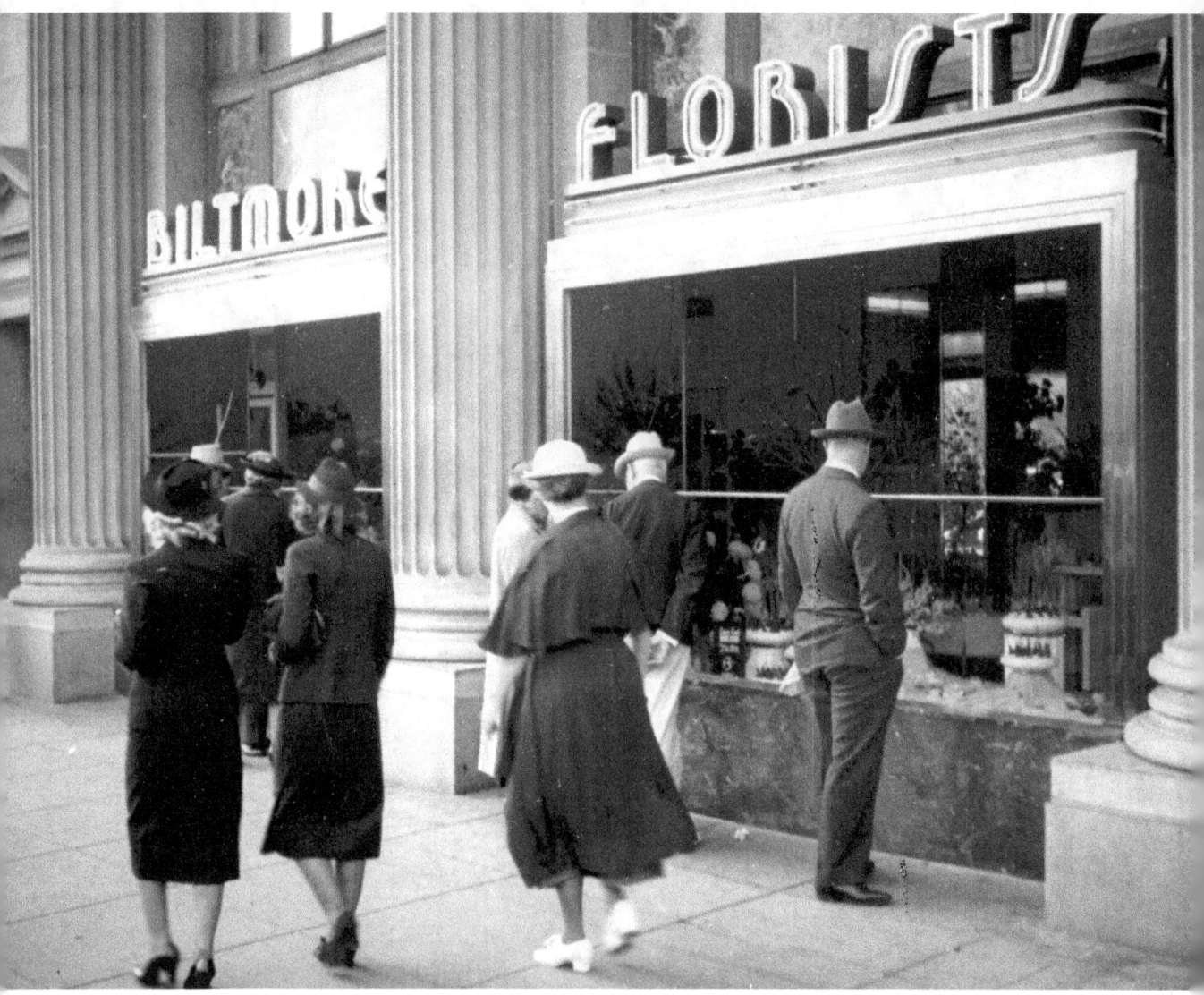

Pedestrians view the goods at the Biltmore Florists, located in the Biltmore Hotel
at Grand Avenue and Olive Street, ca. 1938. (Order #00072157)

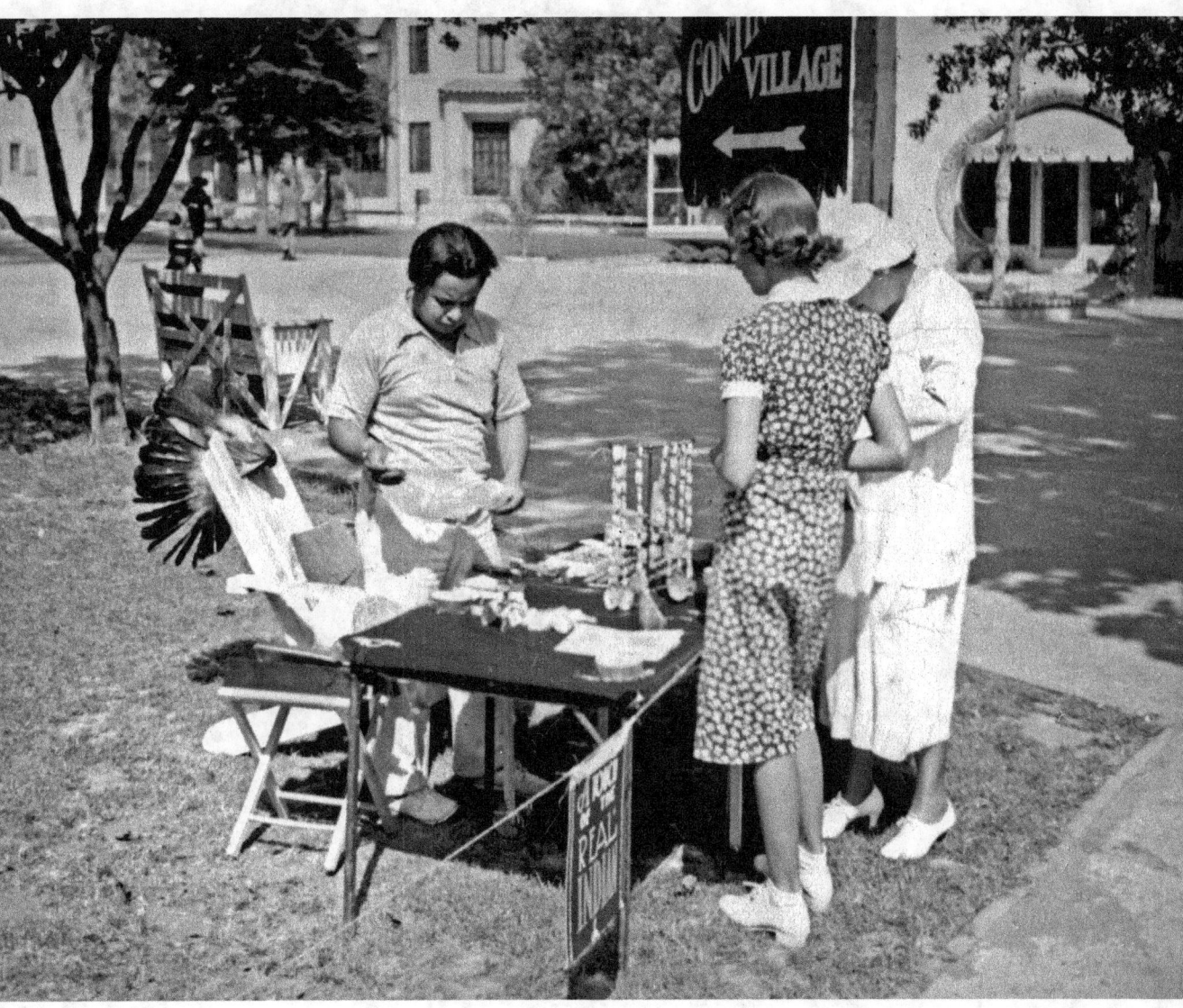

Two women shop for "real Indian" jewelry at Crossroads of the World,
6671 Sunset Boulevard, ca. 1937. (Order #00096866)

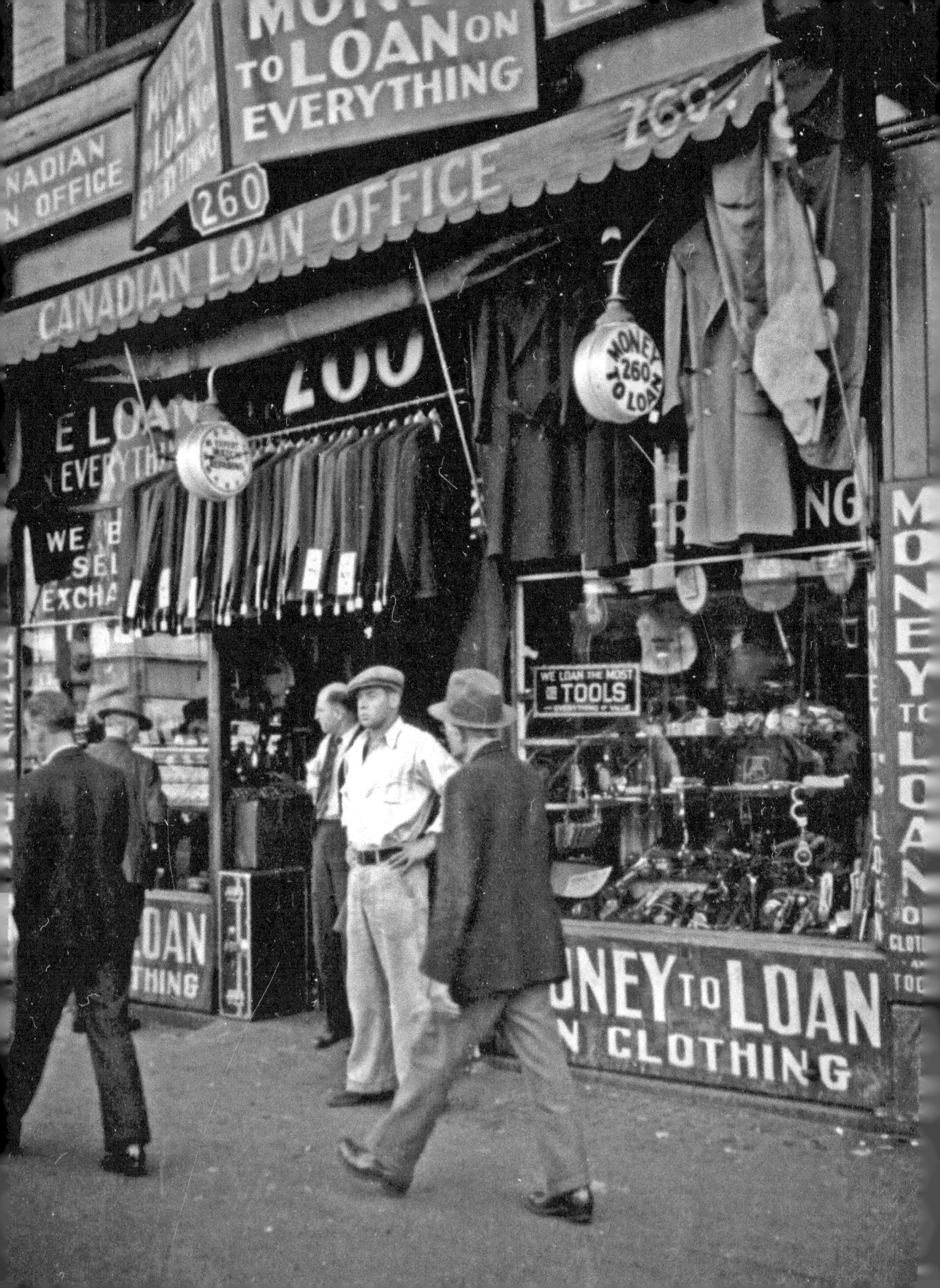
TO LOAN ON
EVERYTHING
260
CANADIAN LOAN OFFICE
MONEY 260 TO LOAN
WE LOAN THE MOST
TOOLS
MONEY TO LOAN
CLOTHING
LOAN
THING
NEY TO LOAN
N CLOTHING

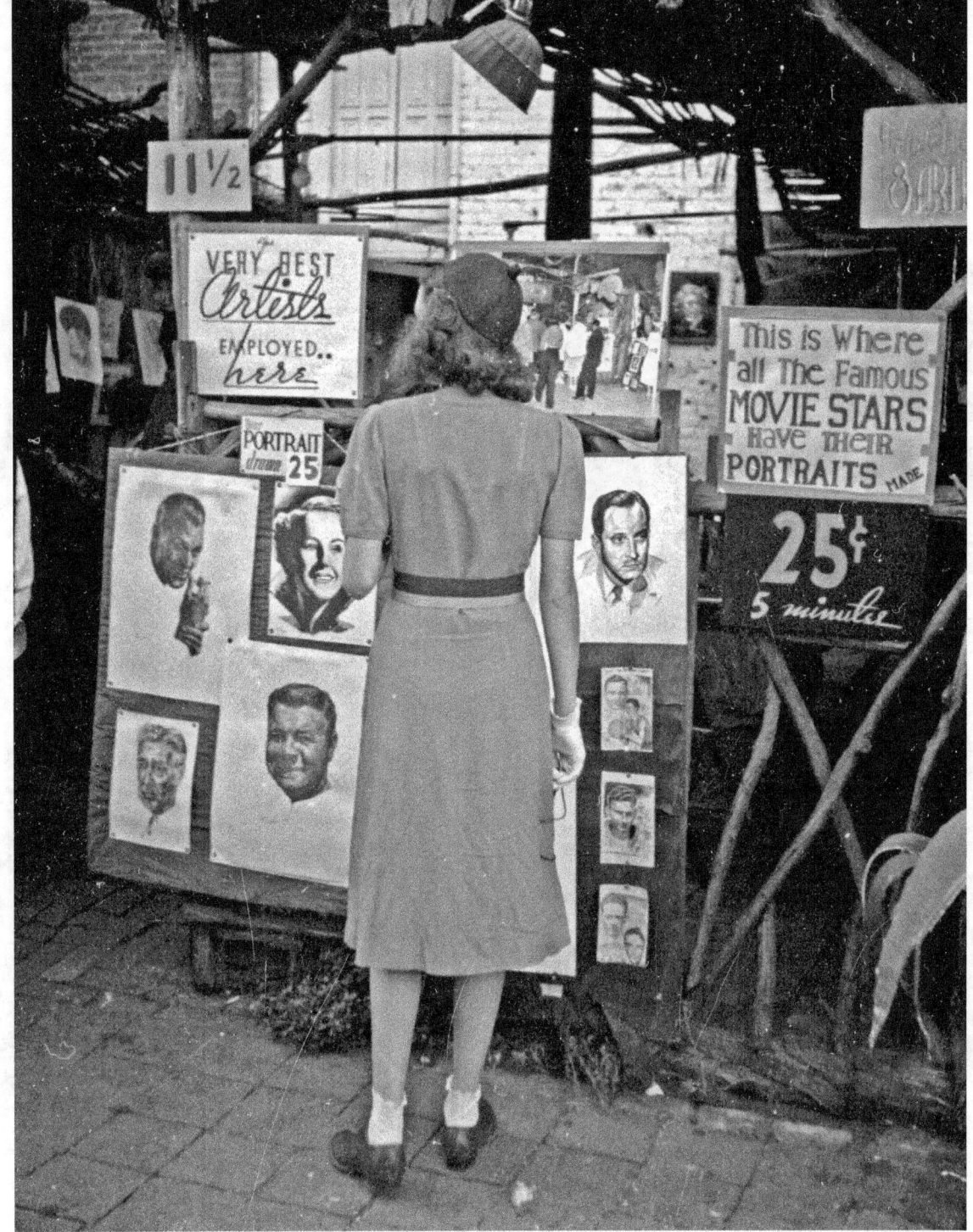

A woman shops for movie star portraits on Olvera Street, ca. 1937.
(Order #00097502)

Opposite: Men walk past the Canadian Loan Office (aka pawnshop)
at 260 East Fifth Street, ca. 1937. (Order #00097196)

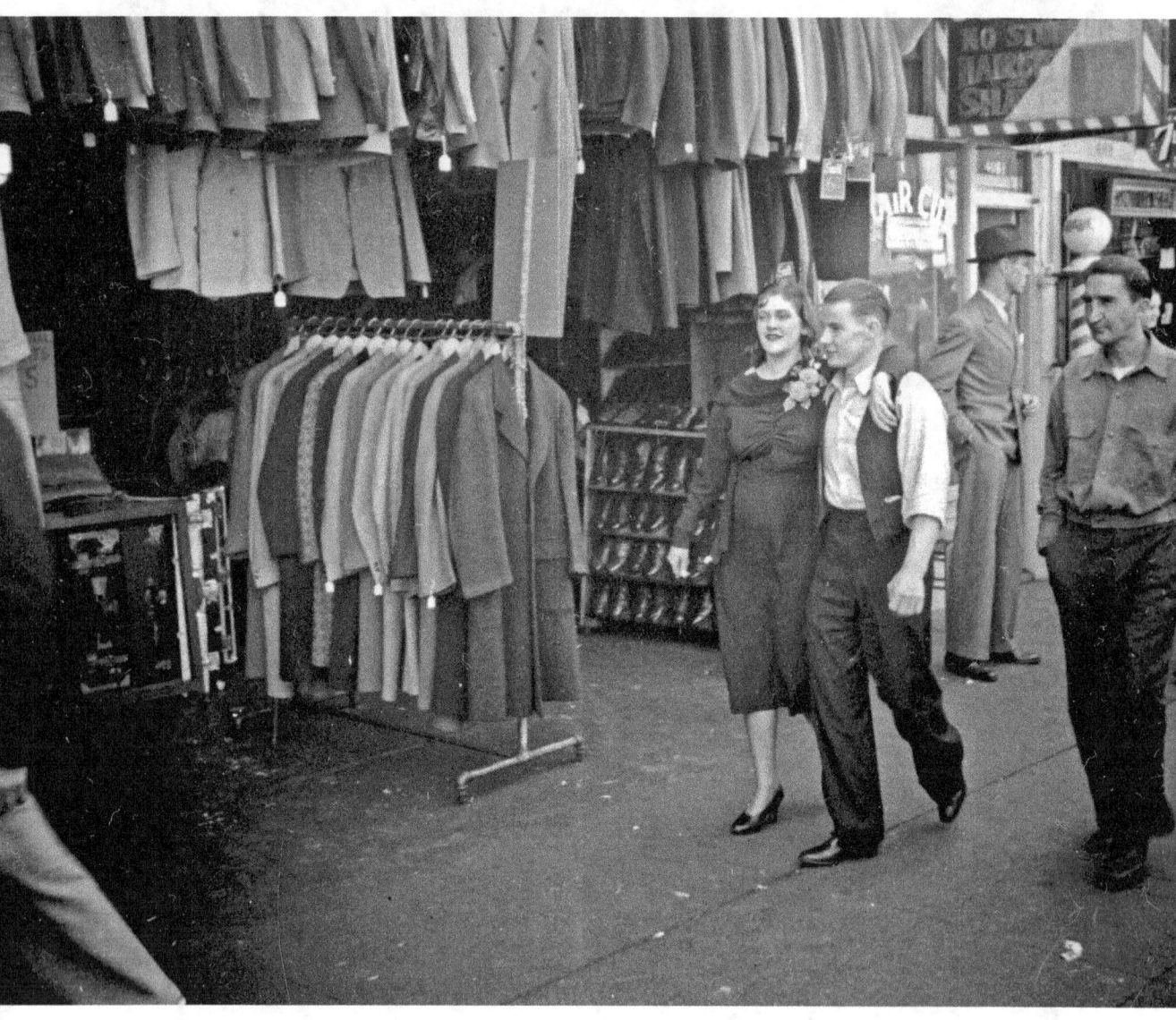

A couple strolls passed Joe Goldes second hand clothing store
at 410 East Fifth Street, ca. 1937. (Order #00097524)

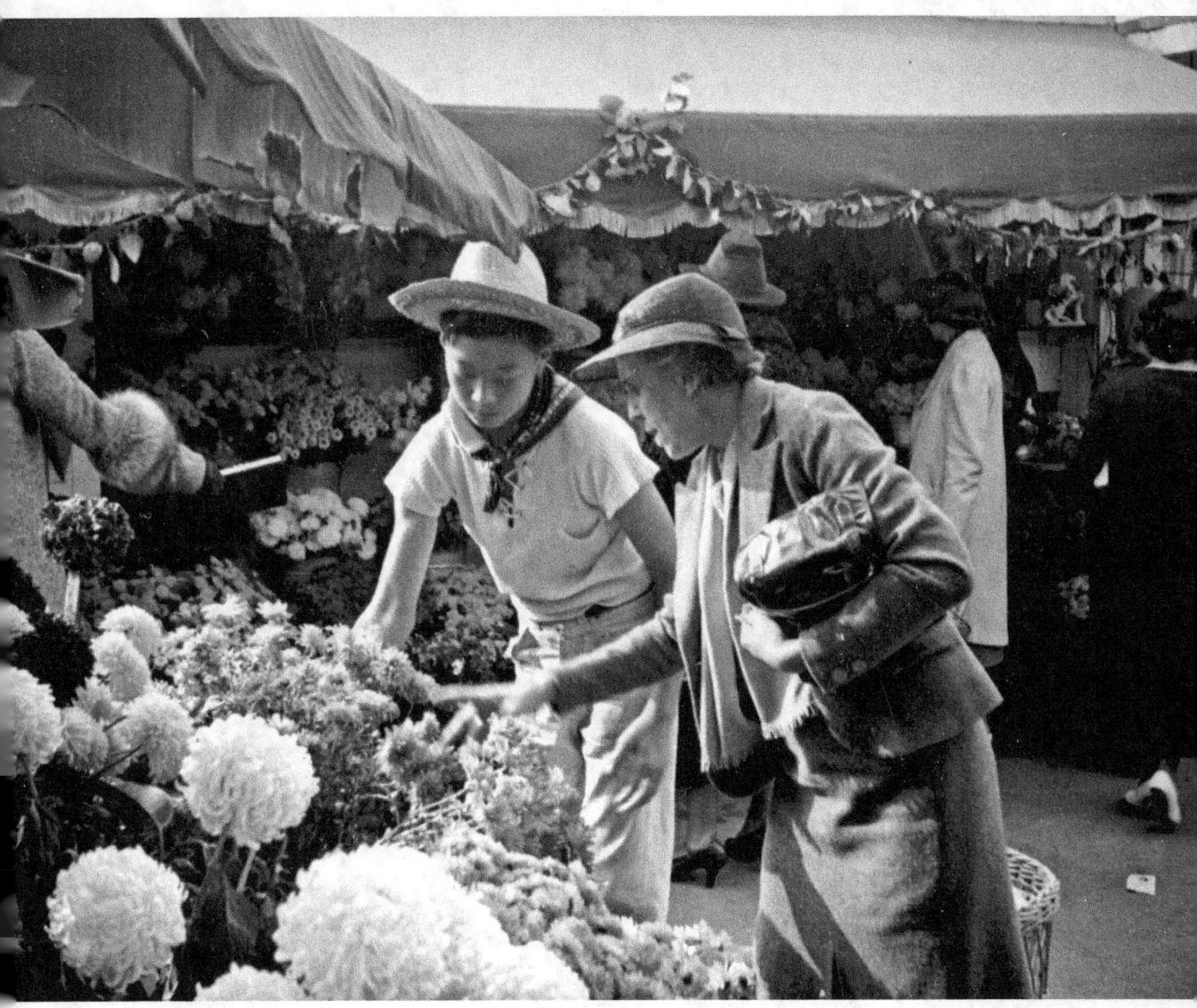

A shopper selects flowers at the Farmers Market at
3rd Street and Fairfax Avenue in 1937. (Order #00097802)

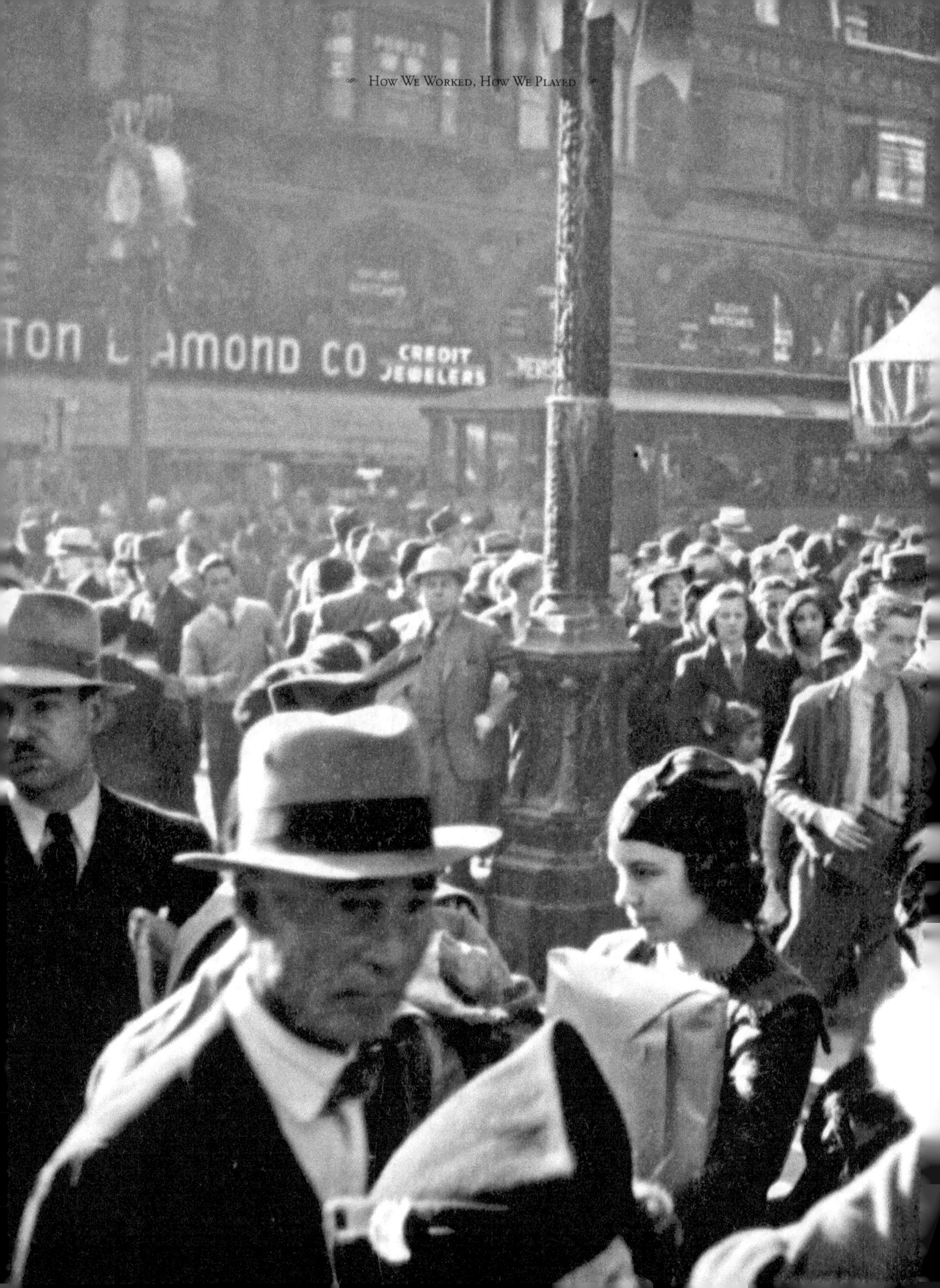
CREDIT
JEWELERS

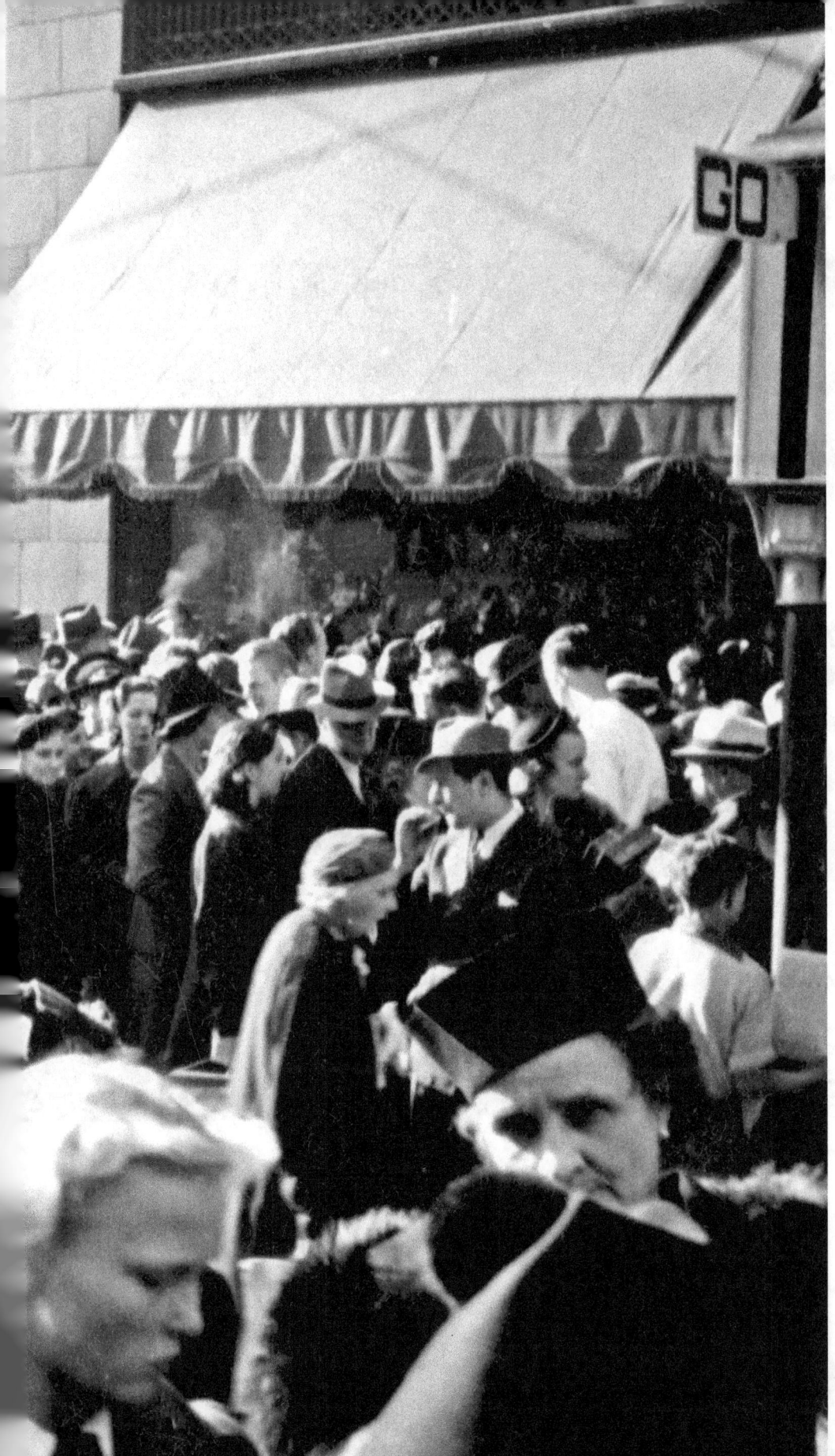

Holiday crowds at 7th Street and Broadway, ca. 1937. (Order #00098749)

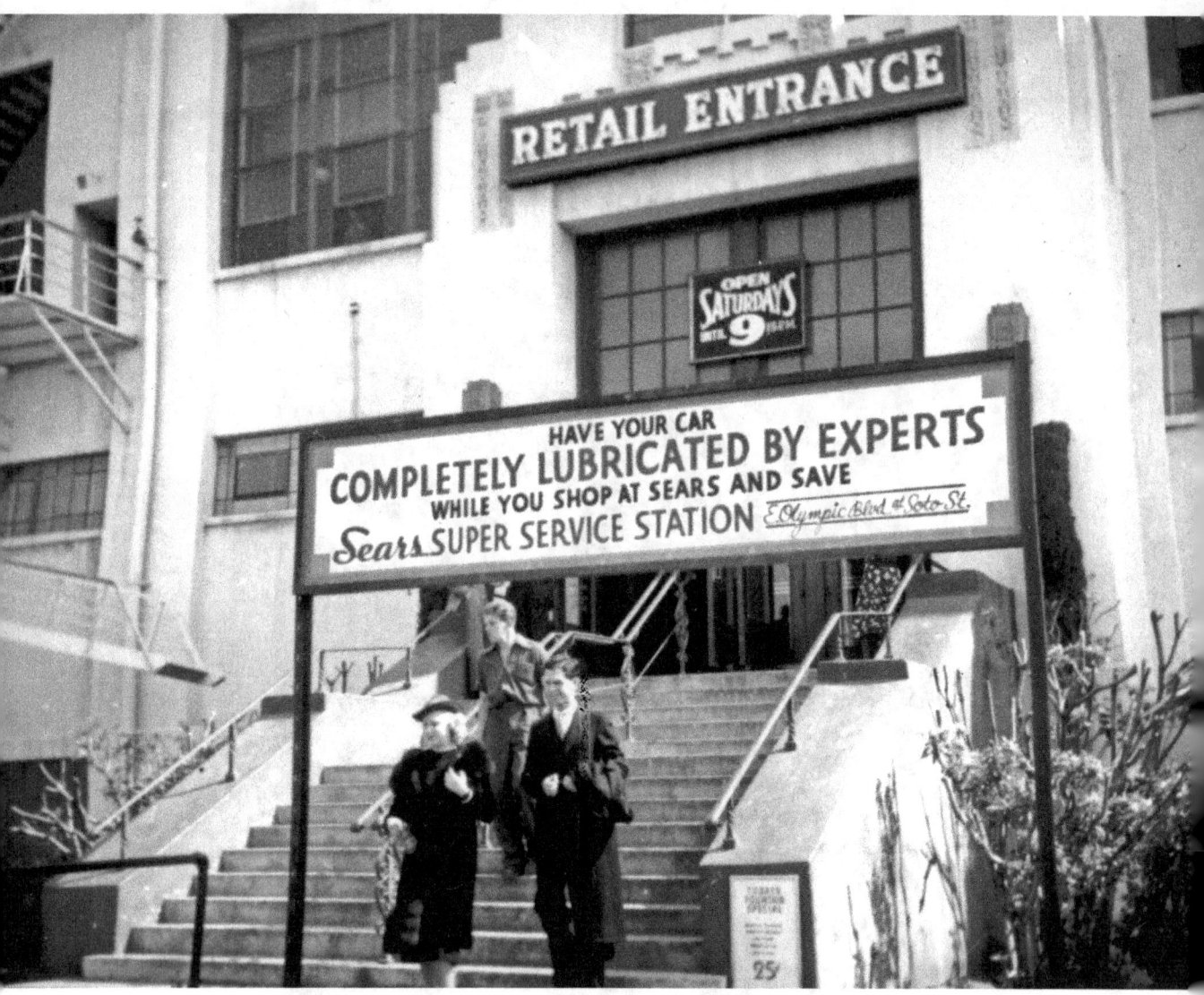

Consumers exit Sears at 2650 East Olympic Boulevard
in Boyle Heights, ca. 1938. (Order #00099123)

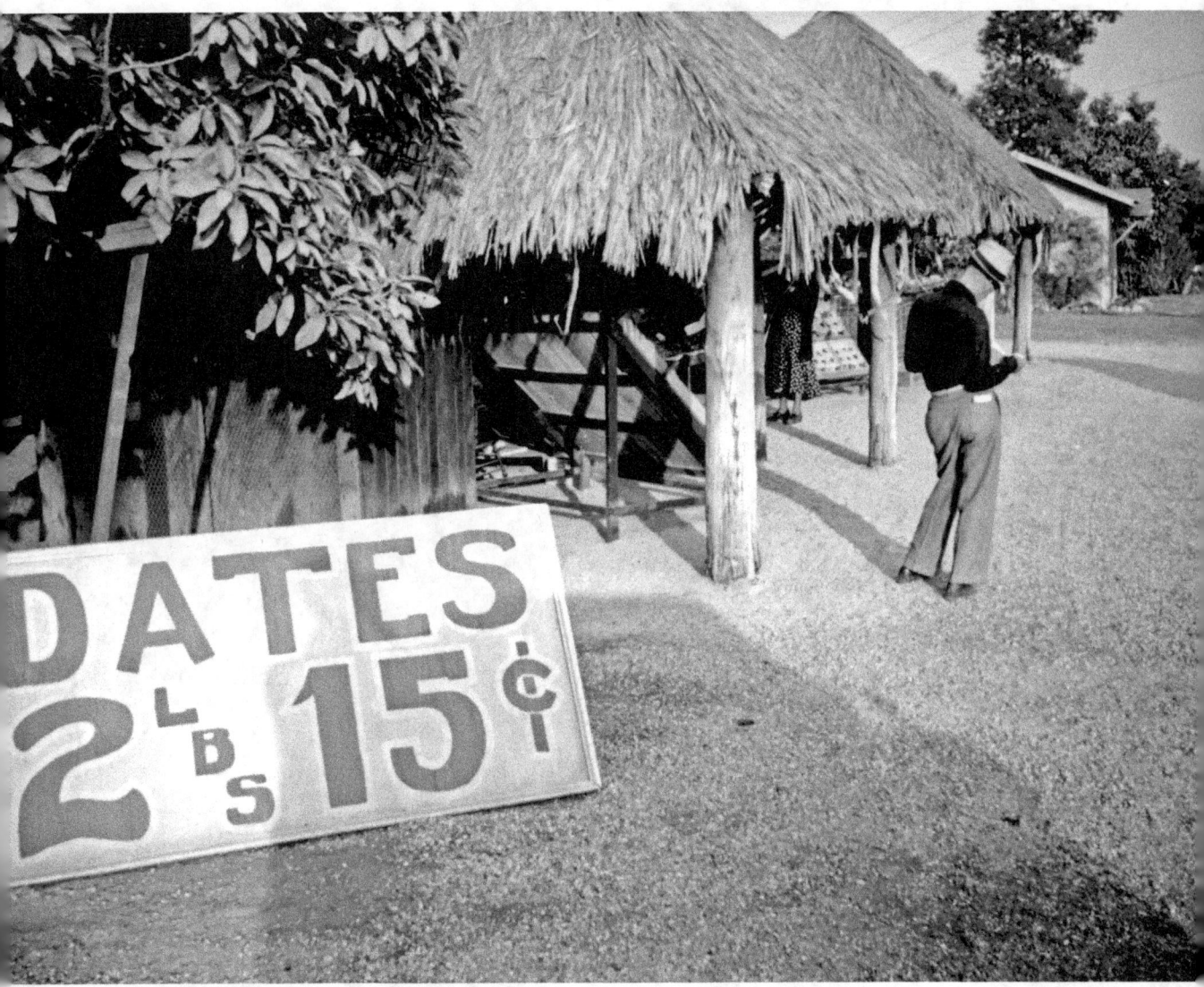

A large sign advertises two pounds of dates for 15 cents at Chase's Avocado Hut,
located at 1813 East Foothill Boulevard in Duarte, ca. 1937. (Order #00097964)

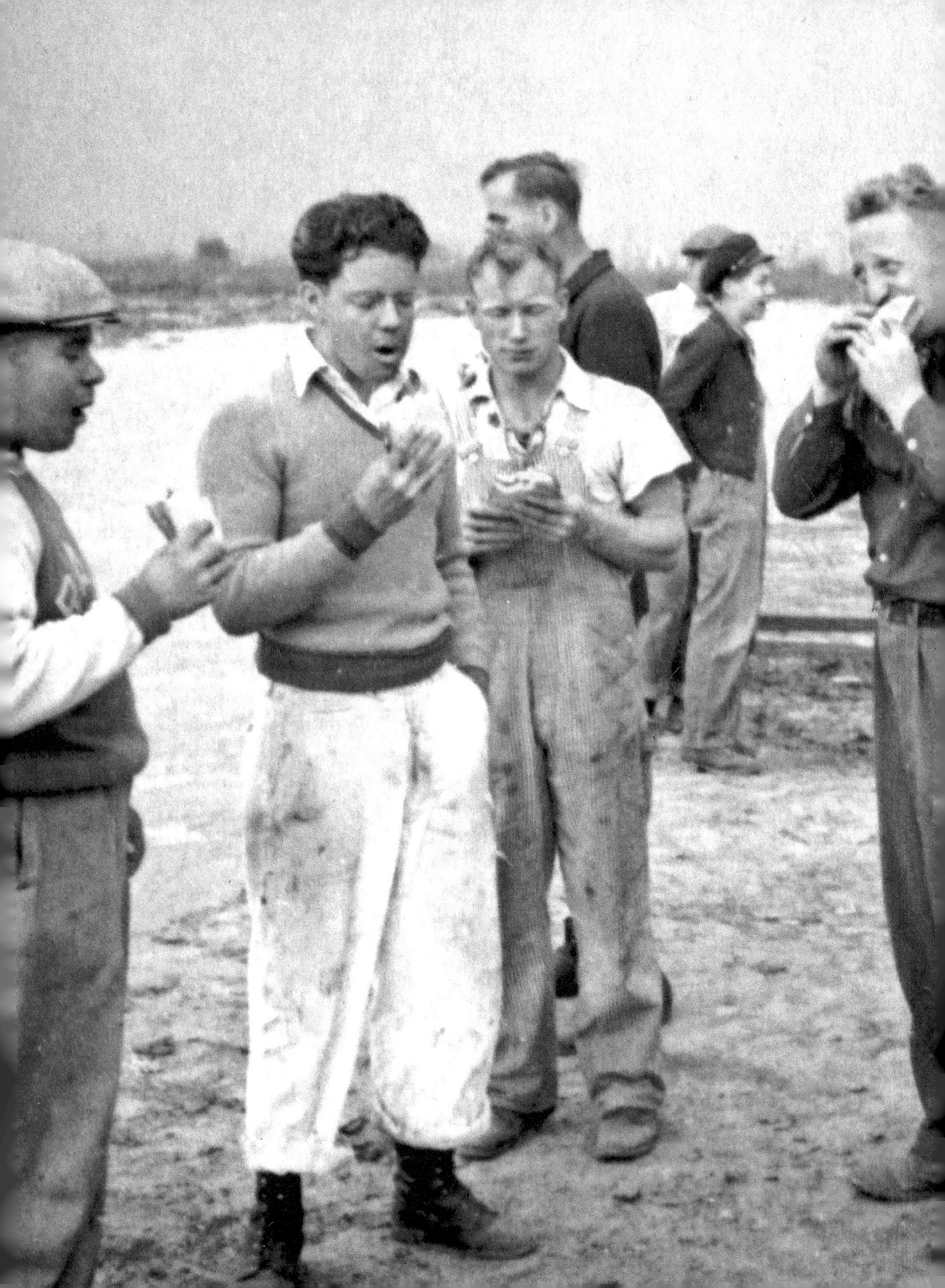

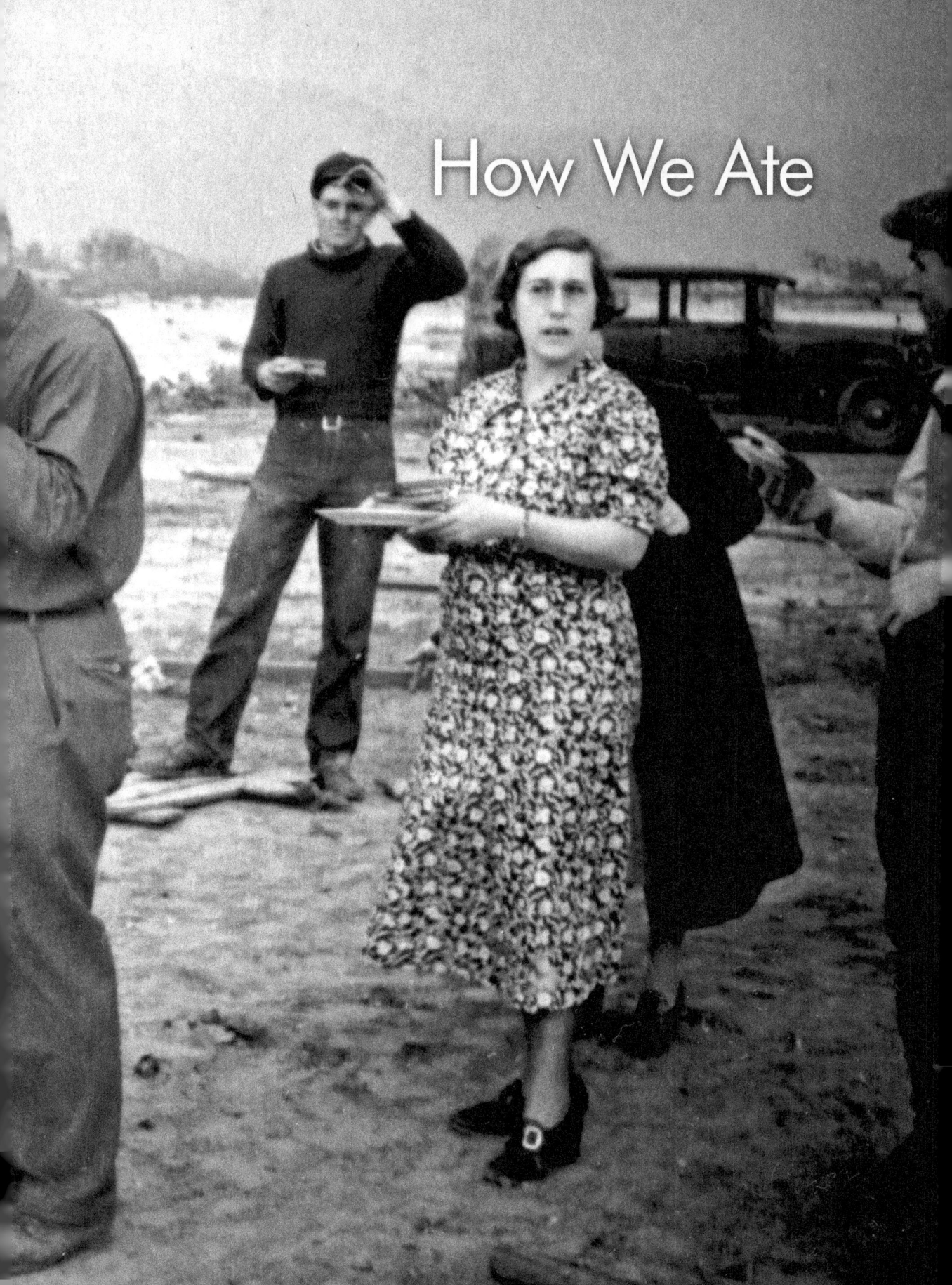

How We Ate

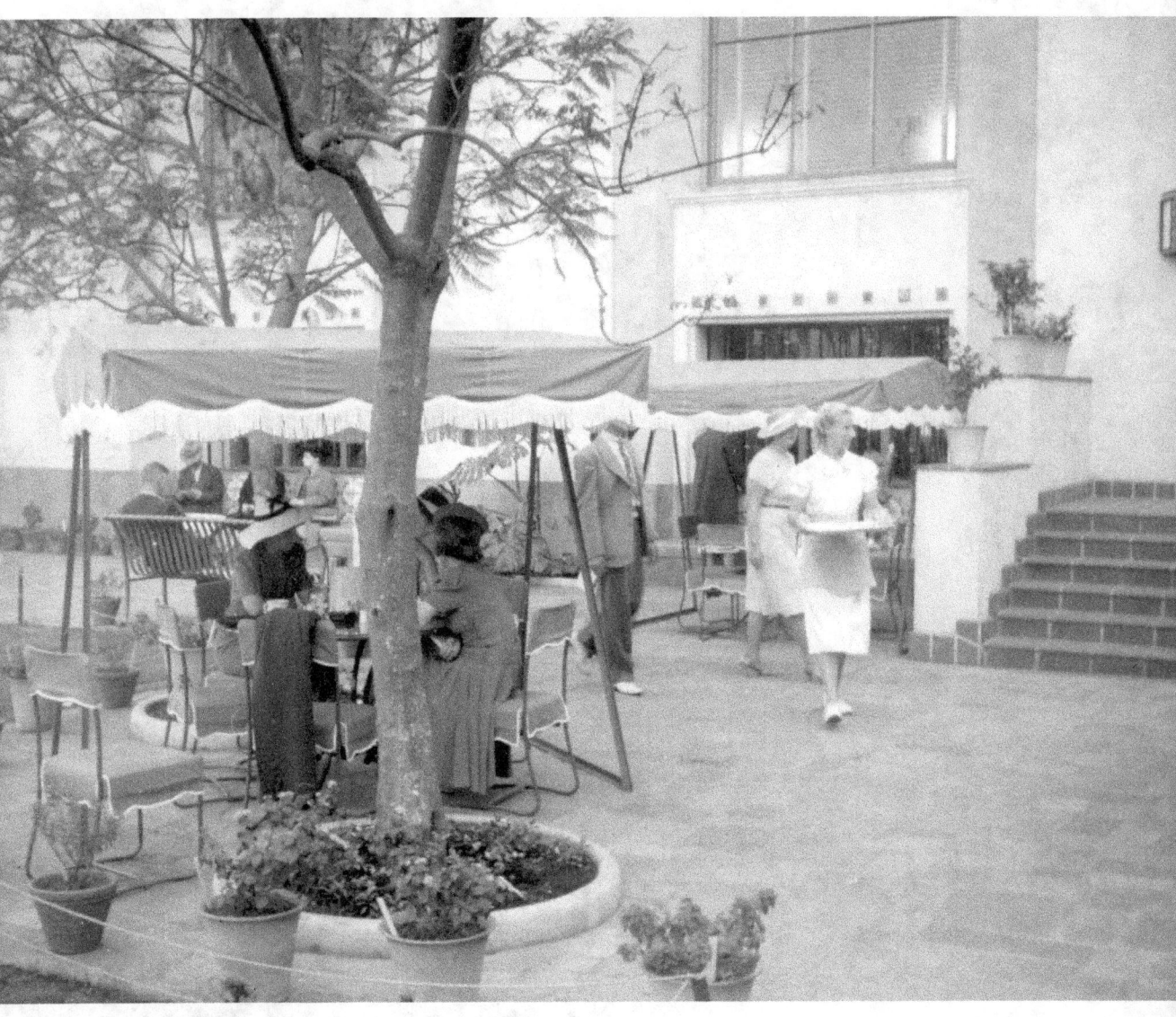

Customers relax at the Union Station courtyard café, ca. 1939.
(Order #00077957)

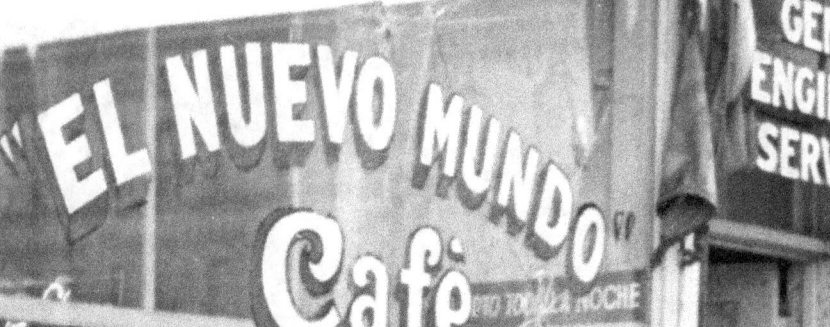
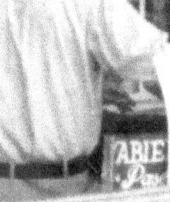

"EL NUEVO MUNDO" Café

112
GENERAL
ENGINEERING
SERVICE CO

COMIDAS CORRIDAS desde 15 20 Y 25

CERVEZA
de Barril
y VINO

ALMUERZO y
LONCHES
PARA AFUERA 15 20

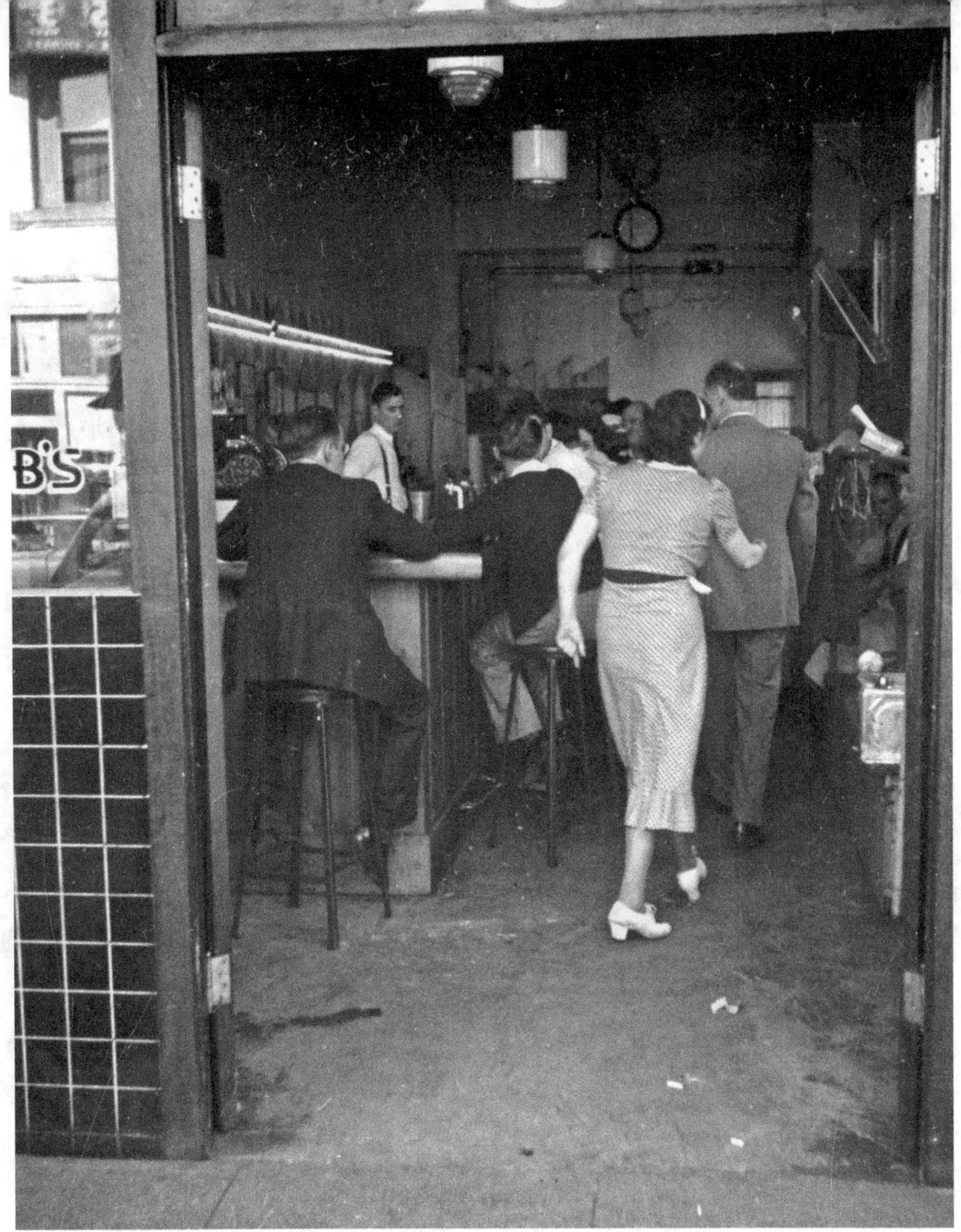

Customers inside a bar on the 200 block of
South Main Street, ca. 1937. (Order #00097523)

Opposite: Offerings advertised outside the El Nuevo Mundo Café,
near 1st and Main Streets, ca. 1937. (Order #00097515)

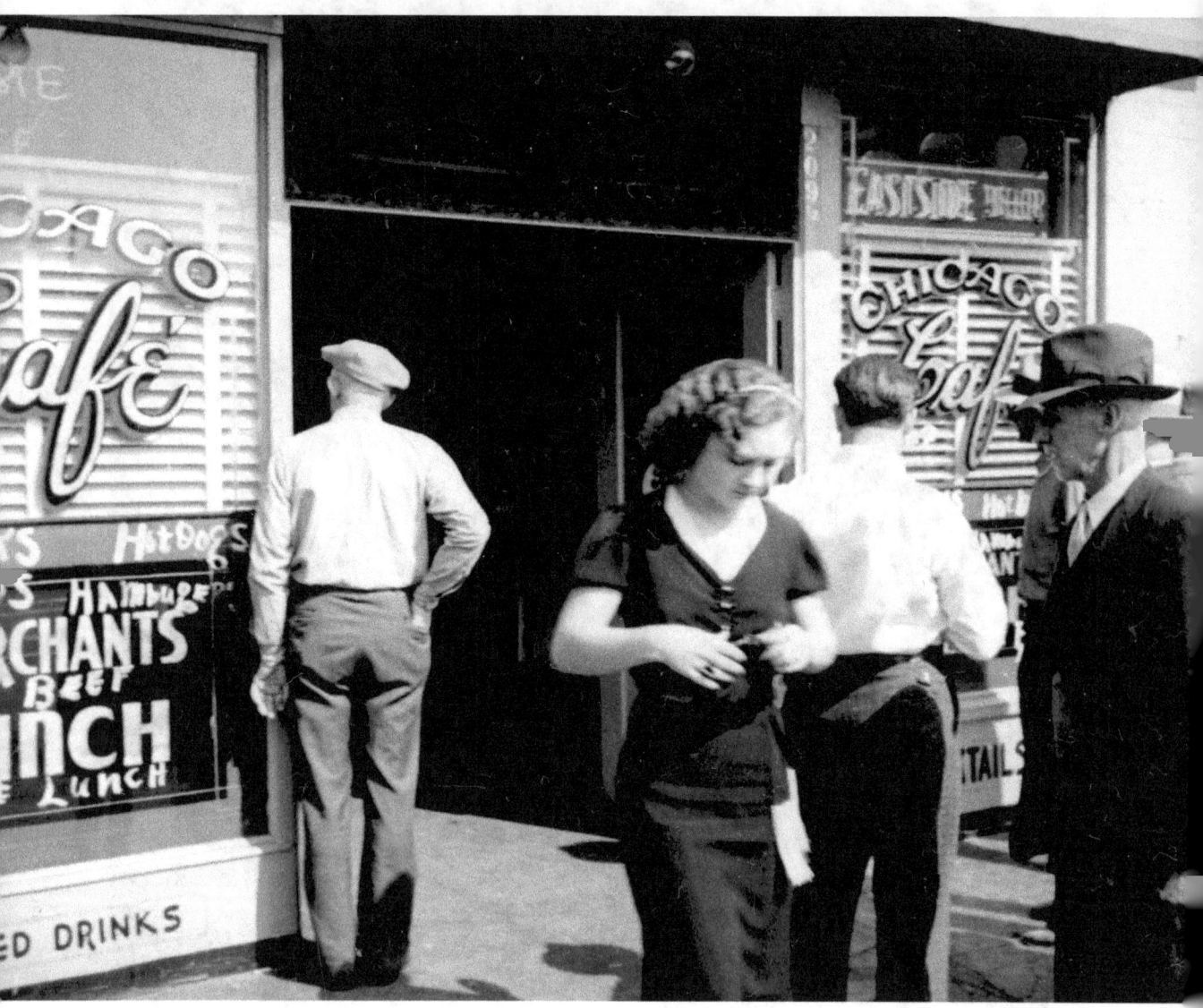

People flow in and out of the Chicago Café at
209 East Fifth Street, ca. 1937. (Order #00097526)

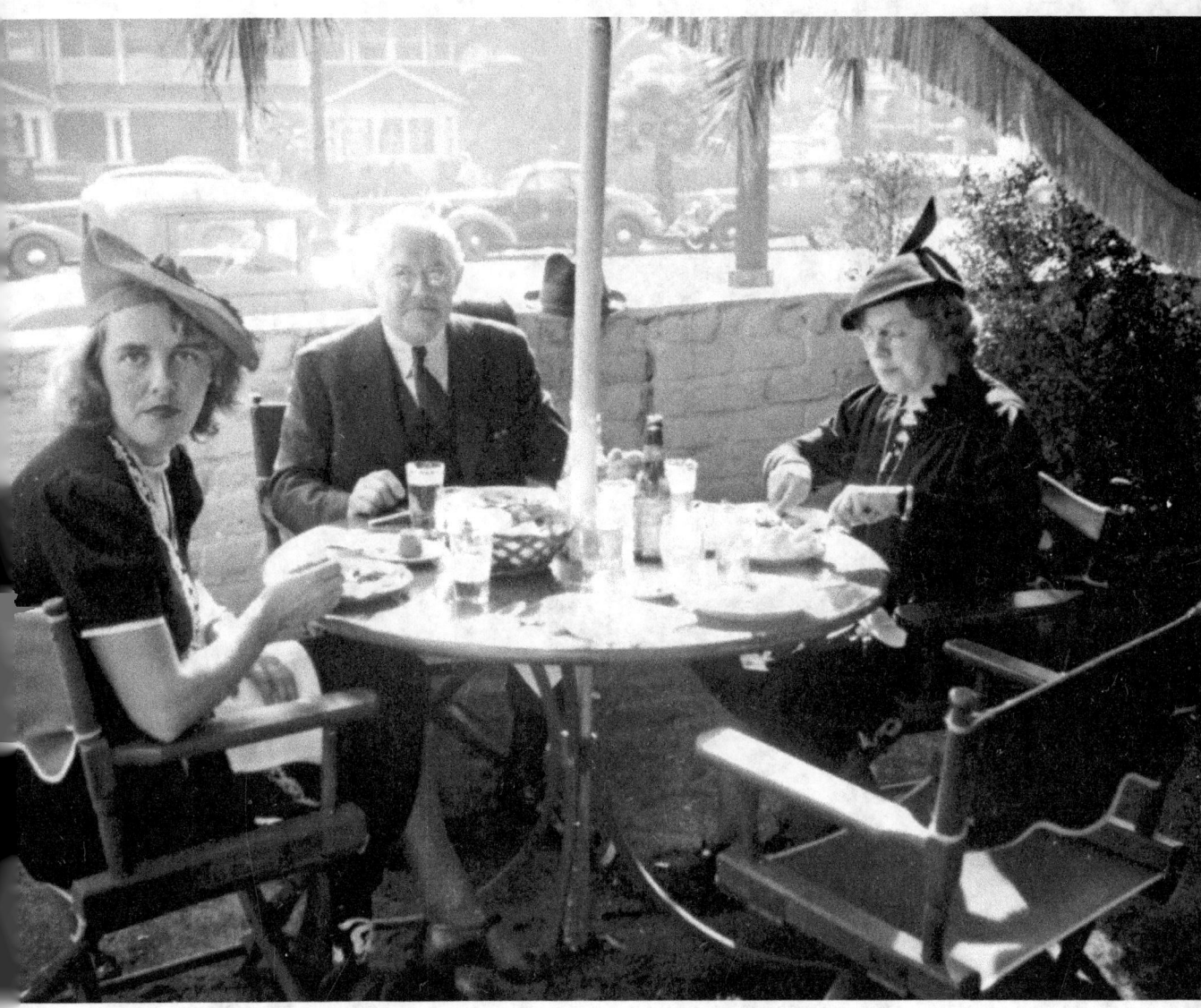

Ethel Schultheis, with parents Theodore and Marie Wisloh, dine on the patio of the Palms Grill at 5931 Hollywood Boulevard, ca. 1937. (Order #00098807)

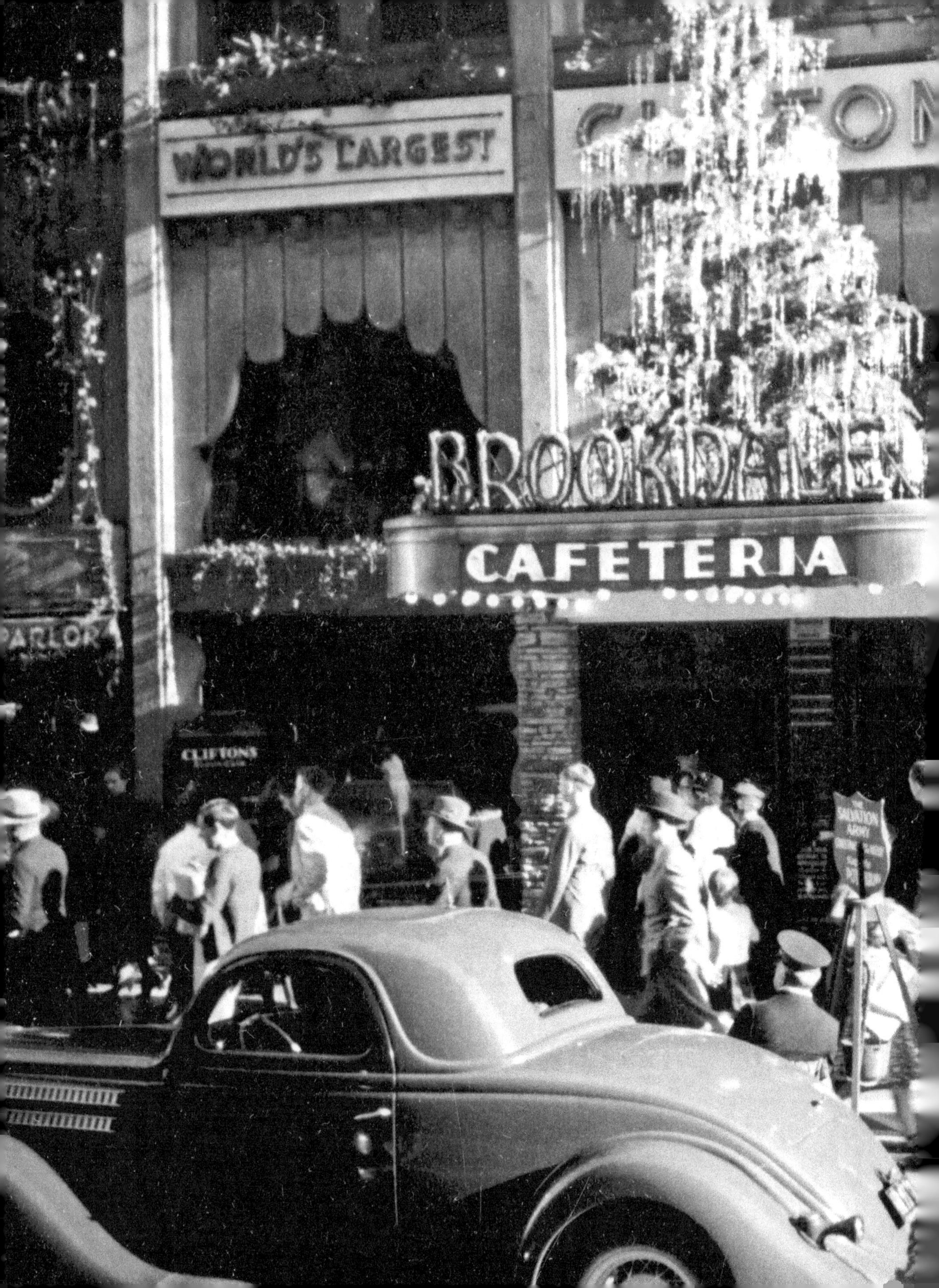
WORLD'S LARGEST
BROOKDALE
CAFETERIA
PARLOR
CLIFTONS
SALVATION ARMY

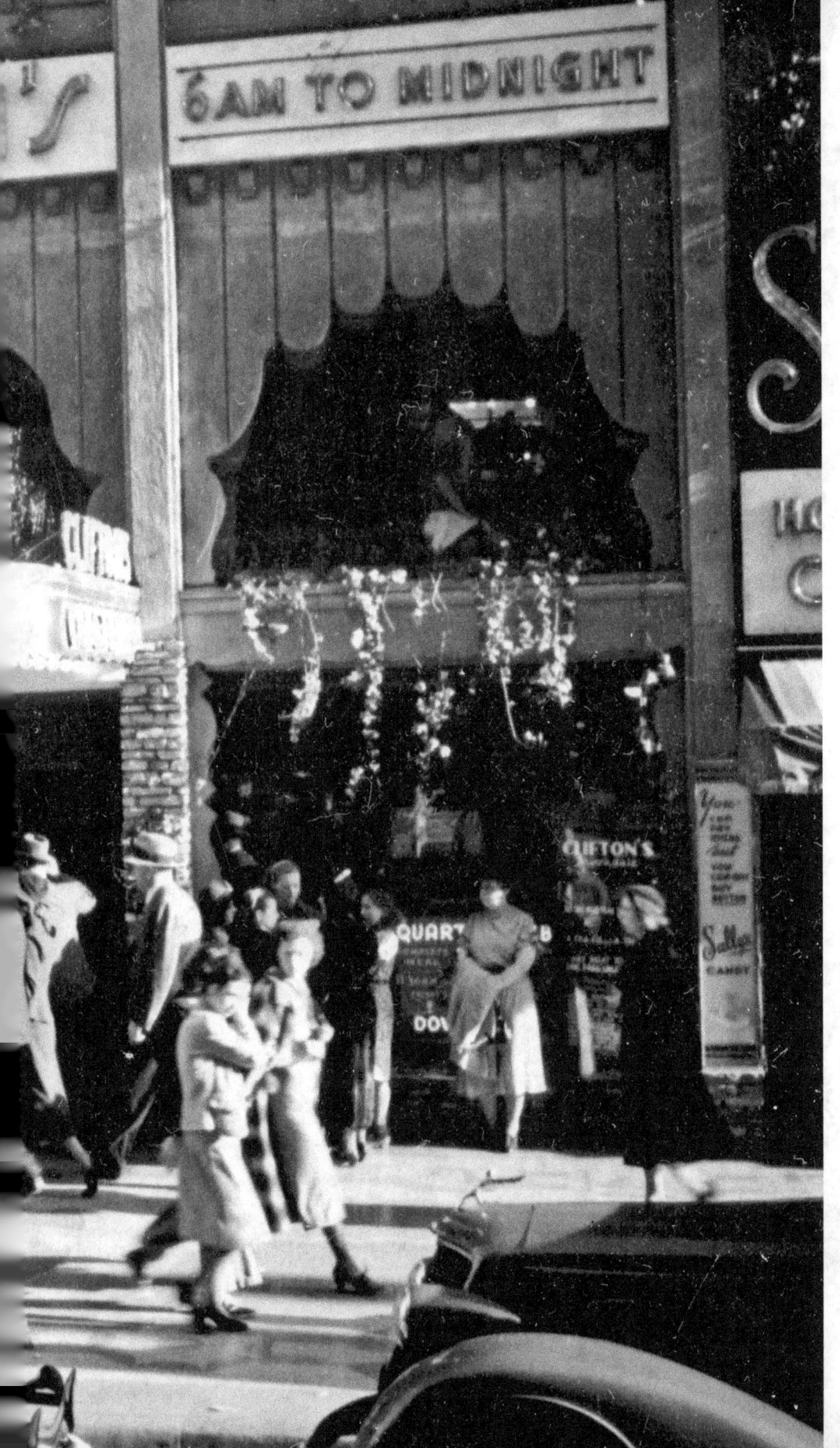

Crowds shopping on Broadway at Christmas walk past Clifton's Brookdale Cafeteria, ca. 1937. (Order #00098746)

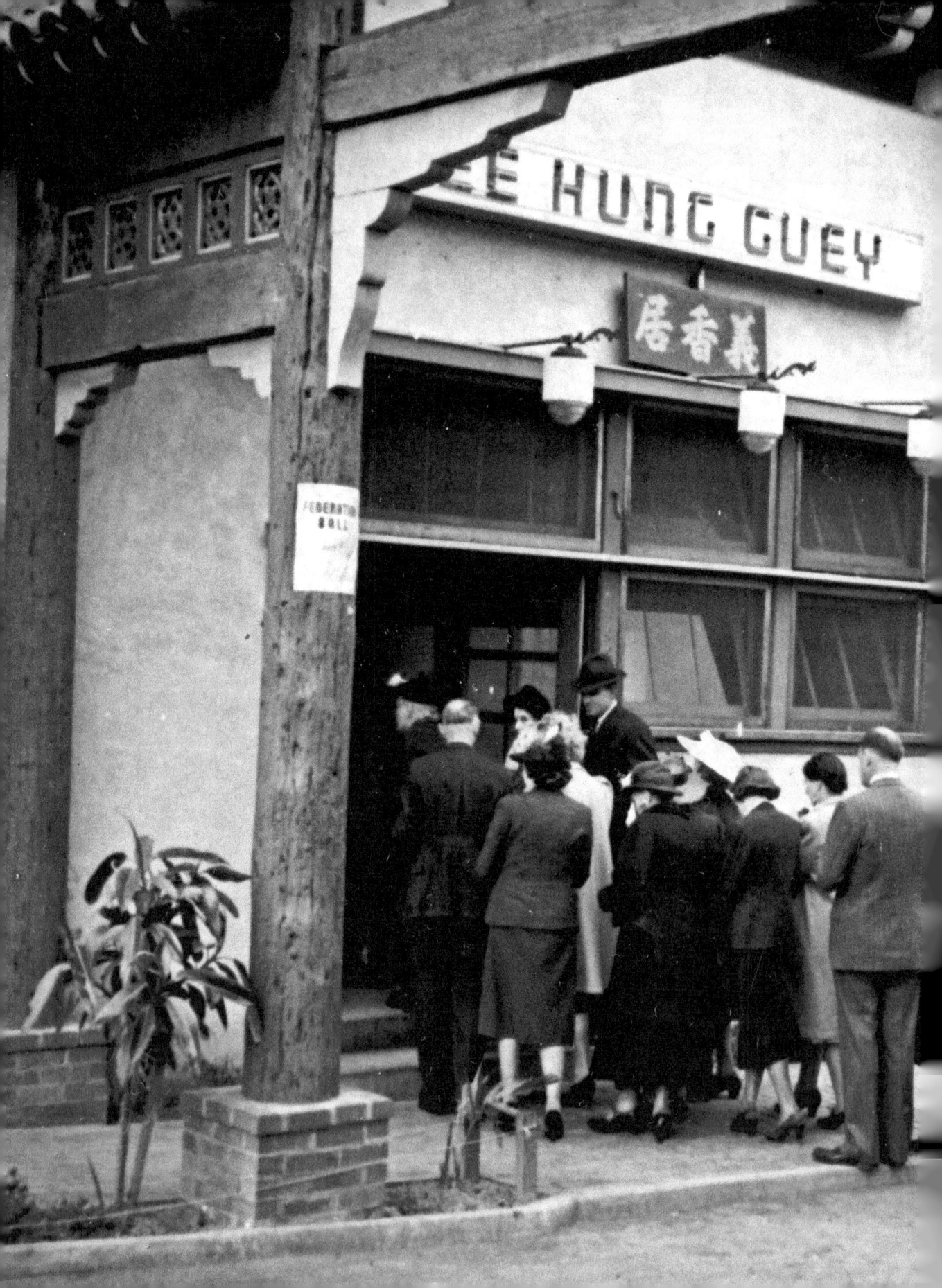

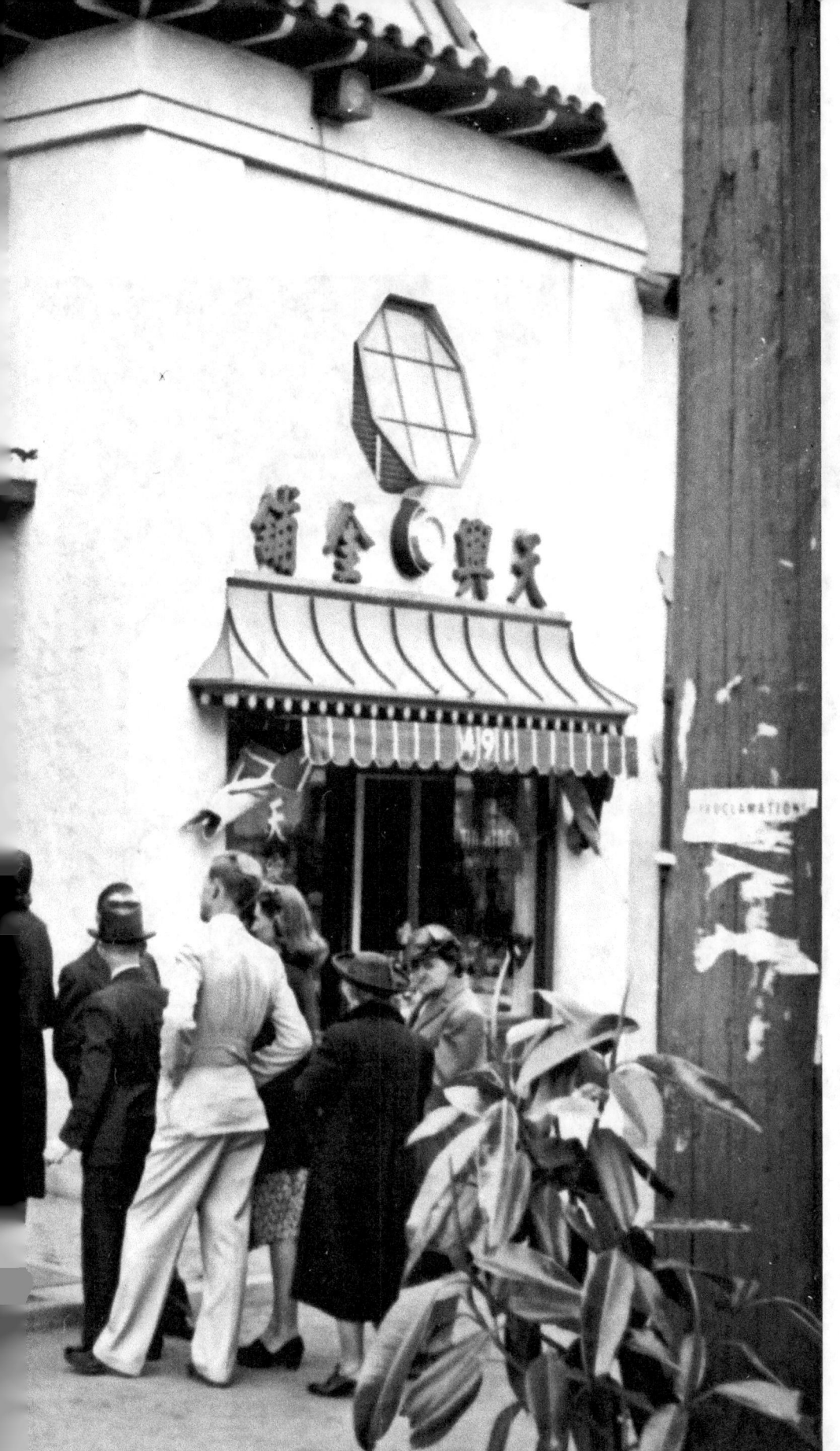

People form a line out the door of the Yee Hung Guey restaurant in New Chinatown, ca. 1937. (Order #00101120)

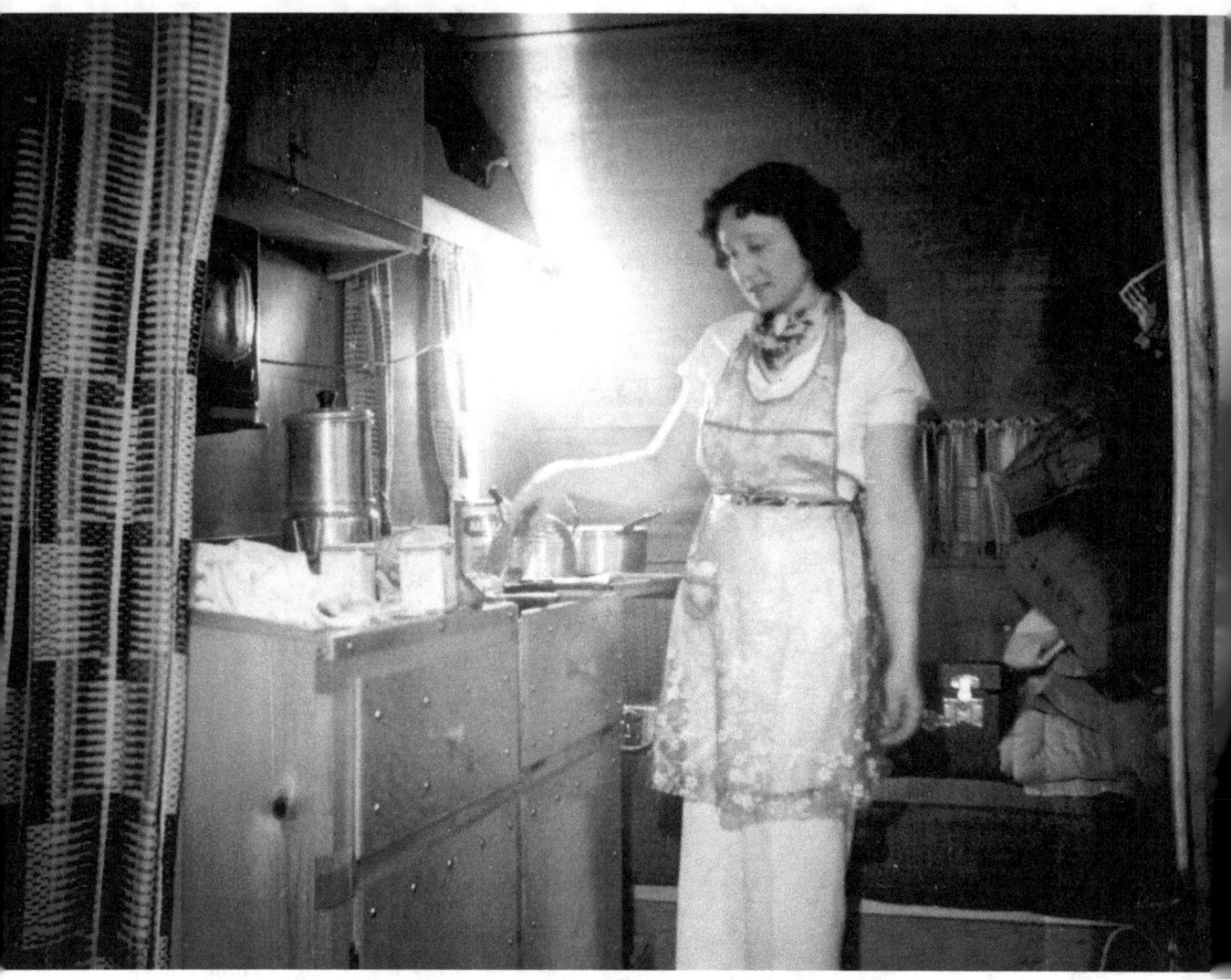

A woman in an apron prepares dinner in a trailer
in Palm Springs, ca. 1938. (Order #00099798)

Opposite: A Schultheis family friend cuts a bun for sandwiches at this picnic style lunch,
possibly near the San Fernando Mission, ca. 1938. (Order #00101371)

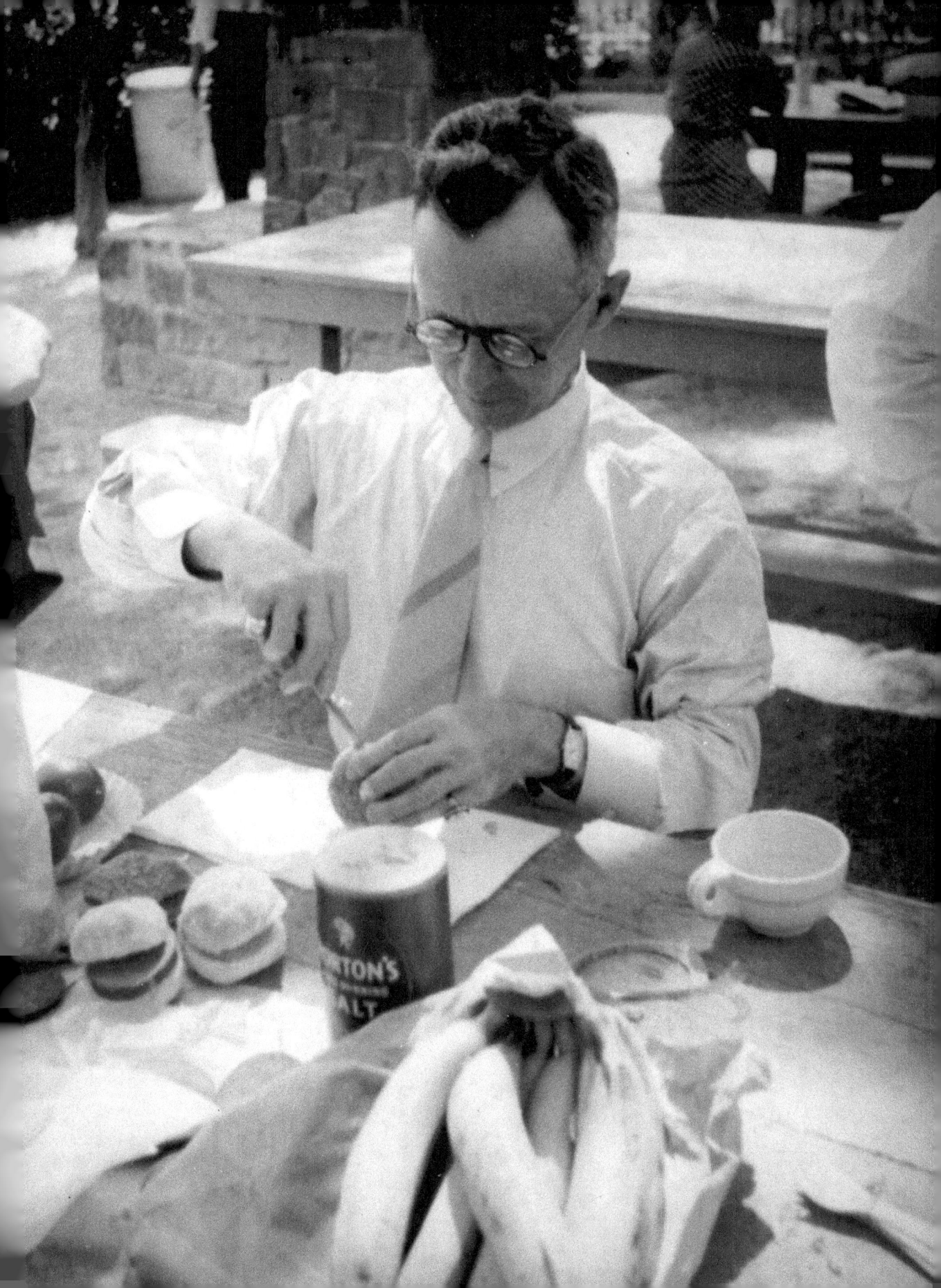

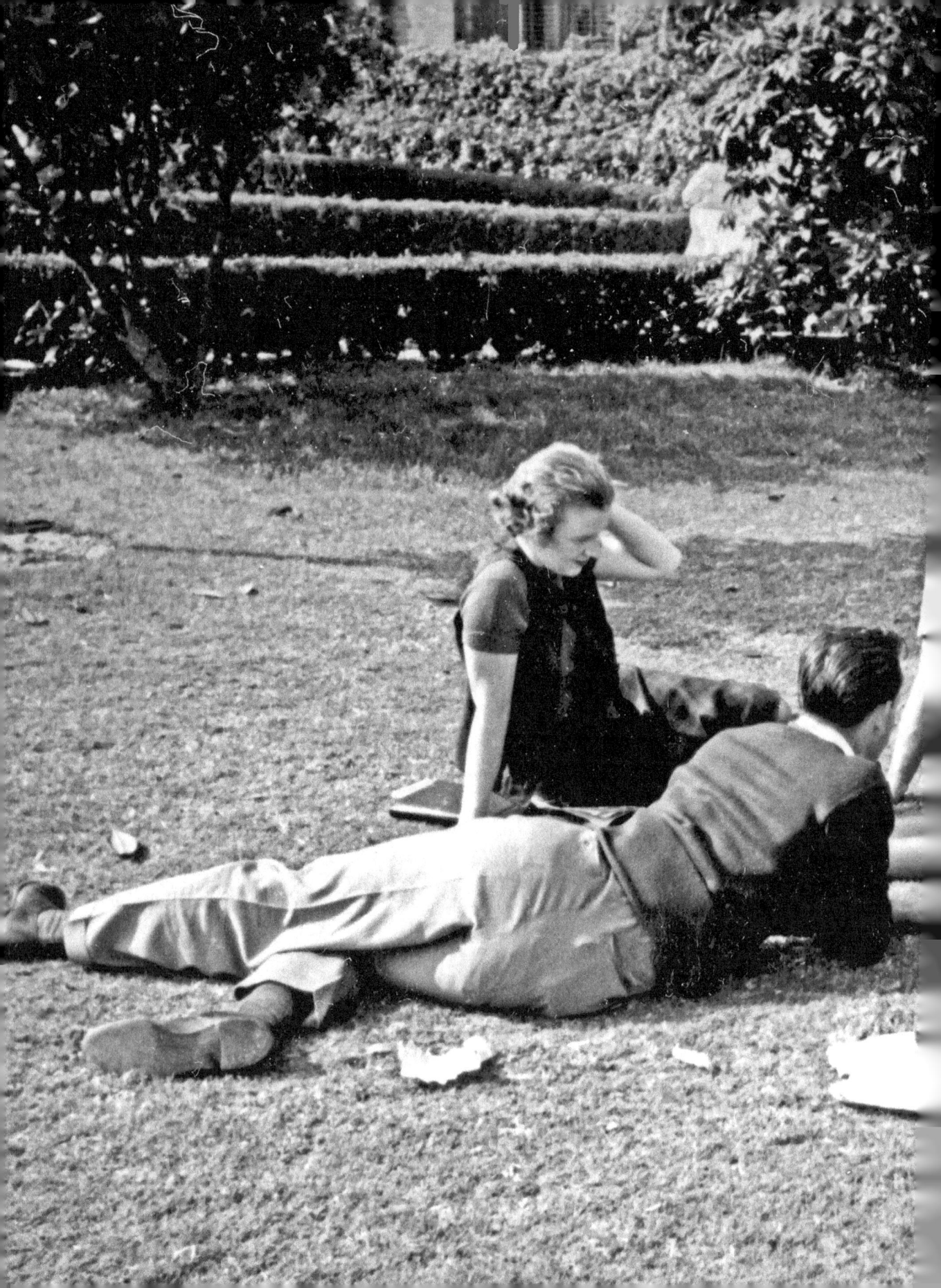

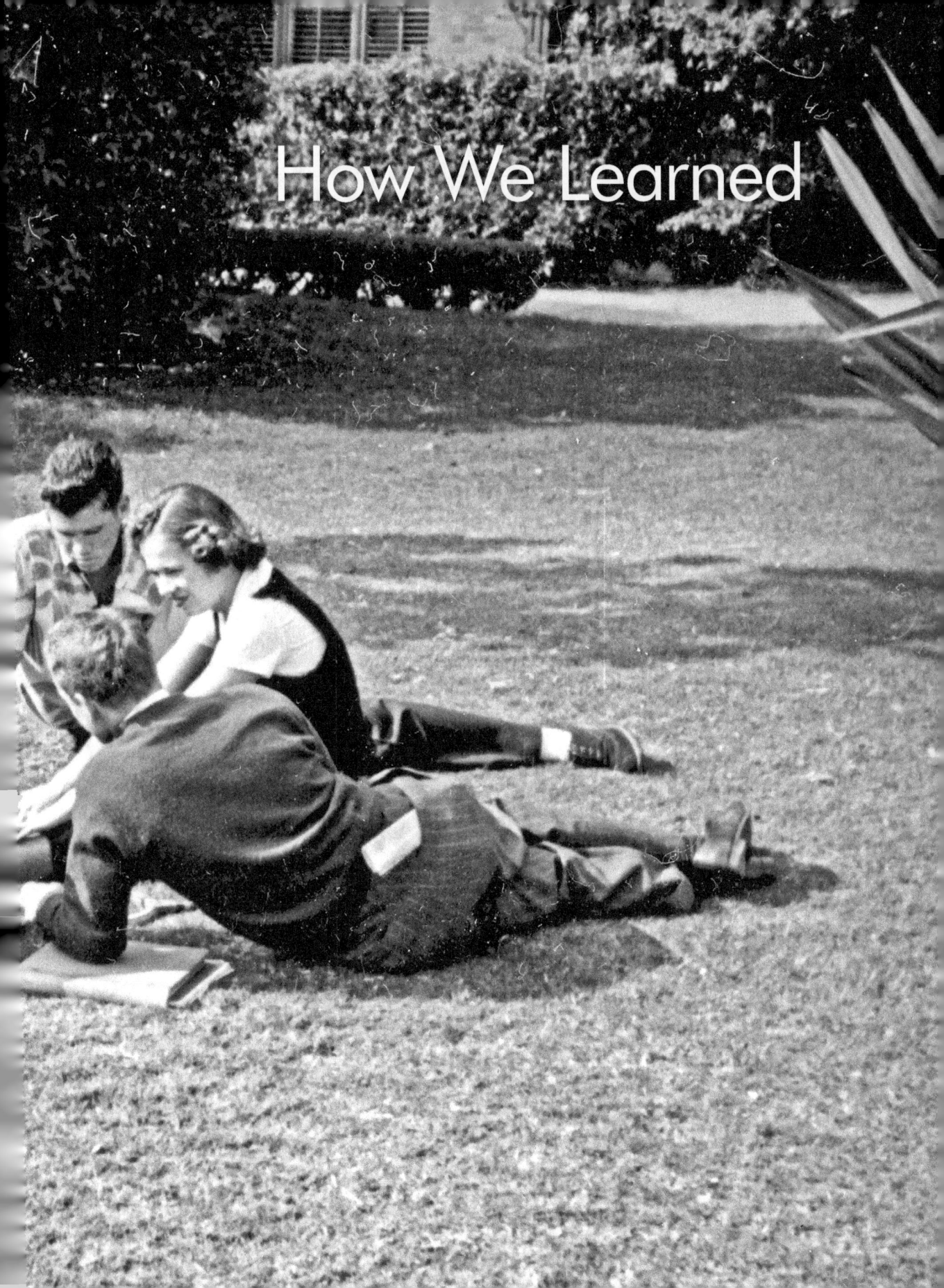

How We Learned

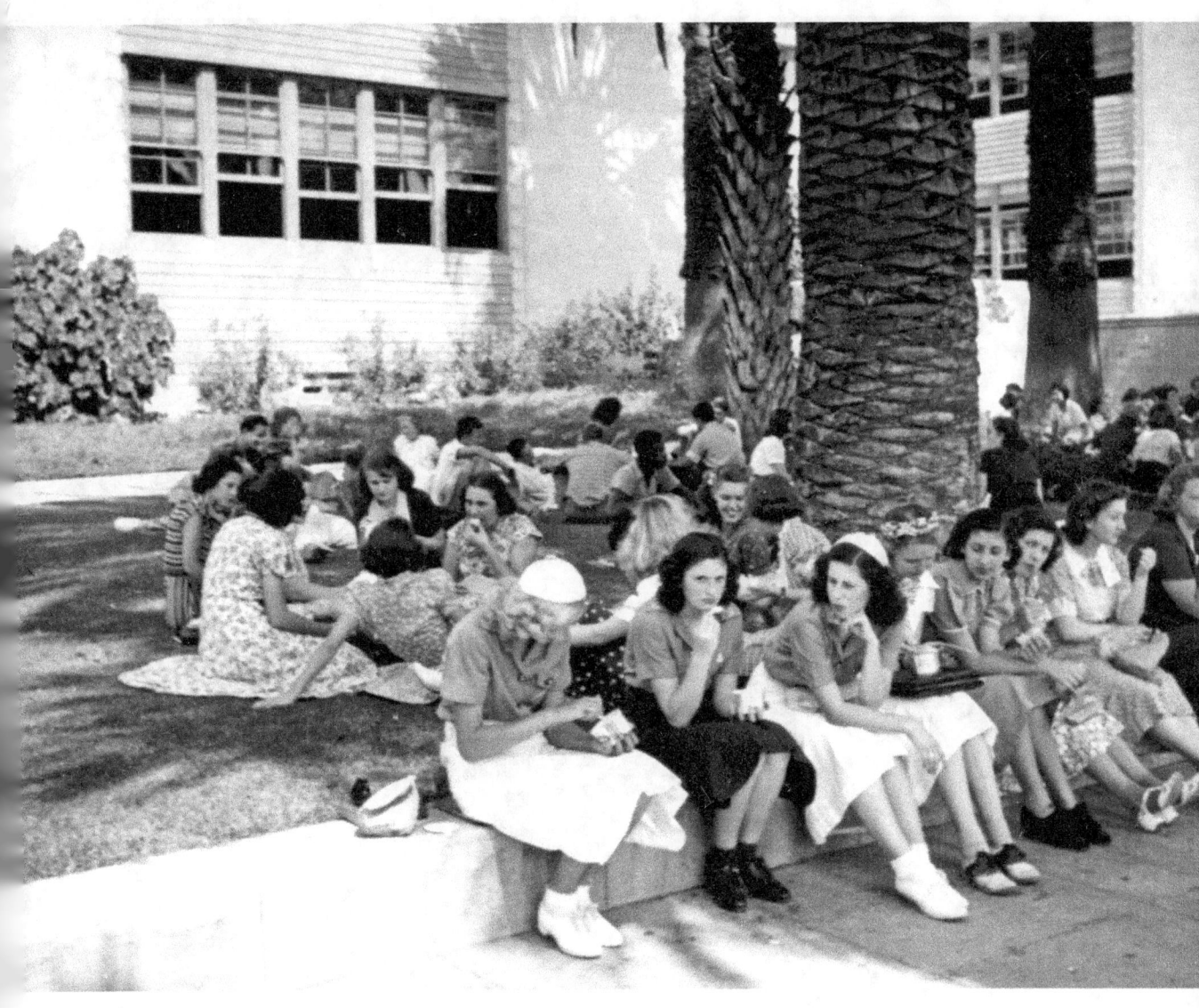

Students during a lunch break at Hollywood High, ca. 1937.
(Order #00071272)

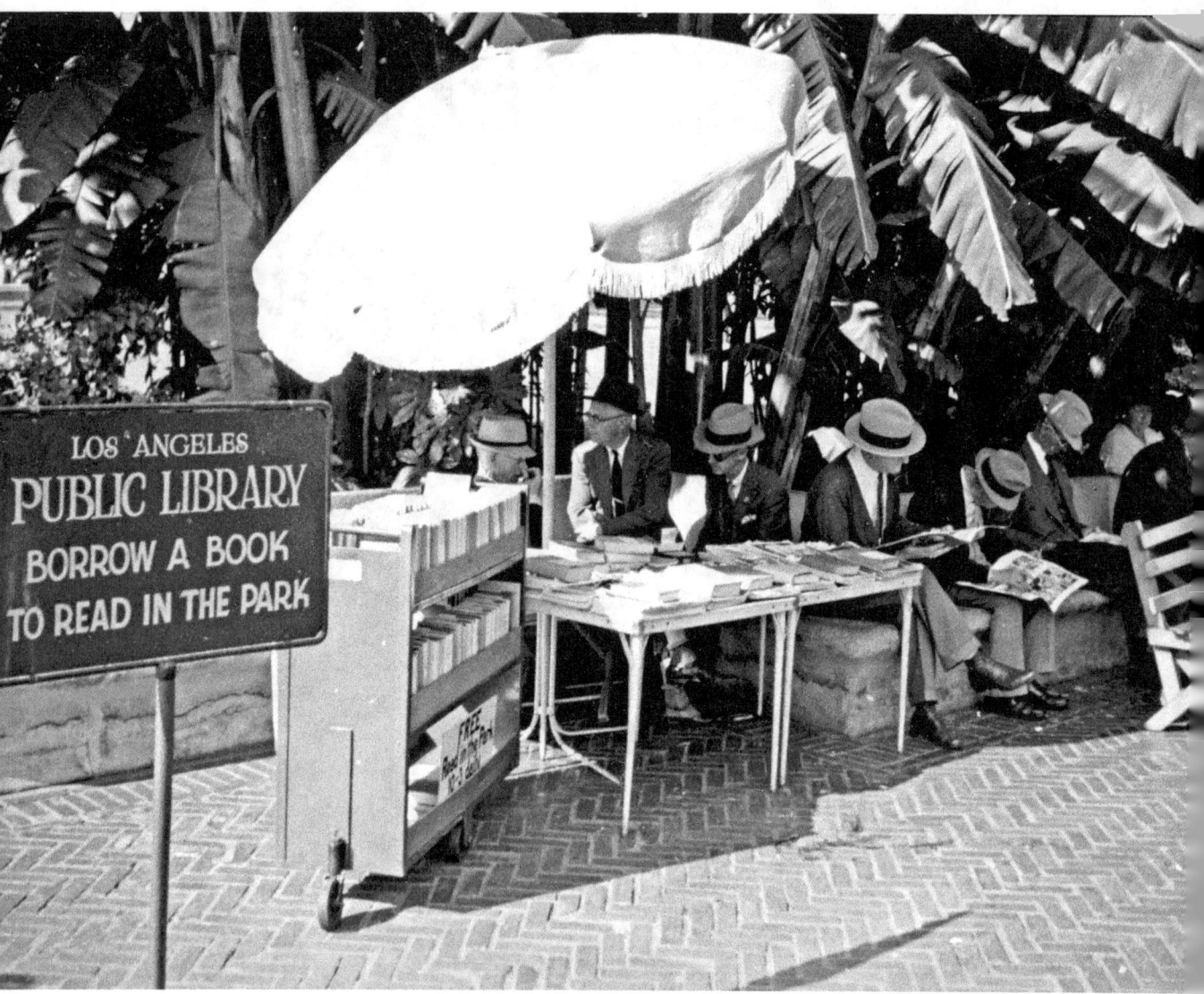

Los Angeles Public Library brings its services to Pershing Square,
offering books and periodicals to park visitors, ca. 1938. (Order #00072146)

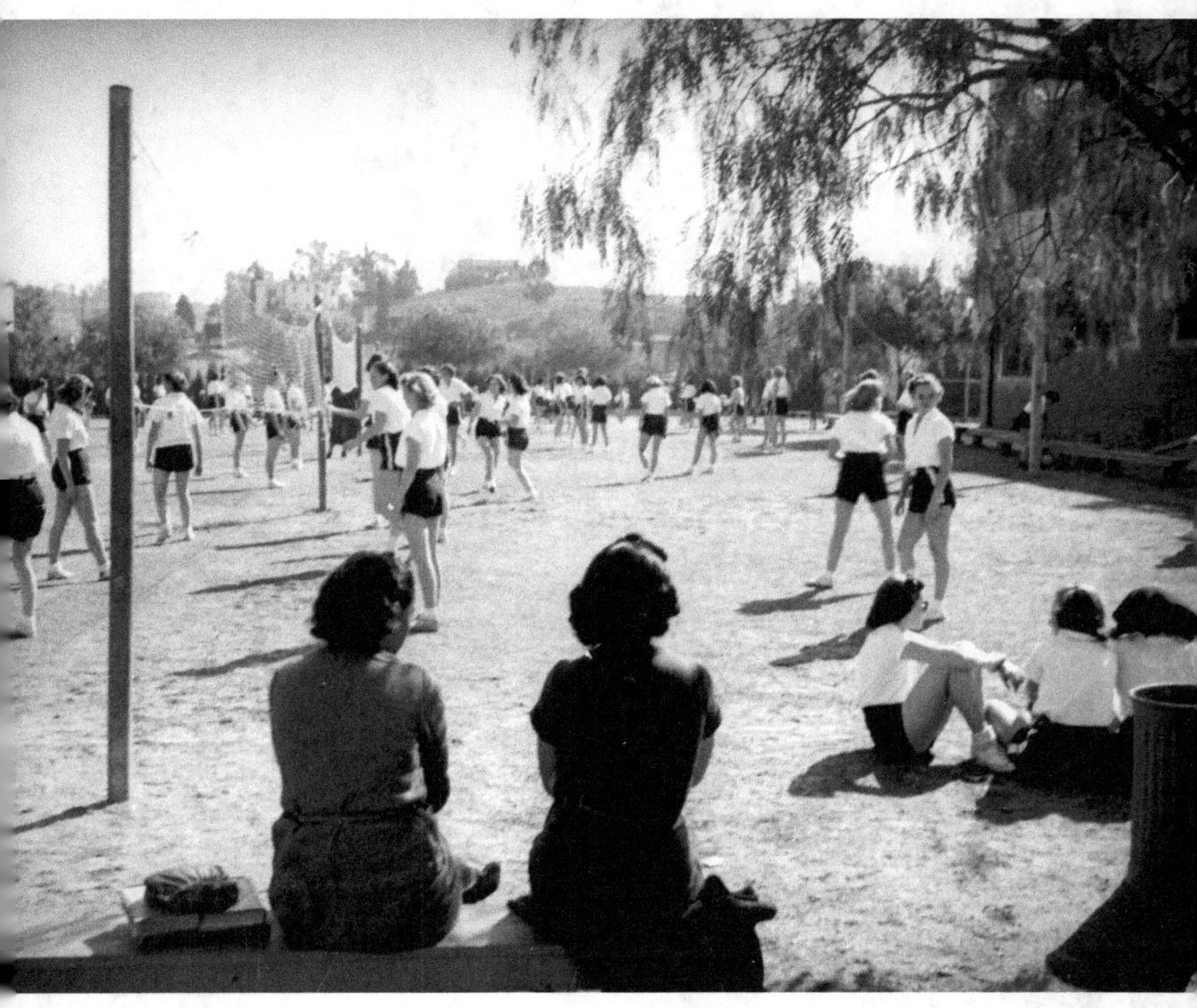

Students play volleyball at John Marshall High, ca. 1937.
(Order #00097974)

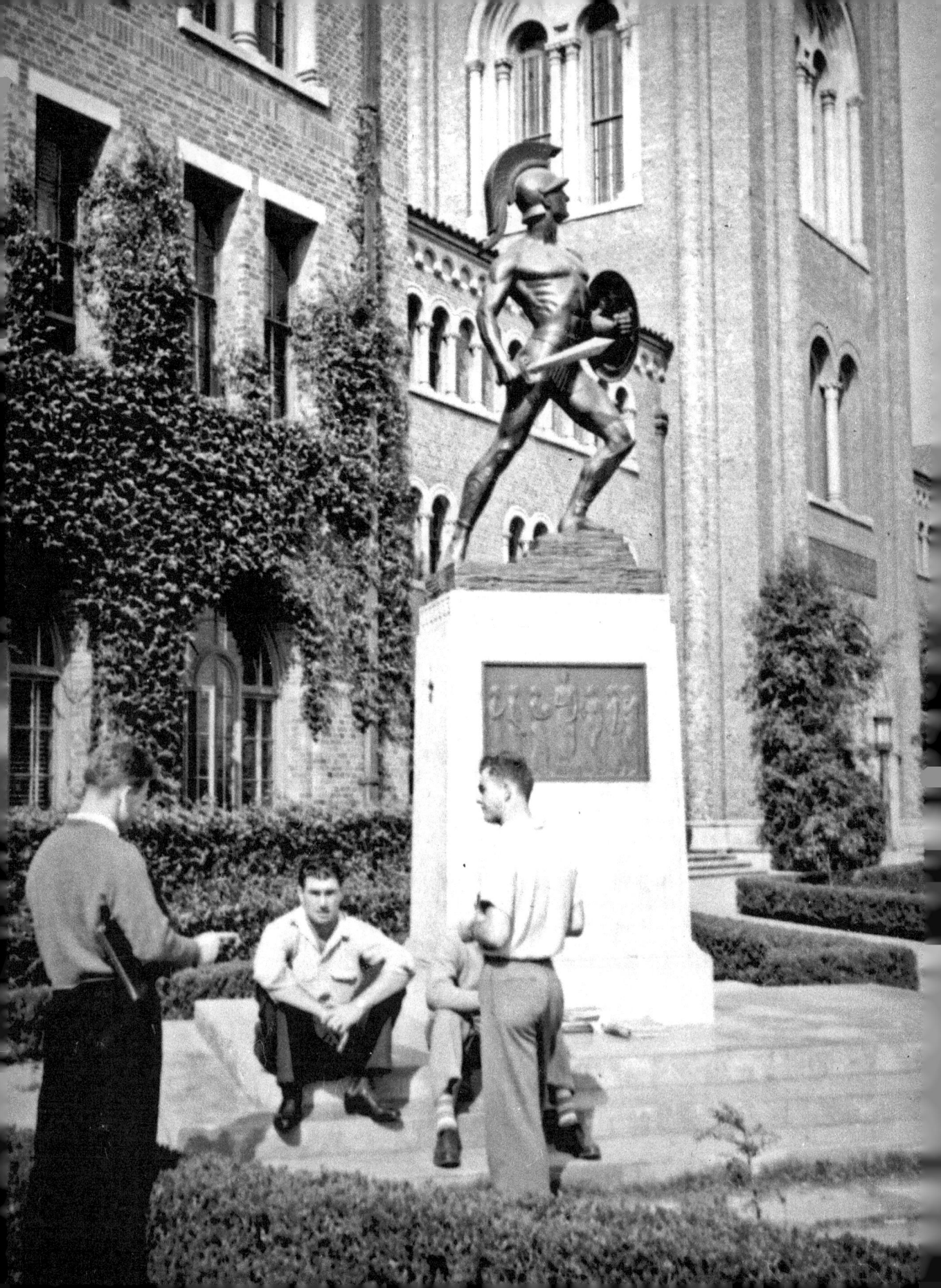

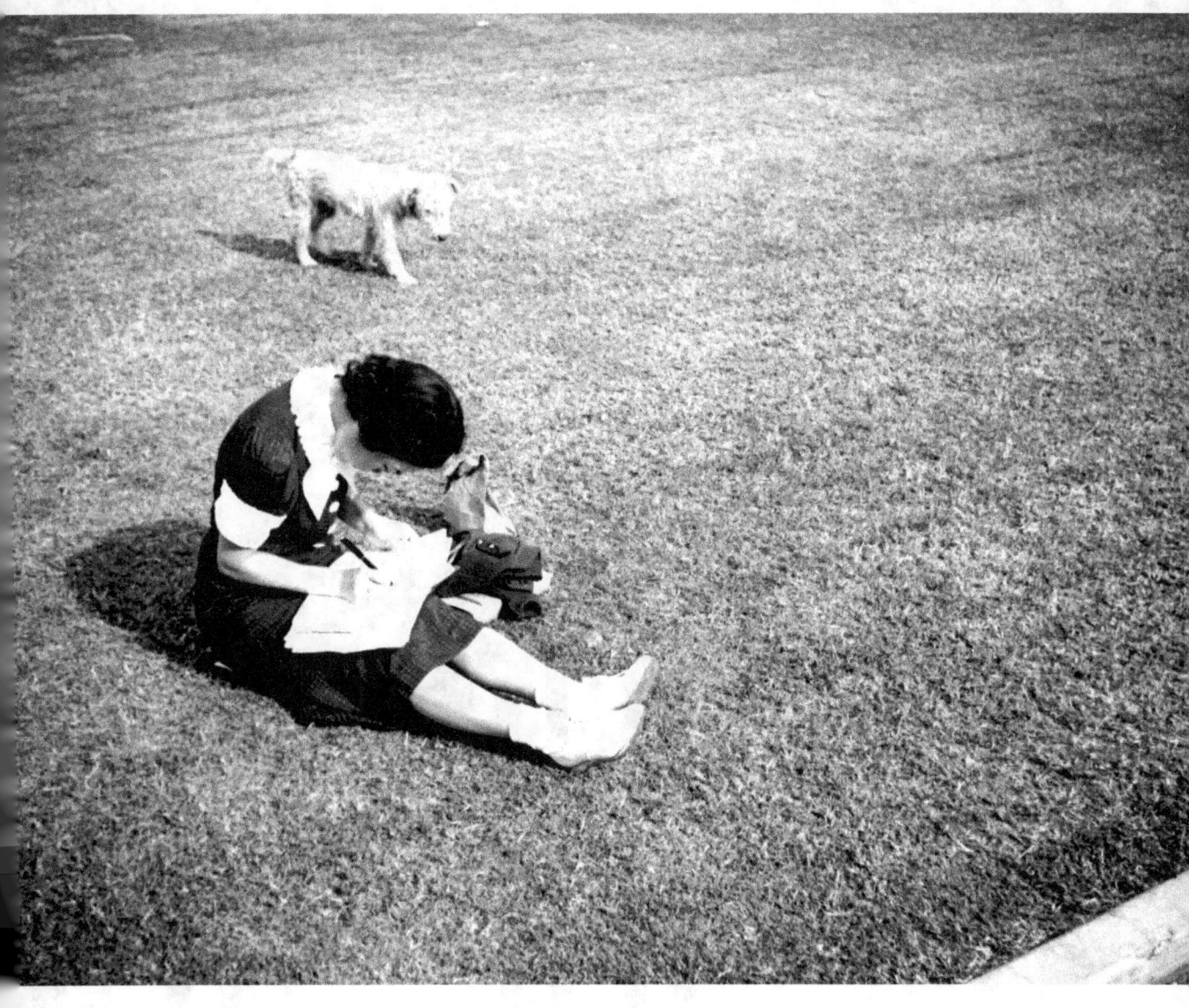

A Los Angeles City College student deep in study, ca. 1937.
(Order #00098230)

Opposite: Students gather around the base of the Tommy Trojan statue at USC
in front of the Bovard Auditorium, ca, 1937. (Order #00098174)

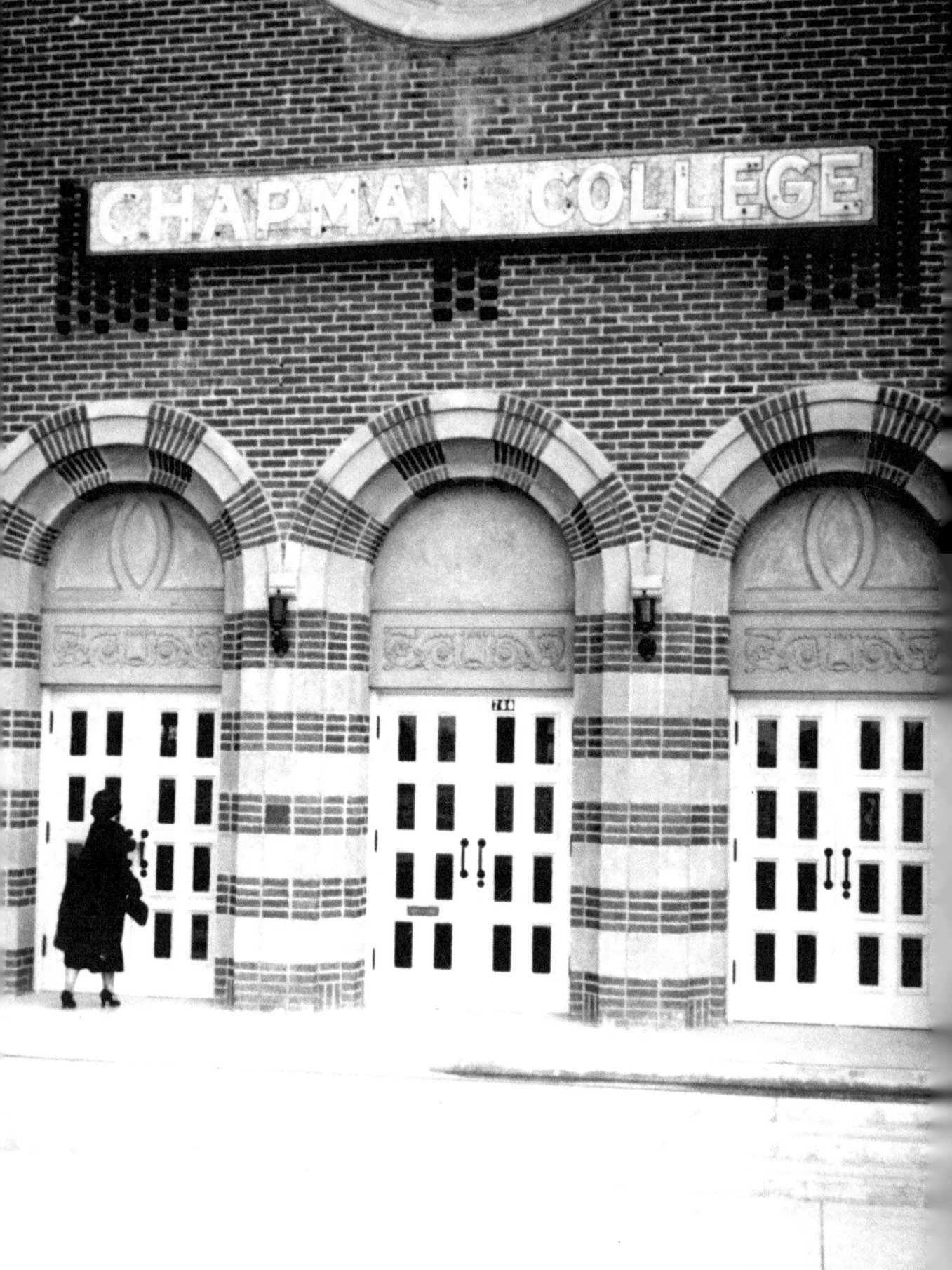

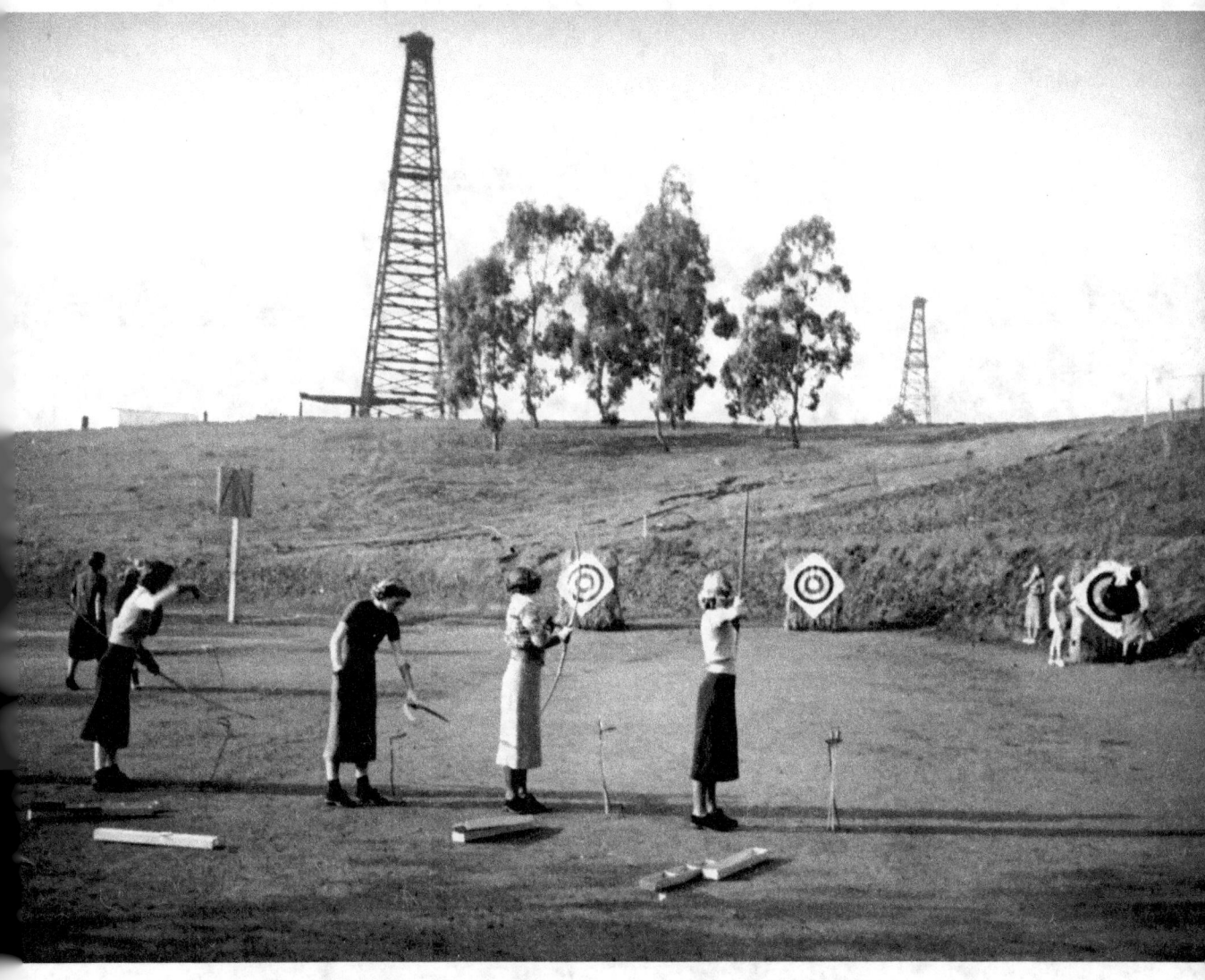

Beverly Hills High School students practice archery, ca. 1937.
(Order #00098241)

Opposite: A woman heads into Chapman College at 766 N. Vermont Avenue,
ca. 1937. (Order #00098234)

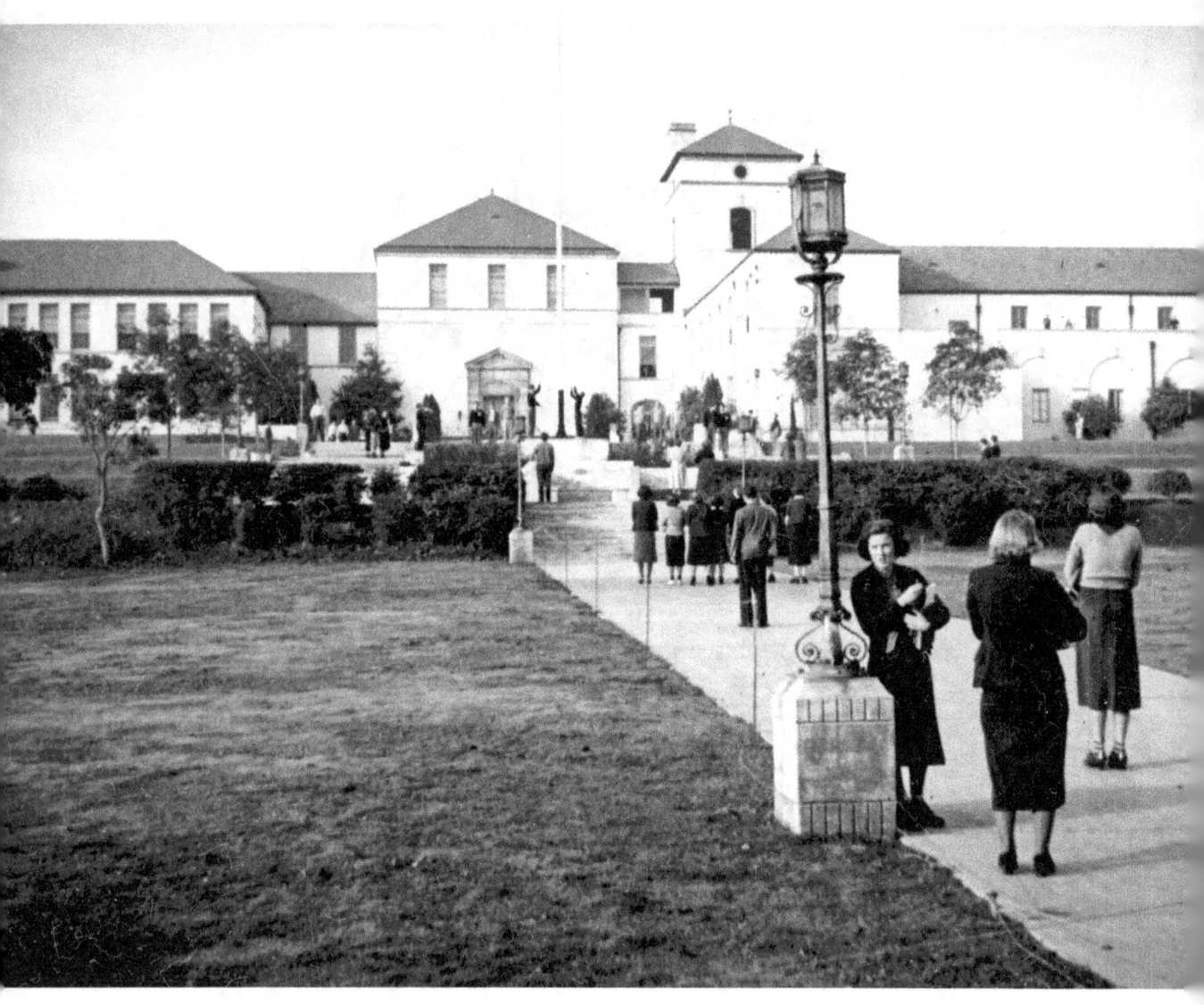

Students descend upon Beverly Hills High School, ca. 1937.
(Order #00098243)

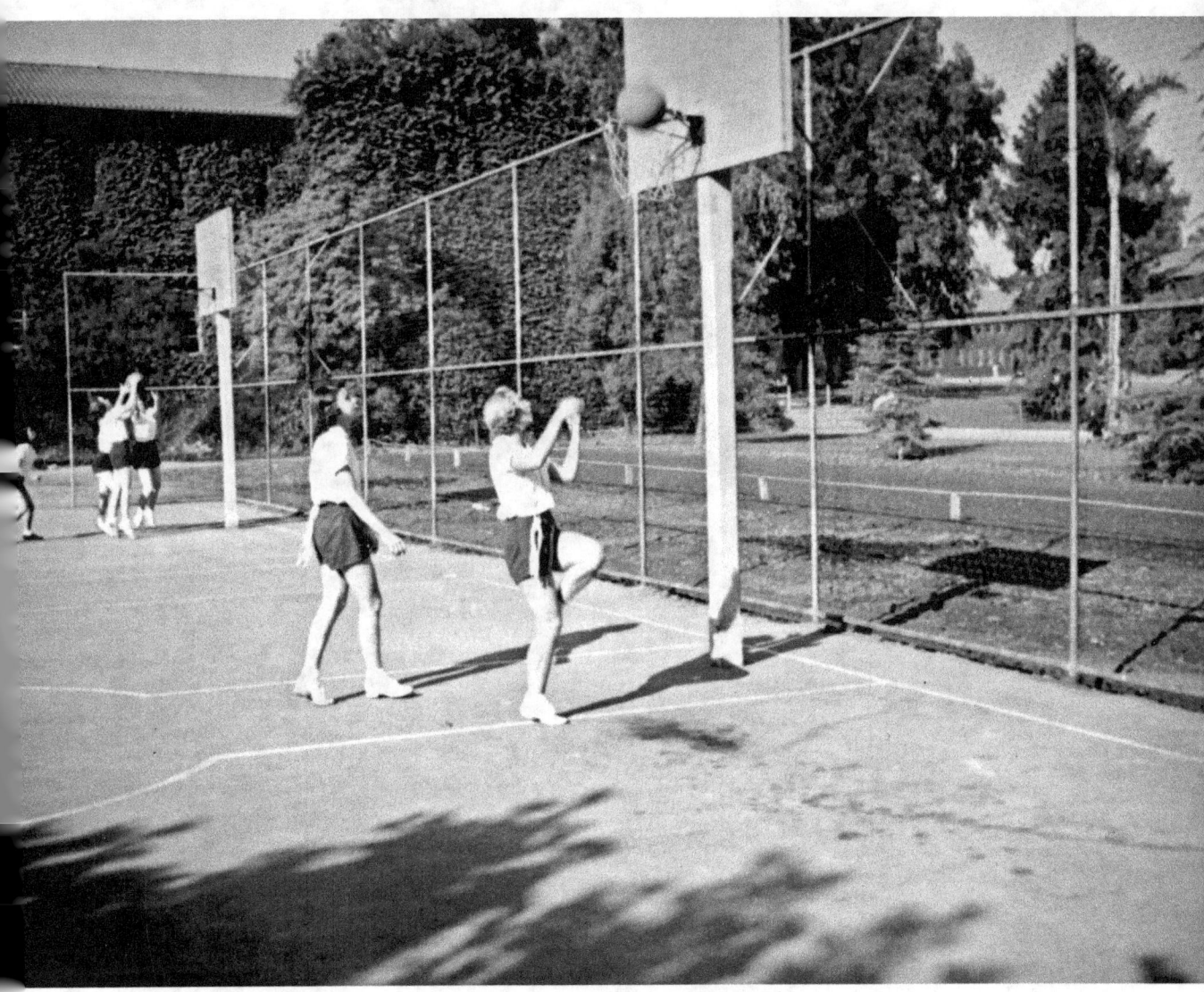

Girls playing basketball at Los Angeles City College, ca. 1937.
(Order #00098246)

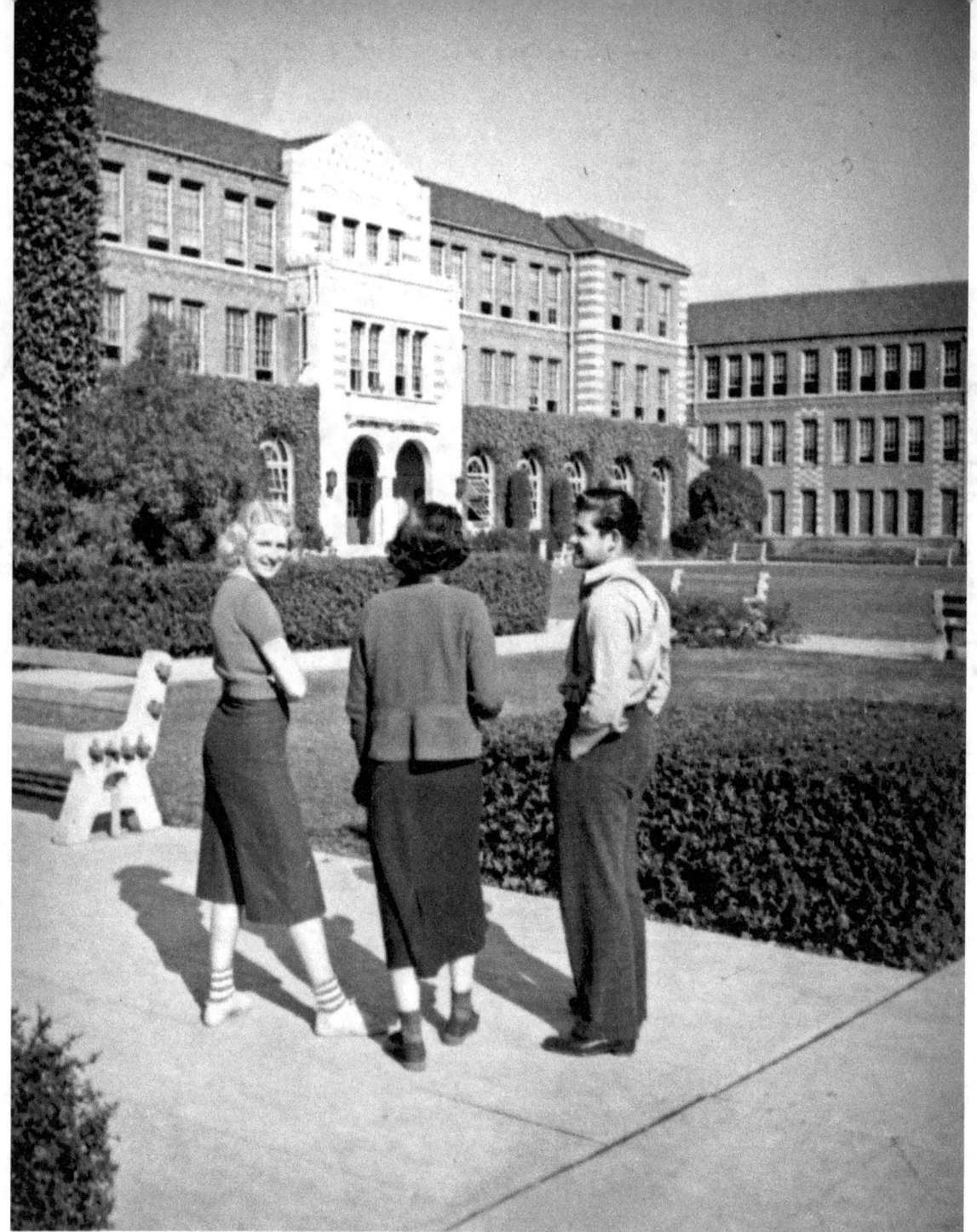

Three students chat in front of Montebello High School, ca. 1938.
(Order #00099241)

Opposite: An art pupil paints a palm tree on the lawn at
Manual Arts High School, ca. 1938. (Order #00100694)

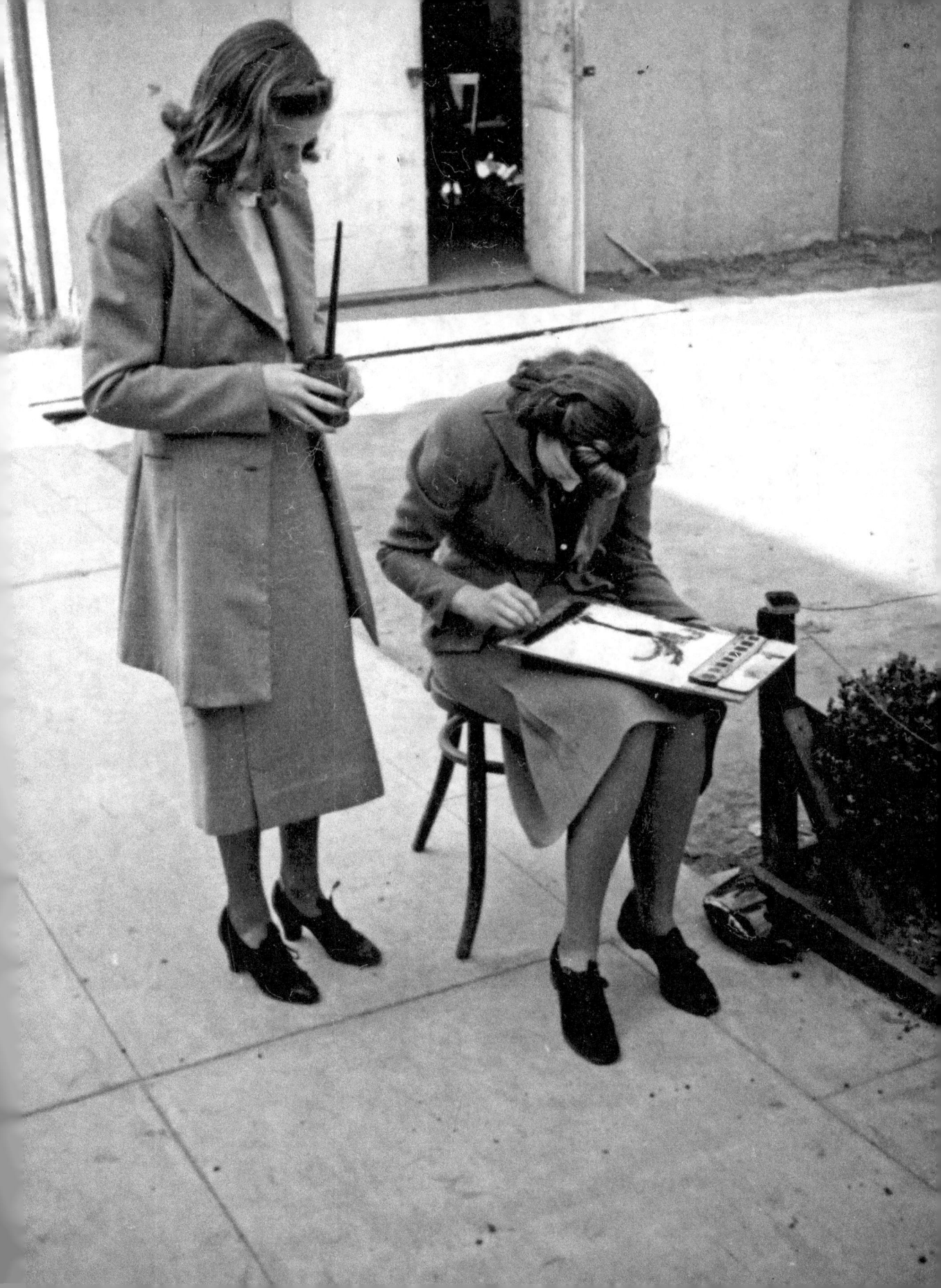

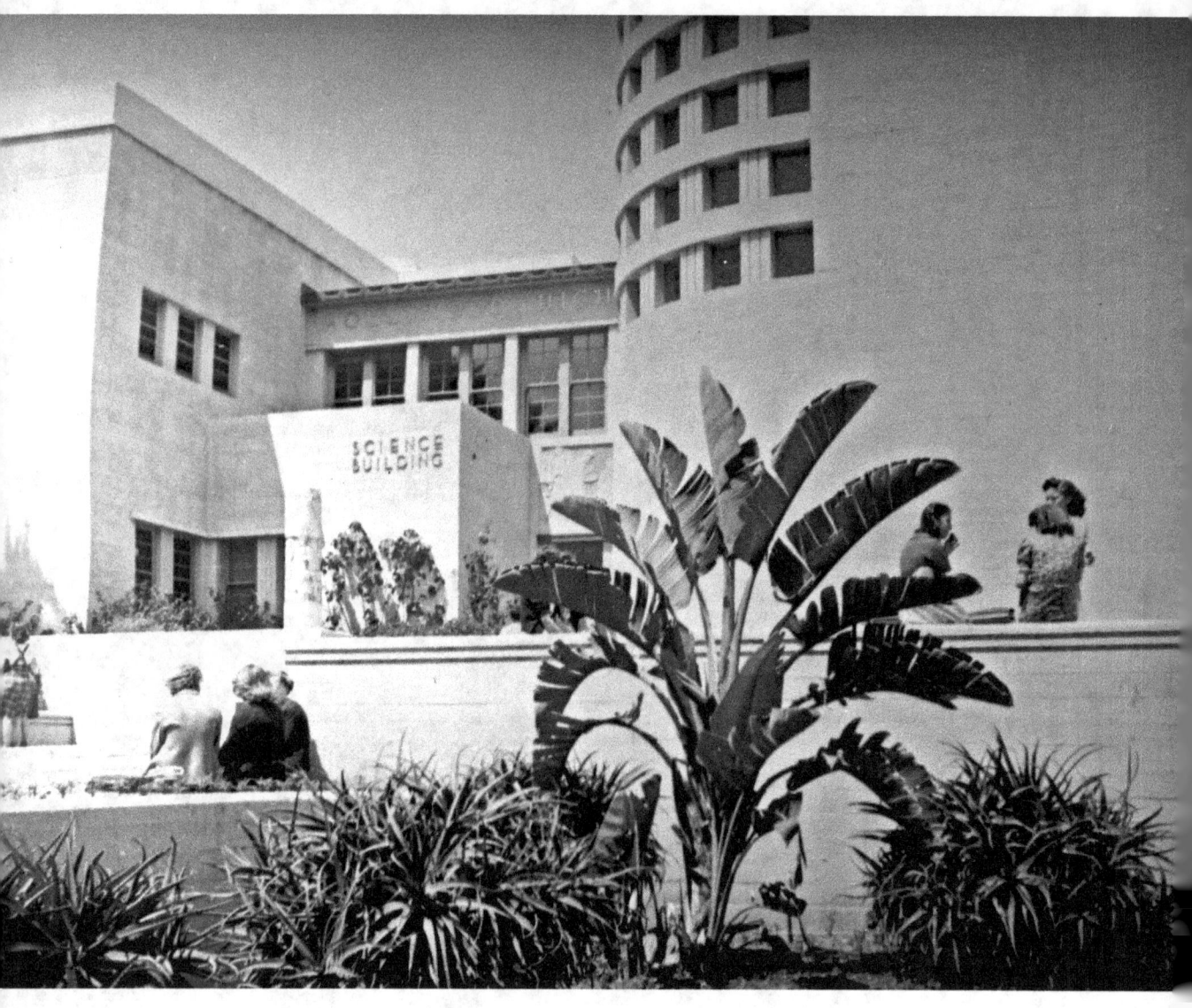

Students hang out in front of the Hollywood High School
Science Building, ca. 1939. (Order #00101091)

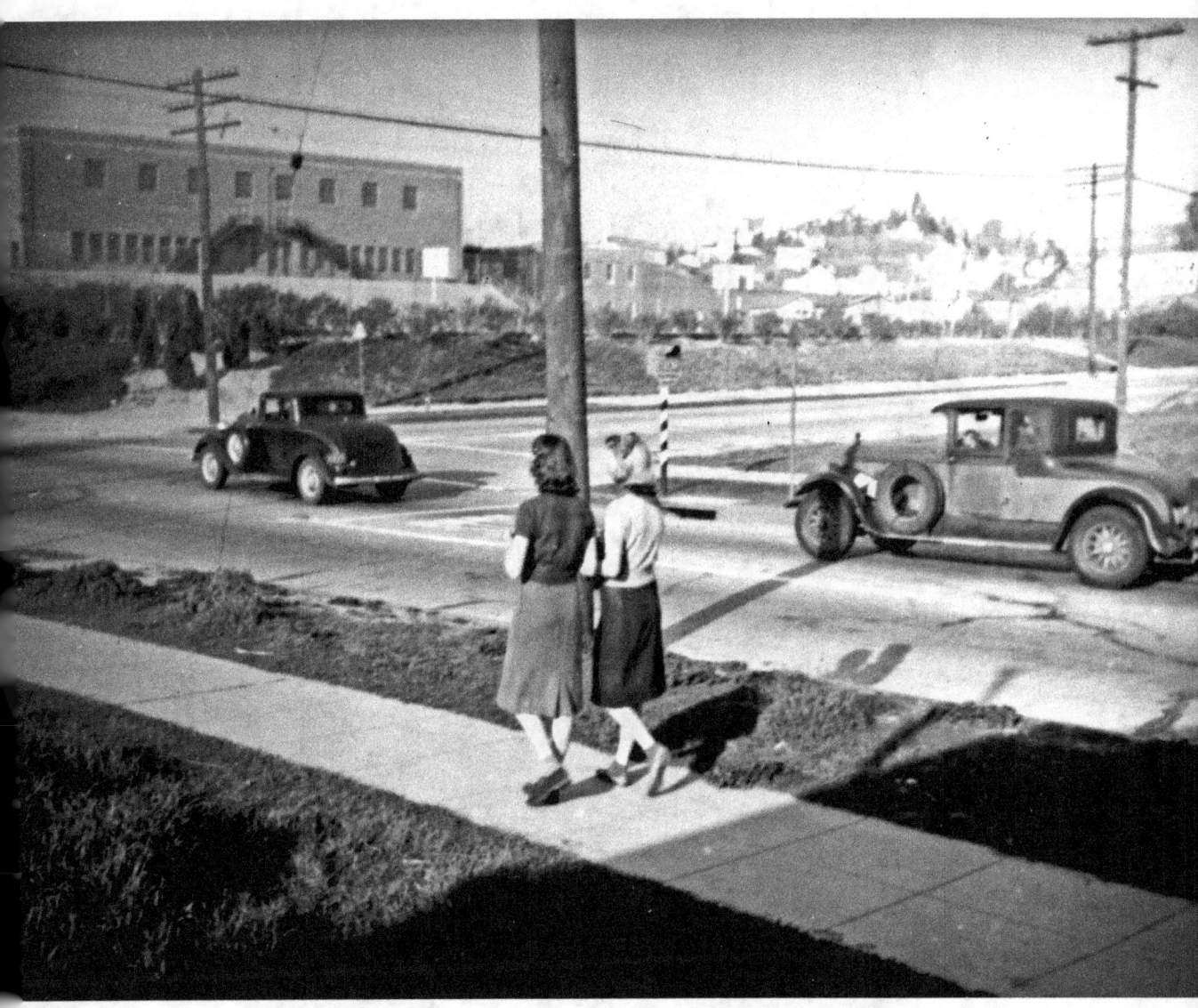

Students walk down St. George towards John Marshall High School, ca. 1938.
(Order #00101318)

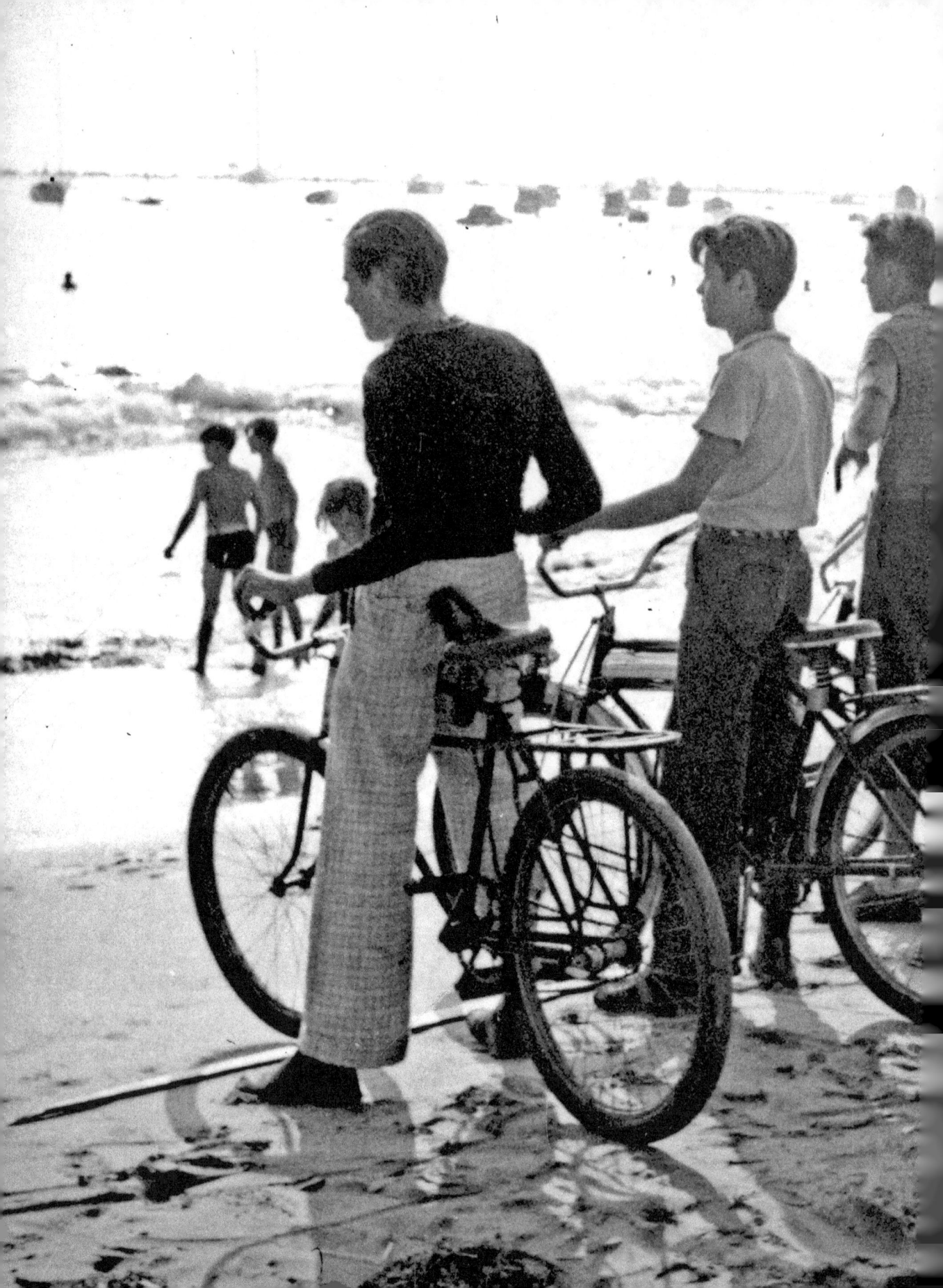

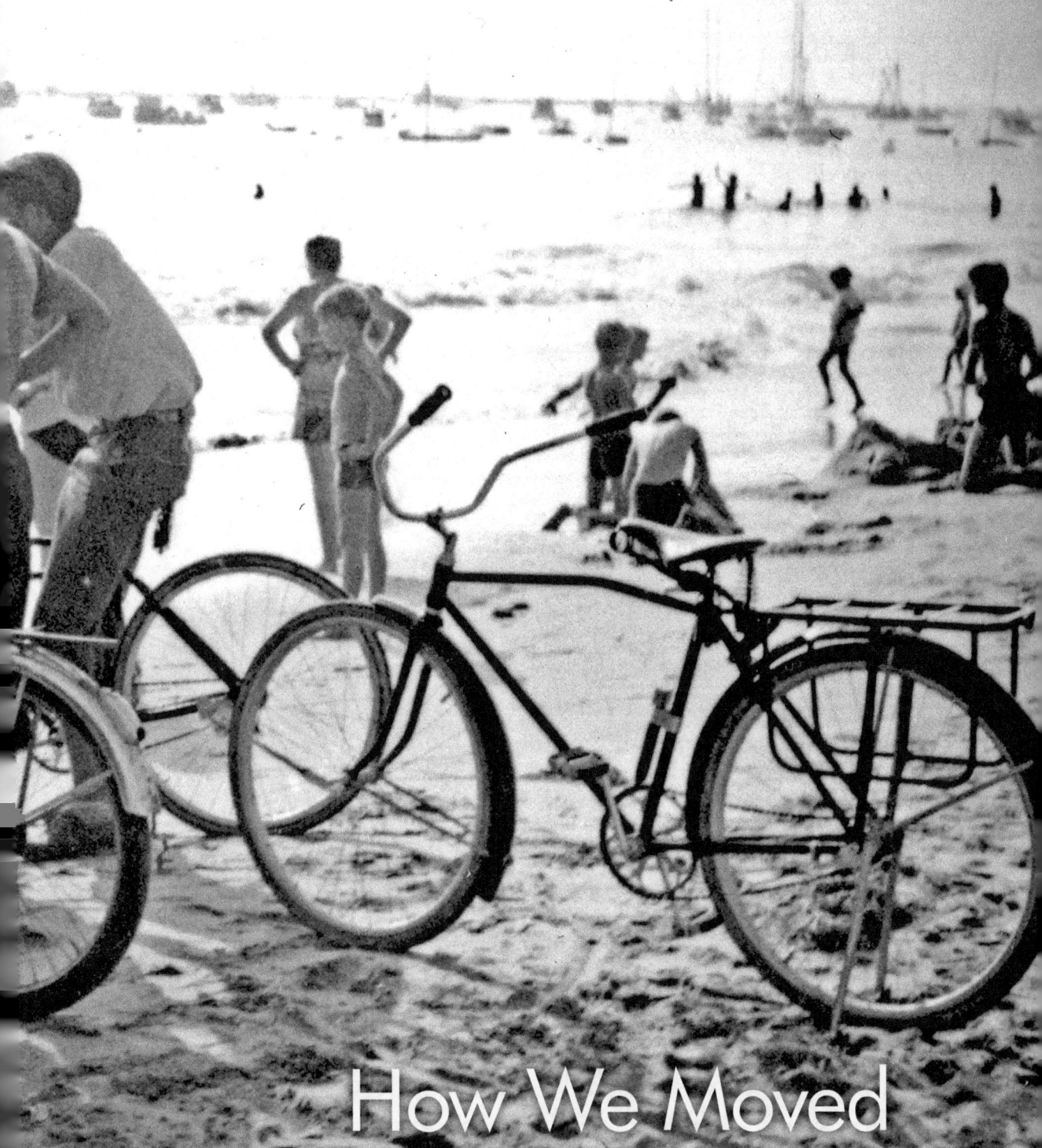

How We Moved

Overleaf:
Bicyclists sit beachside, ca. 1938.
(Order #00070459)

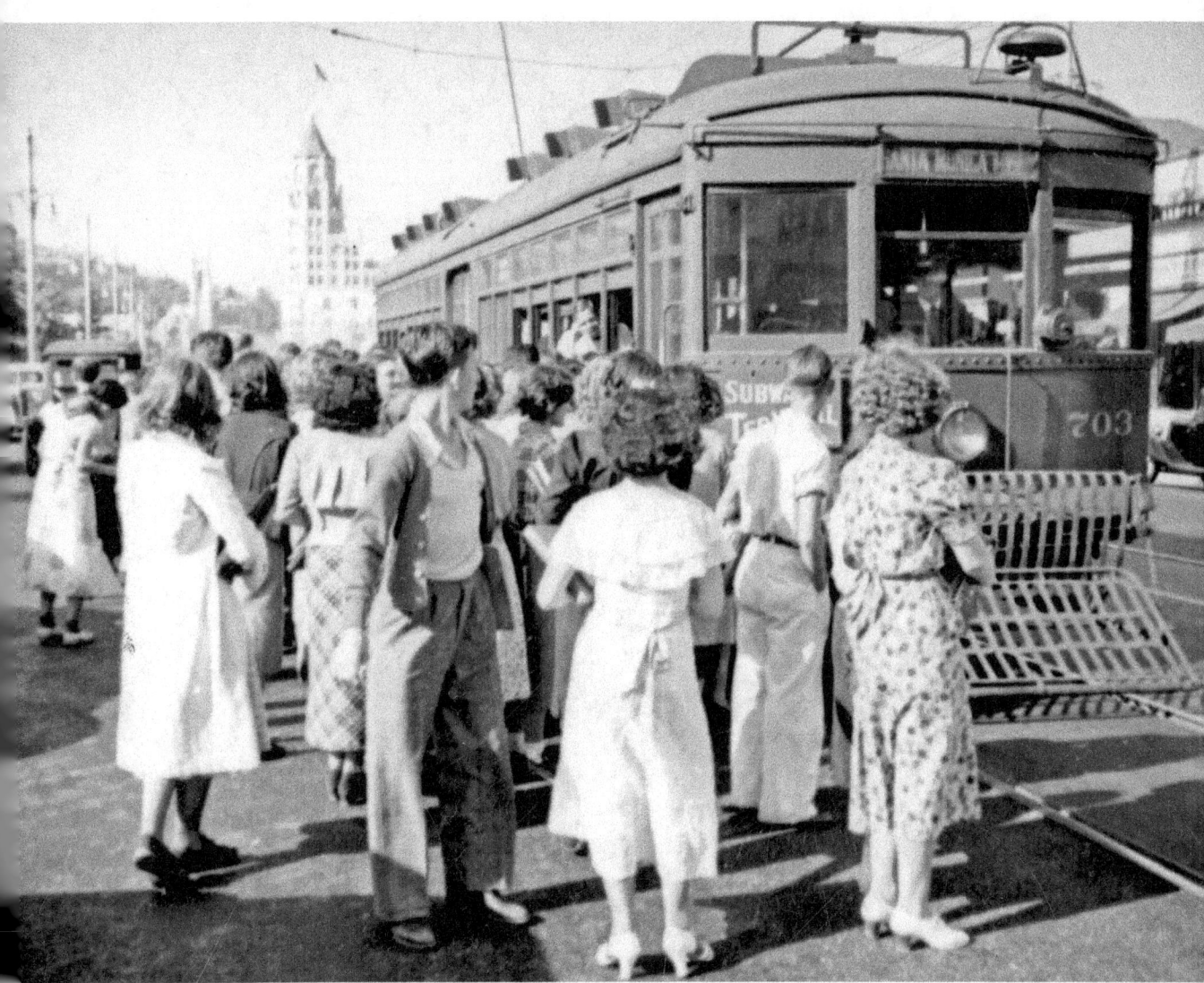

A group waits to board a Pacific Electric Railway car in Hollywood for the
Subway Terminal Building via Santa Monica Boulevard, ca. 1938. (Order #00006891)

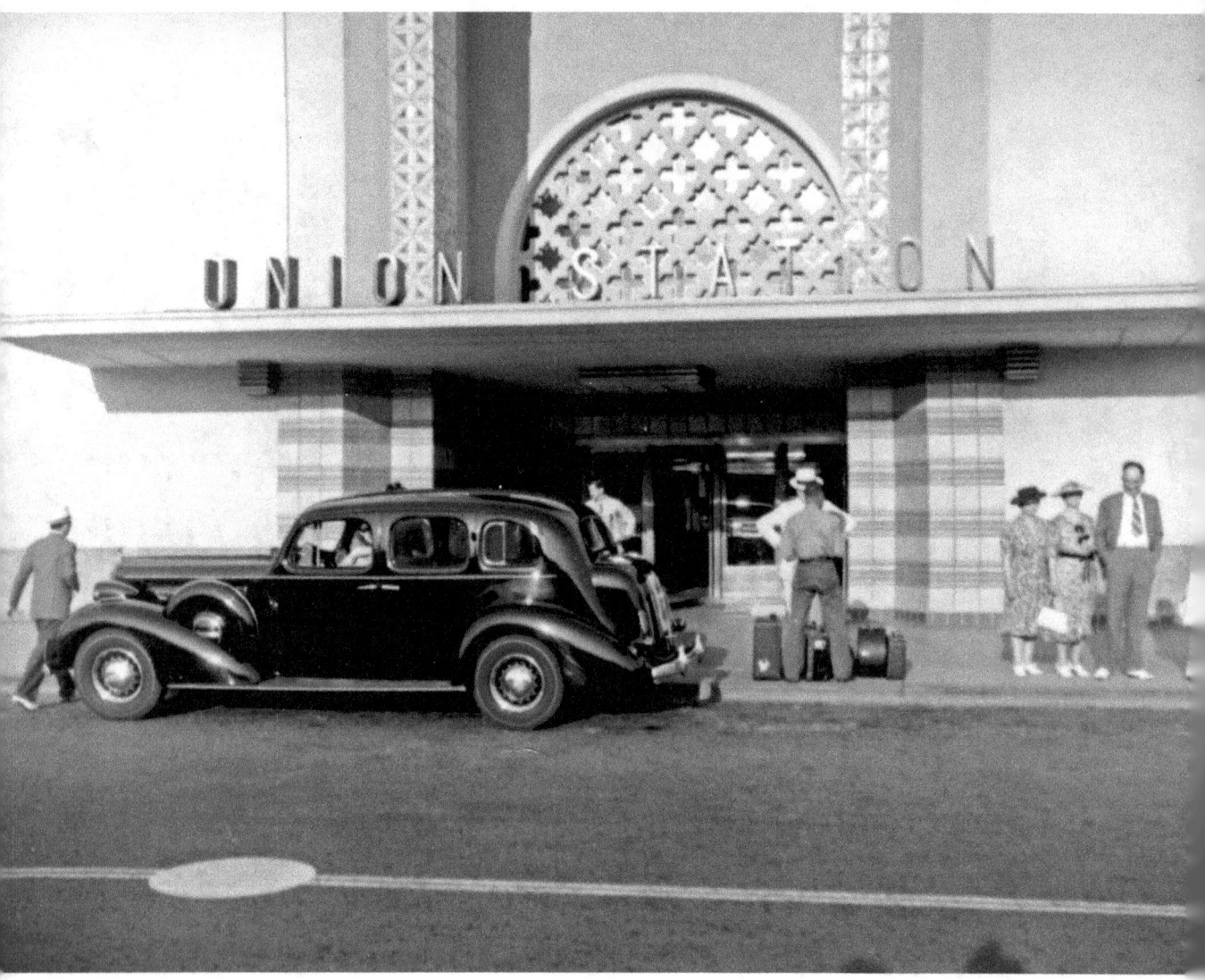

Passengers get dropped off and picked up at the recently completed
Union Station, ca. 1939. (Order #00077963)

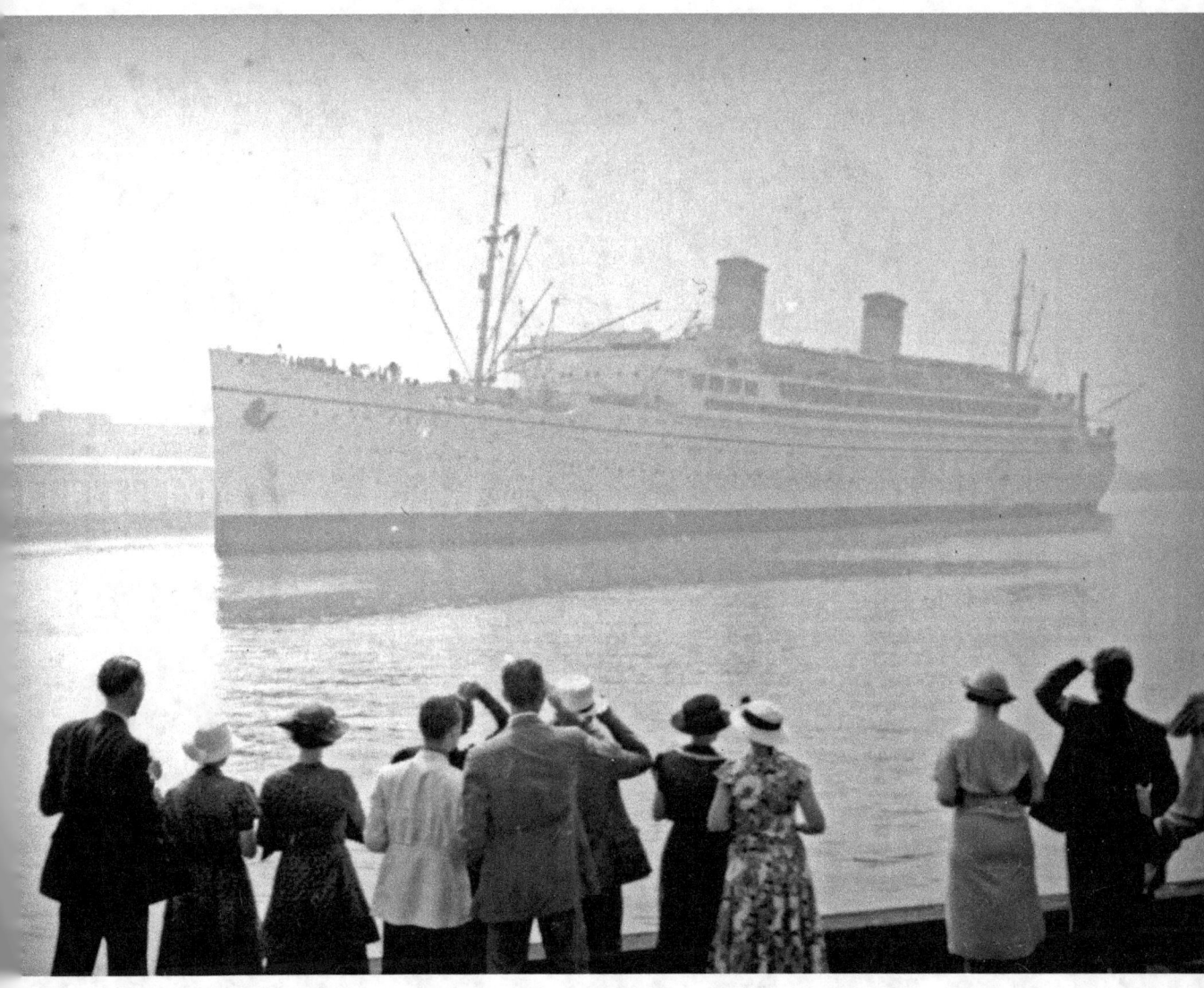

People gathered in the Los Angeles Harbor await the arrival
of the S.S. Monterey, ca. 1937. (Order #00096823)

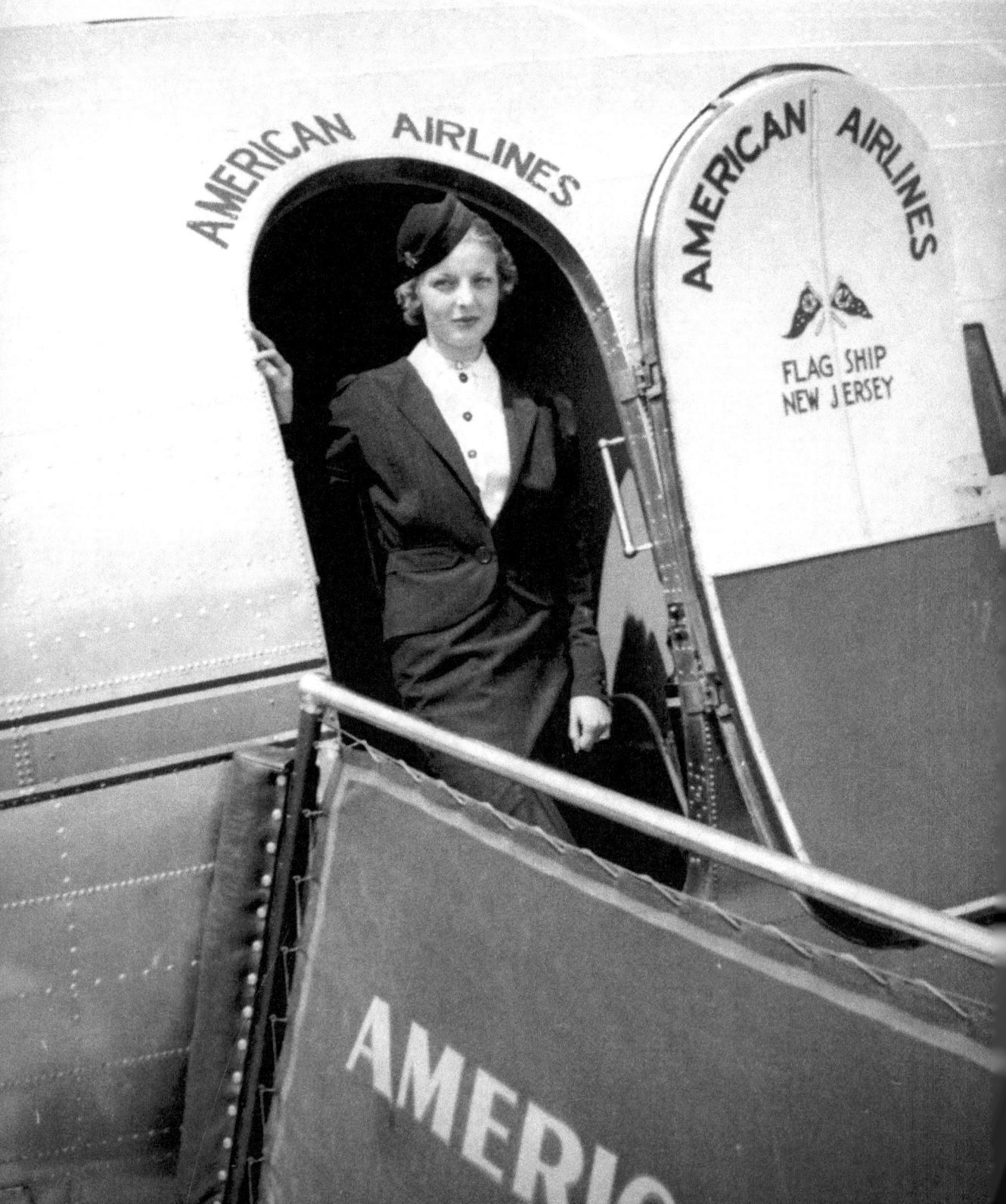

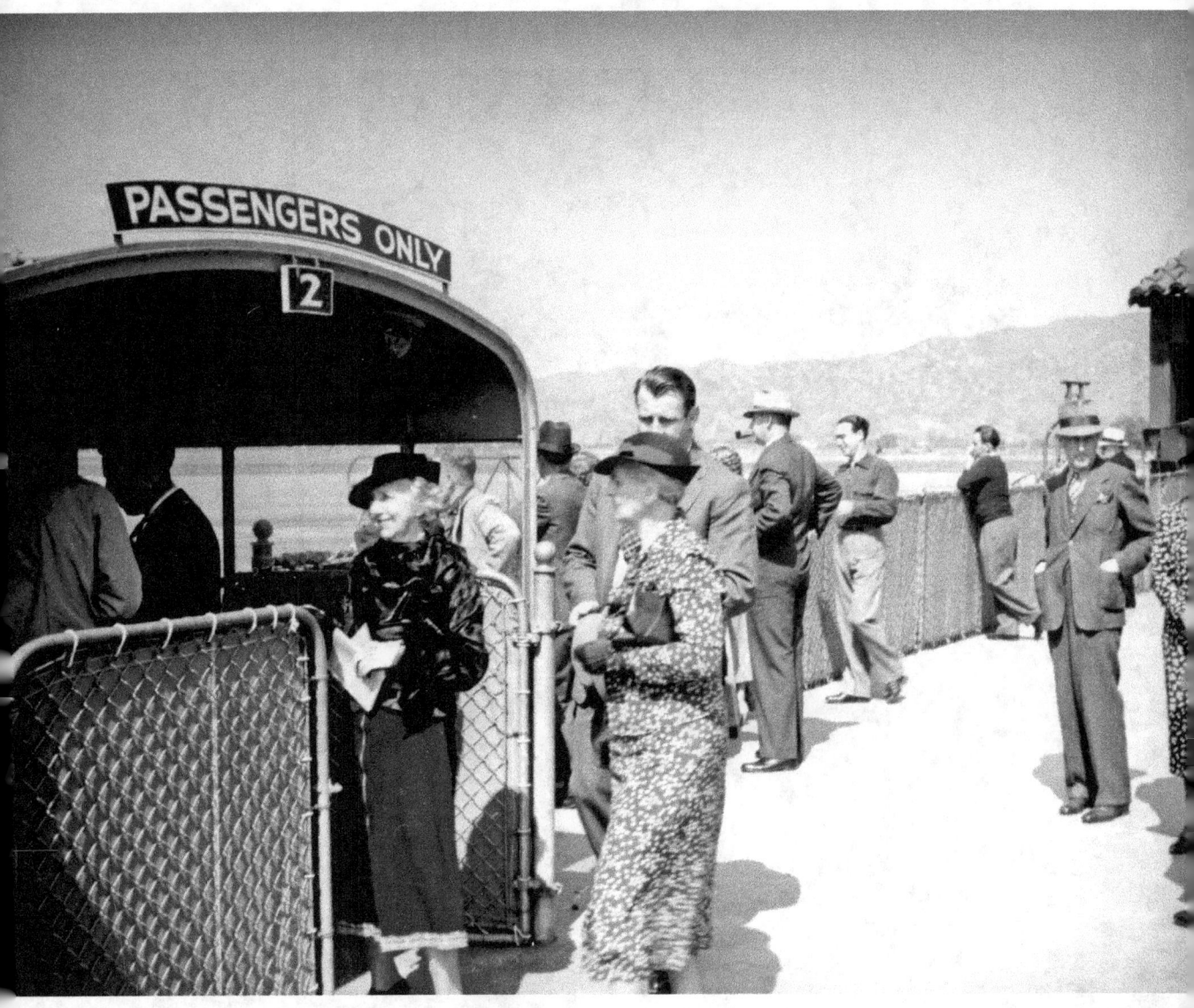

Crowds gather around gate 2 at the Union Air Terminal in Burbank, ca. 1937.
(Order #0097252)

Opposite: A stewardess stands in the doorway of an American Airlines DST
(Douglas Sleeper Transport) at the Grand Central Air Terminal, ca. 1937.
(Order #00097244)

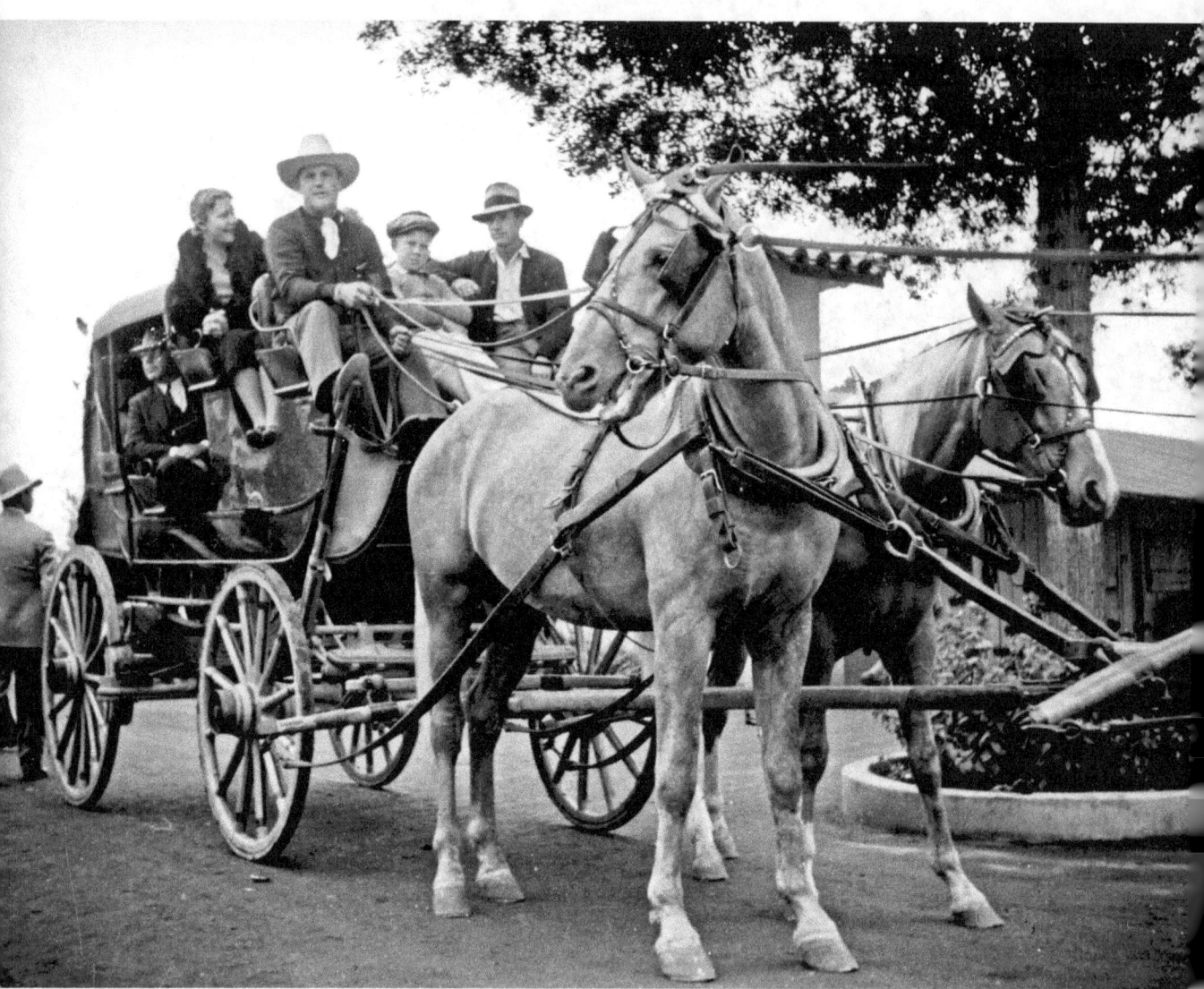

Fair-goers enjoy a trip in a horse-drawn carriage at the
1937 Los Angeles County Fair in Pomona. (Order #00097292)

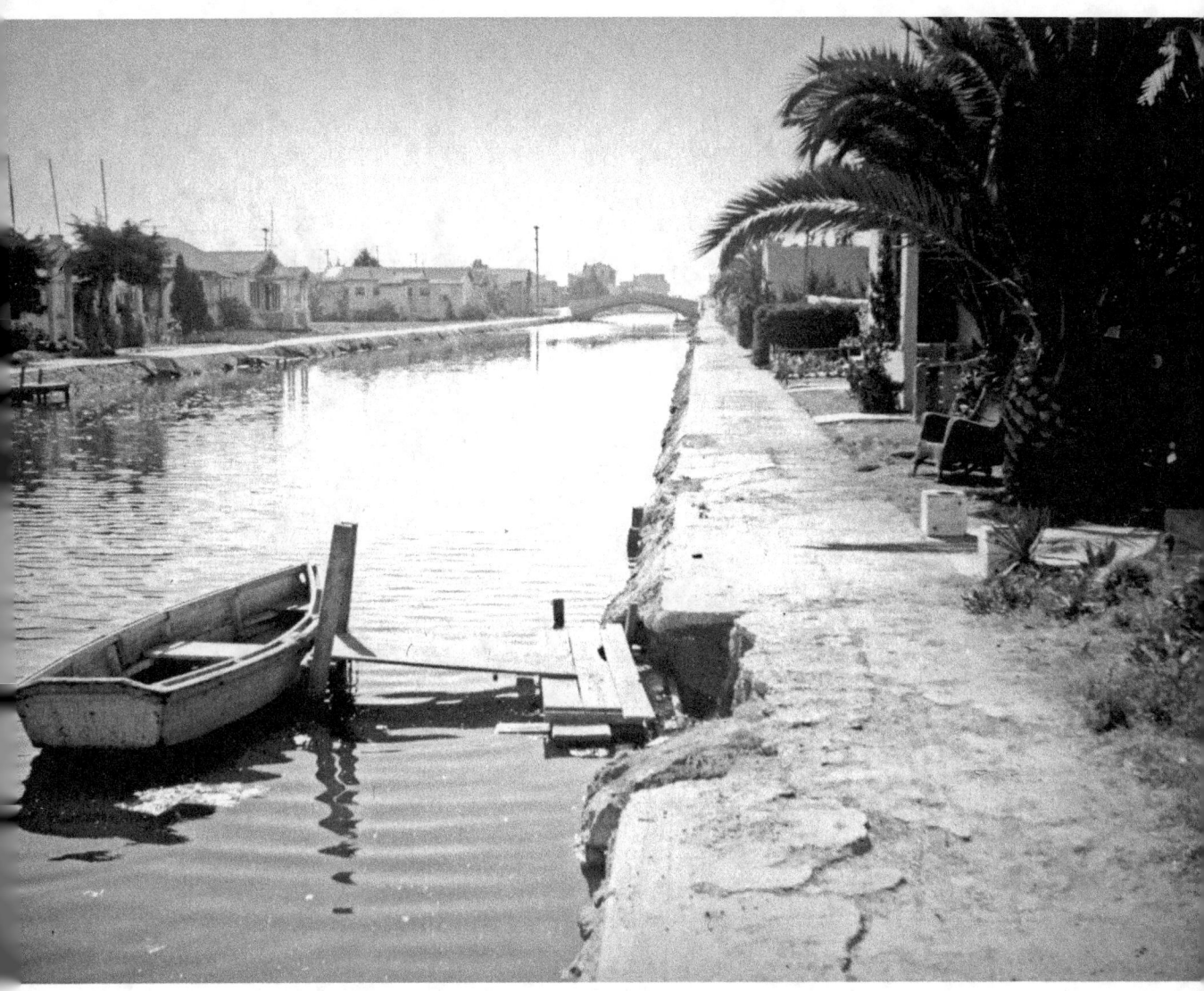

A rowboat is tied to a makeshift dock against the crumbling sidewalk
of a Venice Canal, ca. 1937. (Order #00097398)

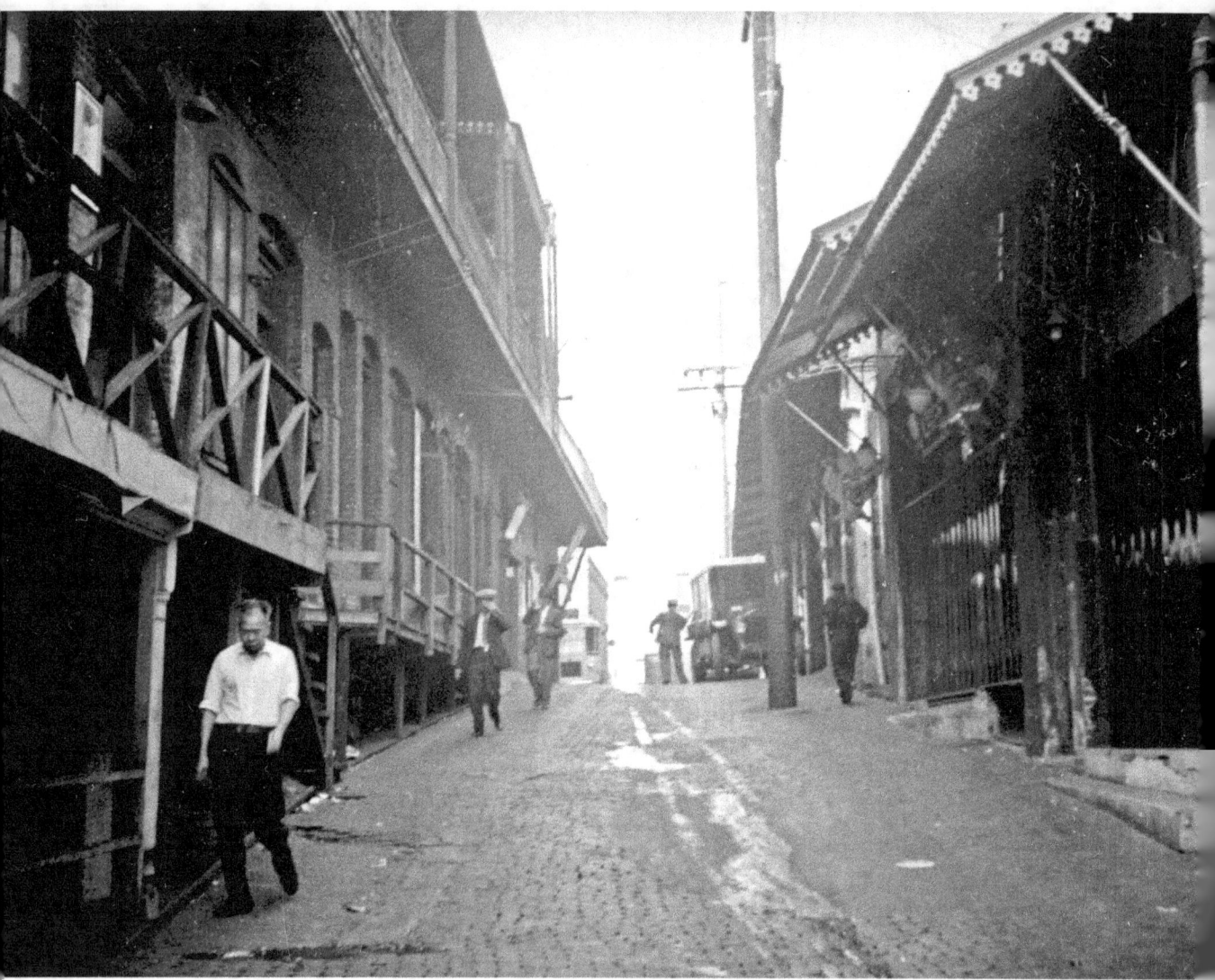

Men walk on the brick road past gated storefronts on Ferguson Alley in old Chinatown.
By 1937, Ferguson Alley was one of the few remnants of the neighborhood,
which was bulldozed to make way for Union Station. (Order #00097512)

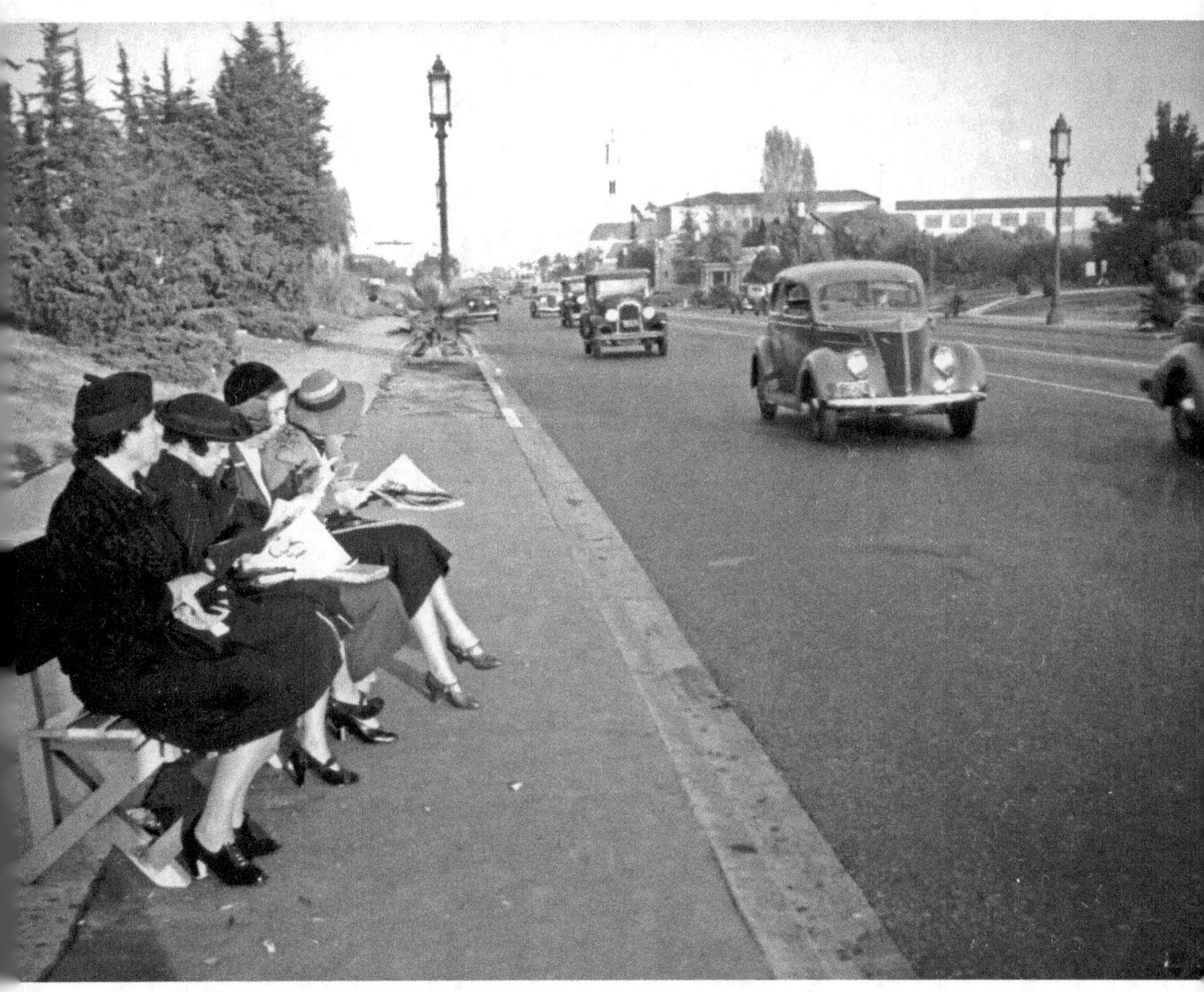

A group of women wait at a bus stop on Wilshire near Rossmore, ca. 1937.
(Order #00097564)

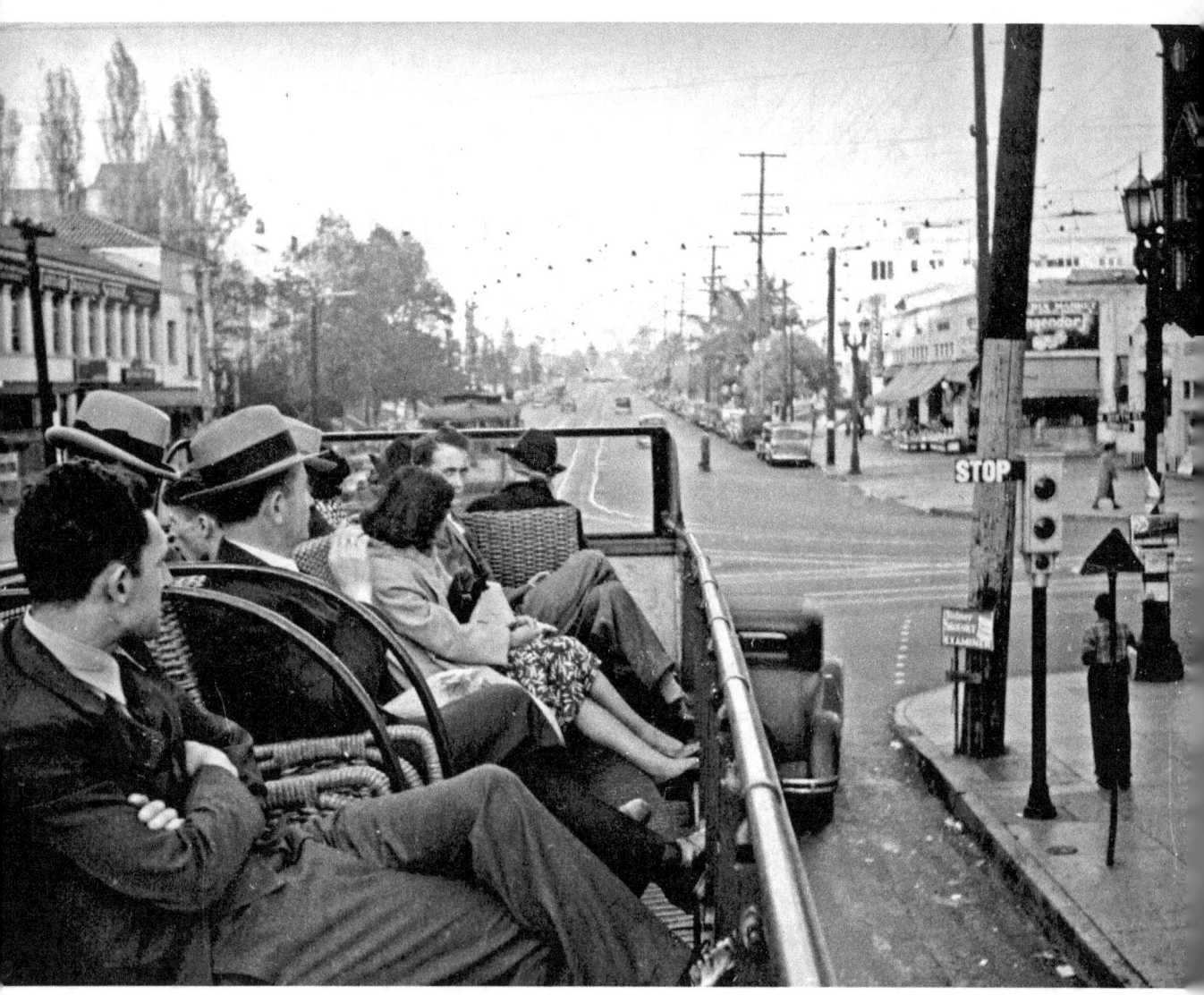

Transit riders on a double-decker bus head north-east on Rampart Boulevard
towards 6th Street, ca. 1937. (Order #0097818)

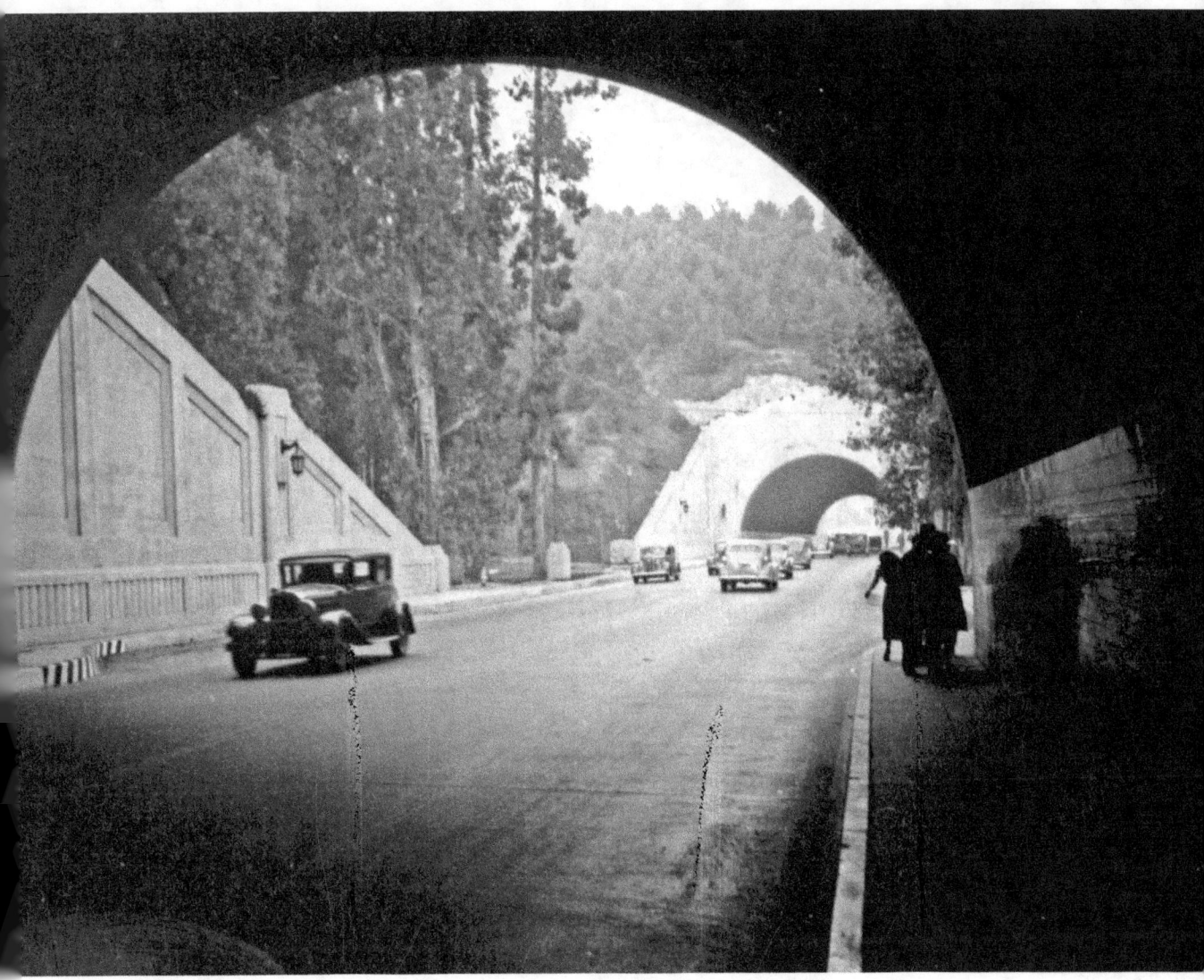

Automobiles and pedestrians travel through the Figueroa Tunnels near Elysian Park, ca. 1937.
This roadway would eventually be incorporated into California State Route 110/
Arroyo Seco Parkway (Pasadena Freeway). (Order #00098289)

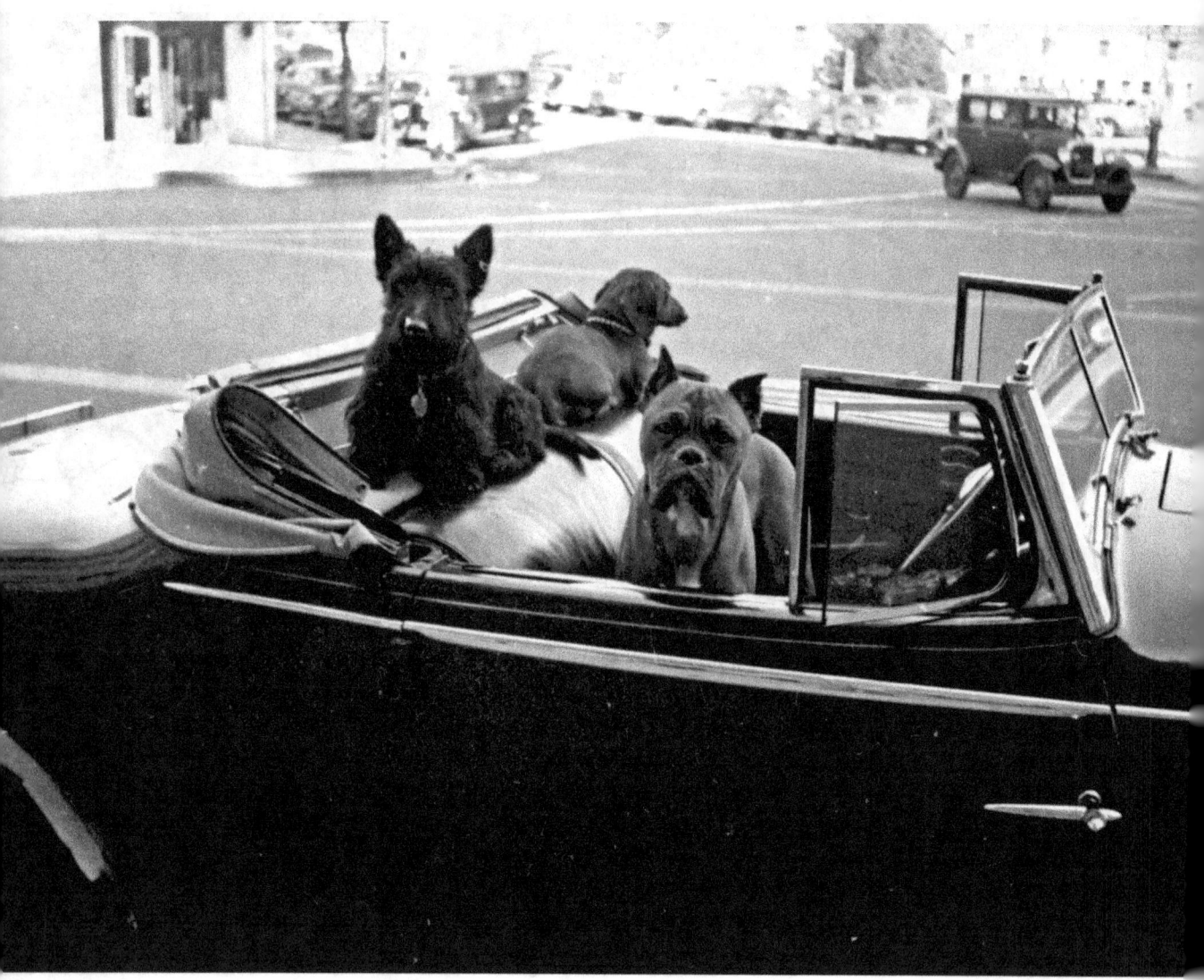

Three Beverly Hills pooches lounge in a parked convertible, ca. 1937.
(Order #00098577)

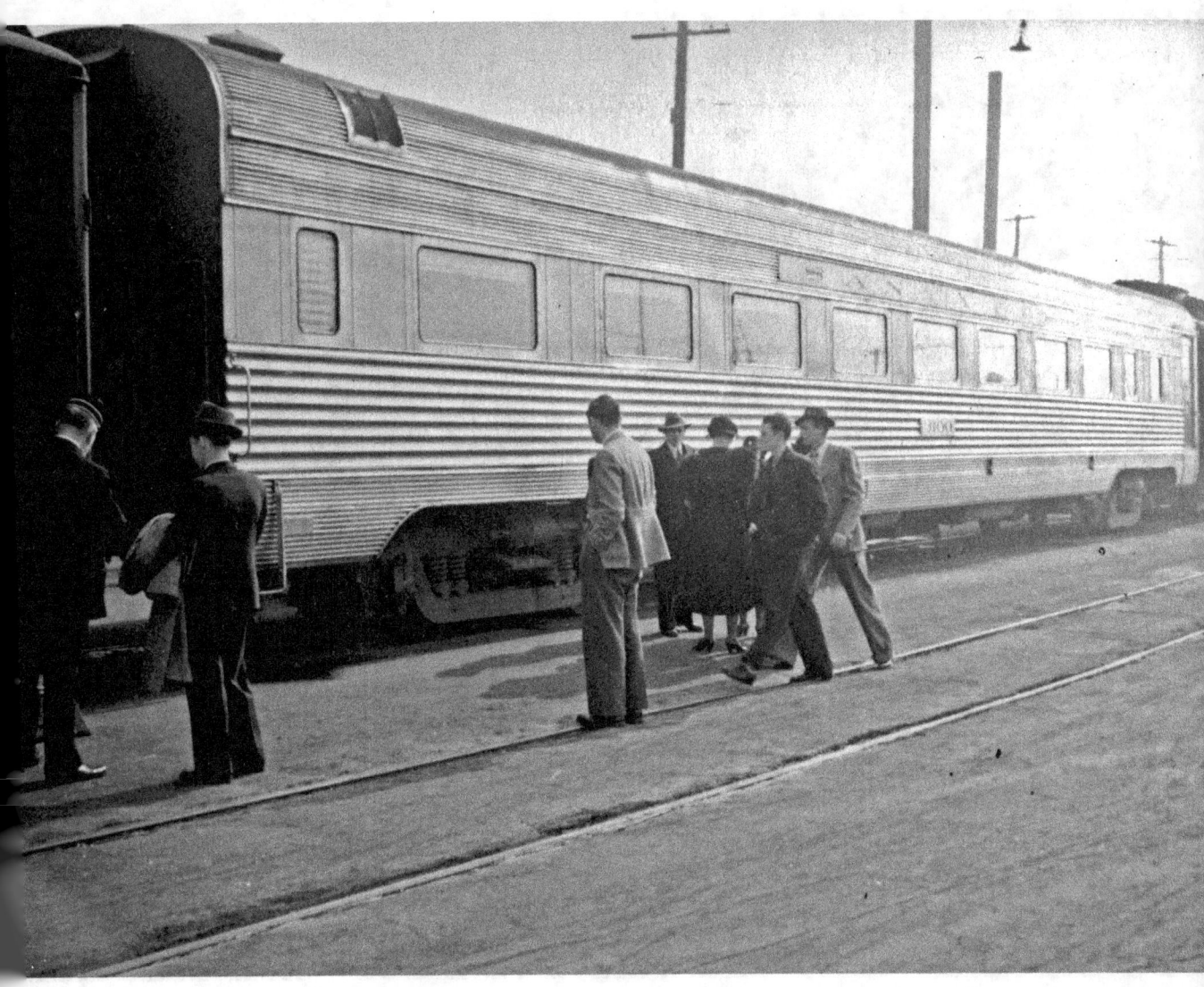

Passengers prepare to board a train at La Grange Station, ca. 1937.
(Order #00098731)

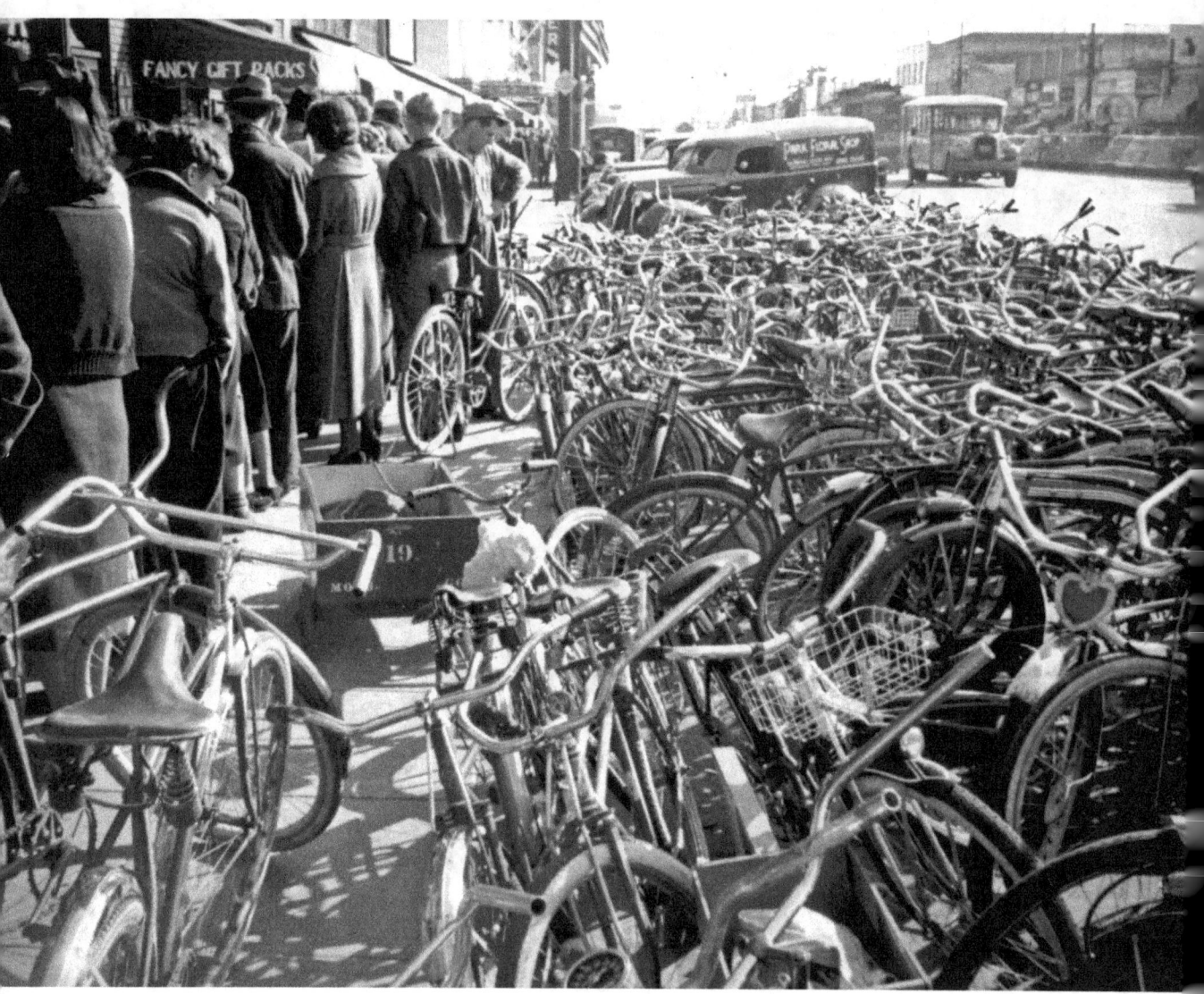

Filmgoers and bikes are gathered in front of the Fox California Theater
in Huntington Park, ca. 1938. (Order #00099036)

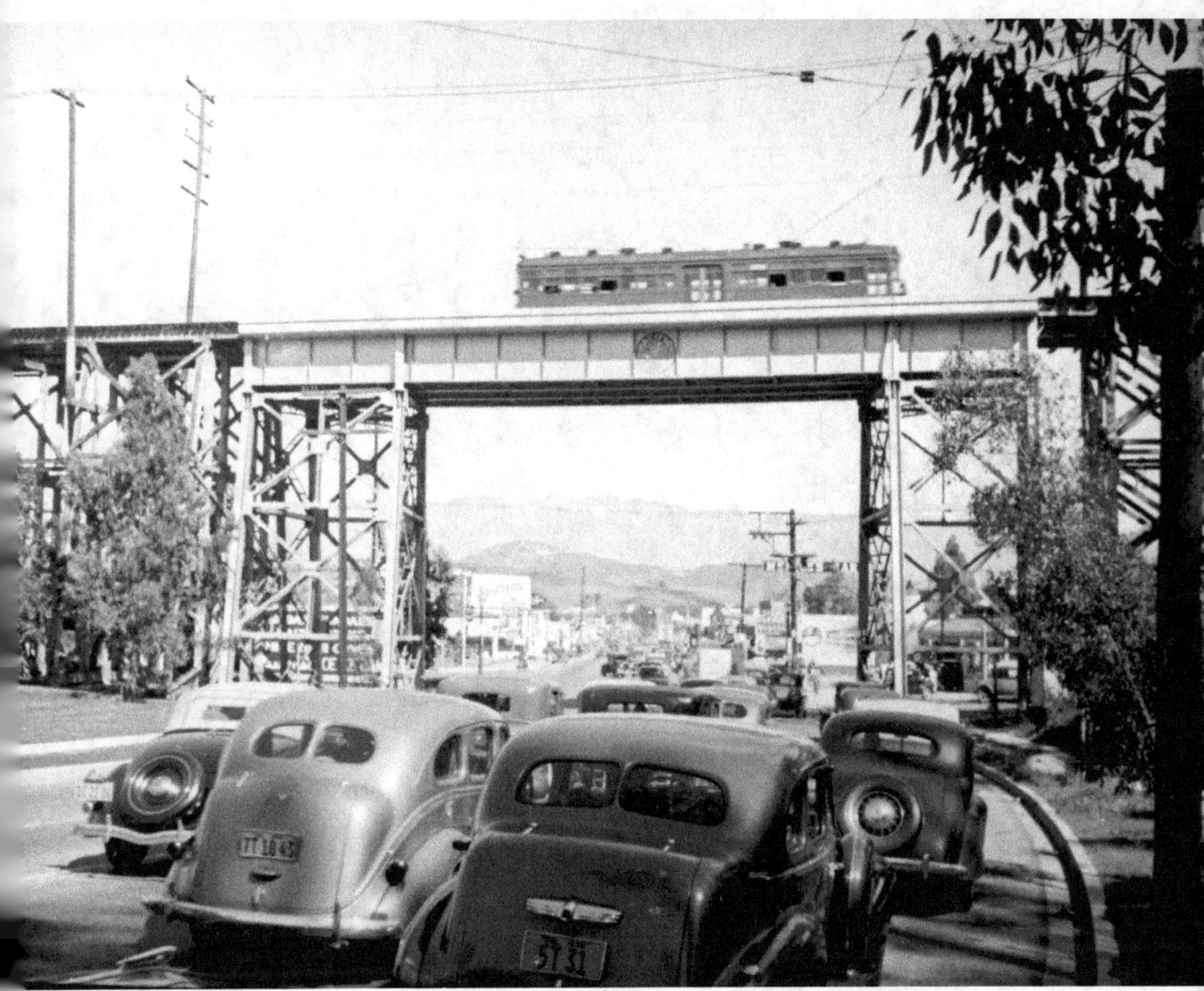

Cars drive under the Pacific Electric railroad tracks crossing Fletcher Drive, ca. 1938.
(Order #00099084)

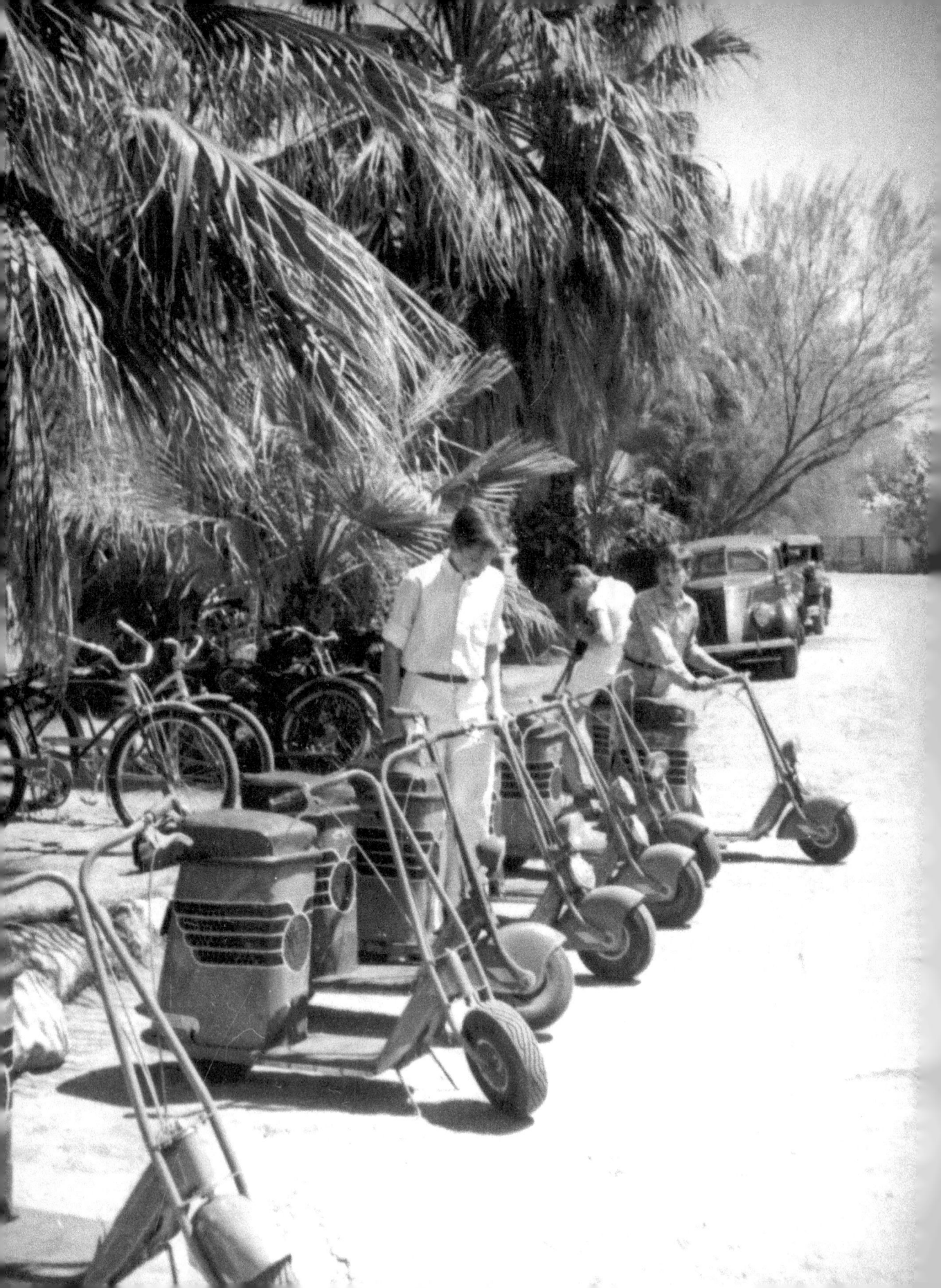

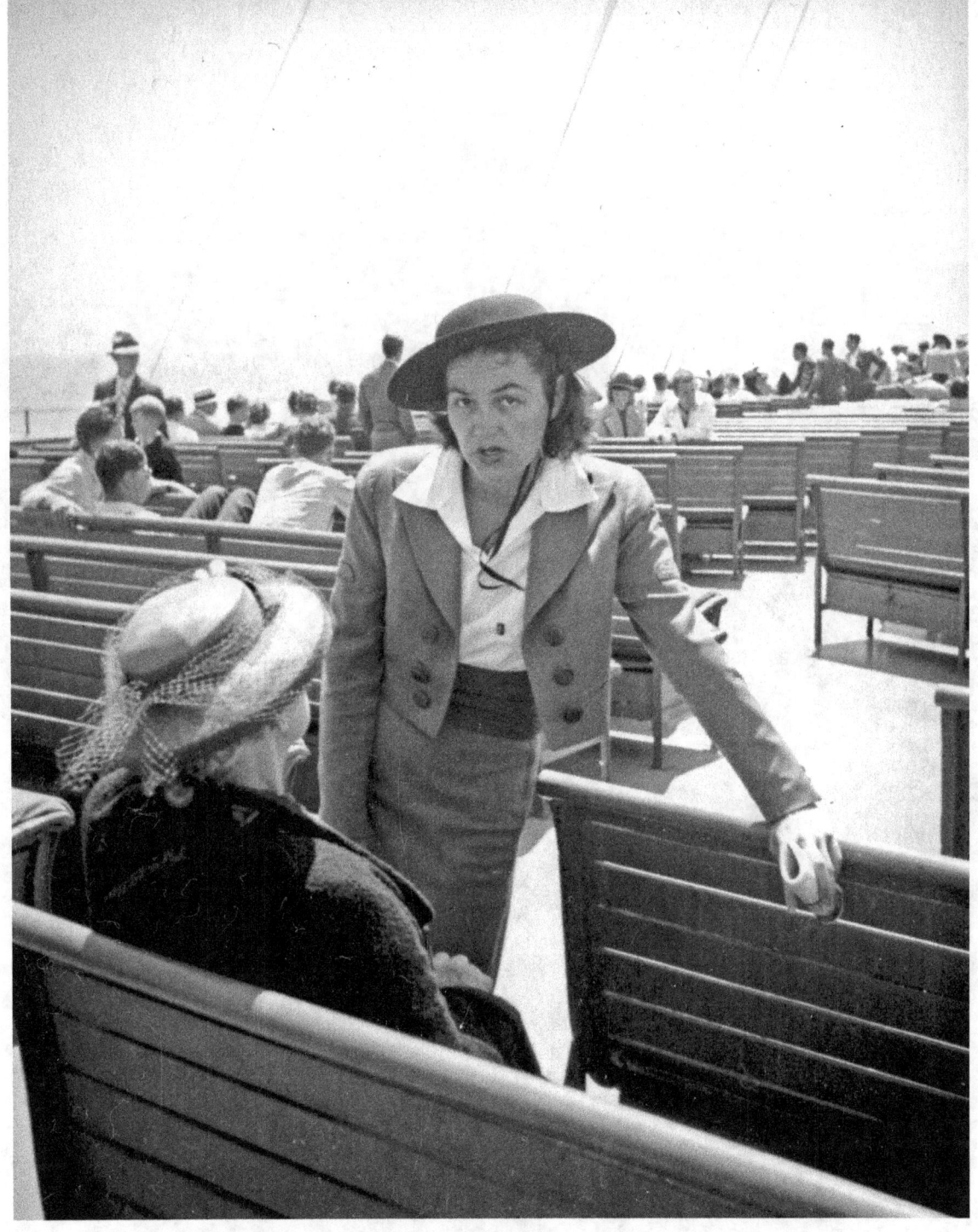

Passengers en route to Catalina Island aboard the S.S. Catalina, ca. 1938.
(Order #00100571)

Opposite: Bike and motor scooters lined up in Palm Springs, ca. 1938.
(Order #00099836)

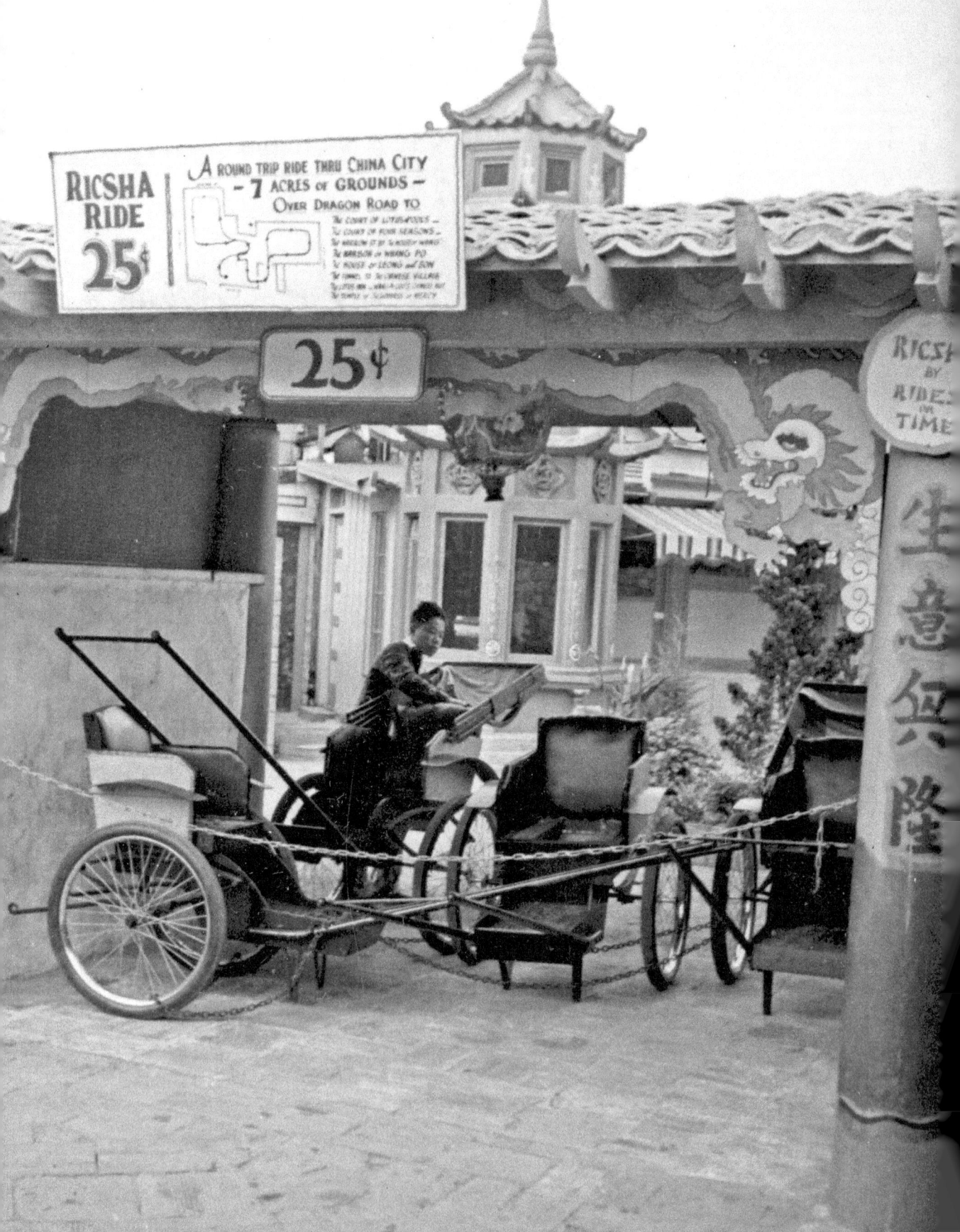

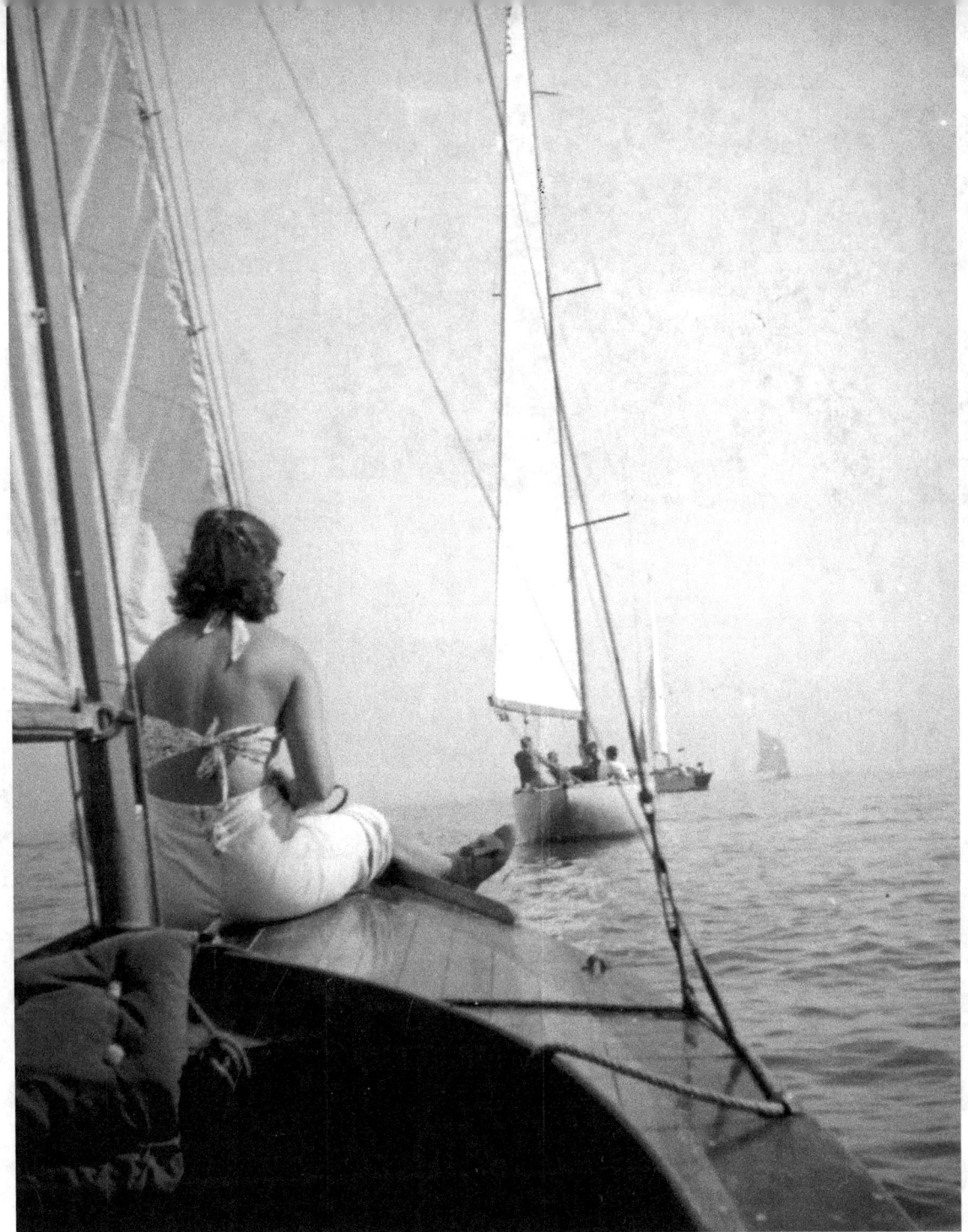

Boats sail near Newport Beach, ca. 1937.
(Order #00101300)

Opposite: A man gets ready for business at a rickshaw stand in China City, ca. 1939.
(Order #00101130)

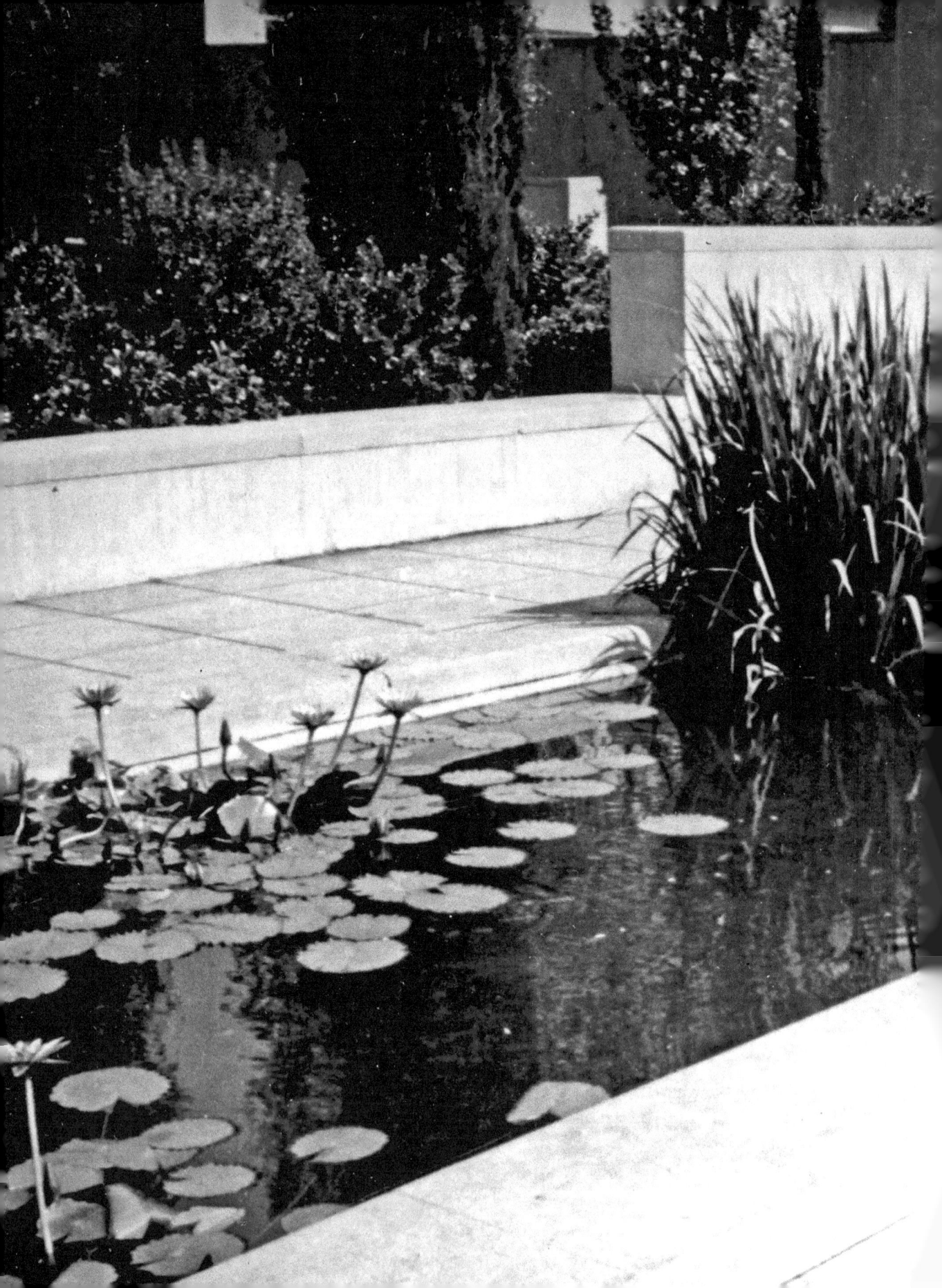

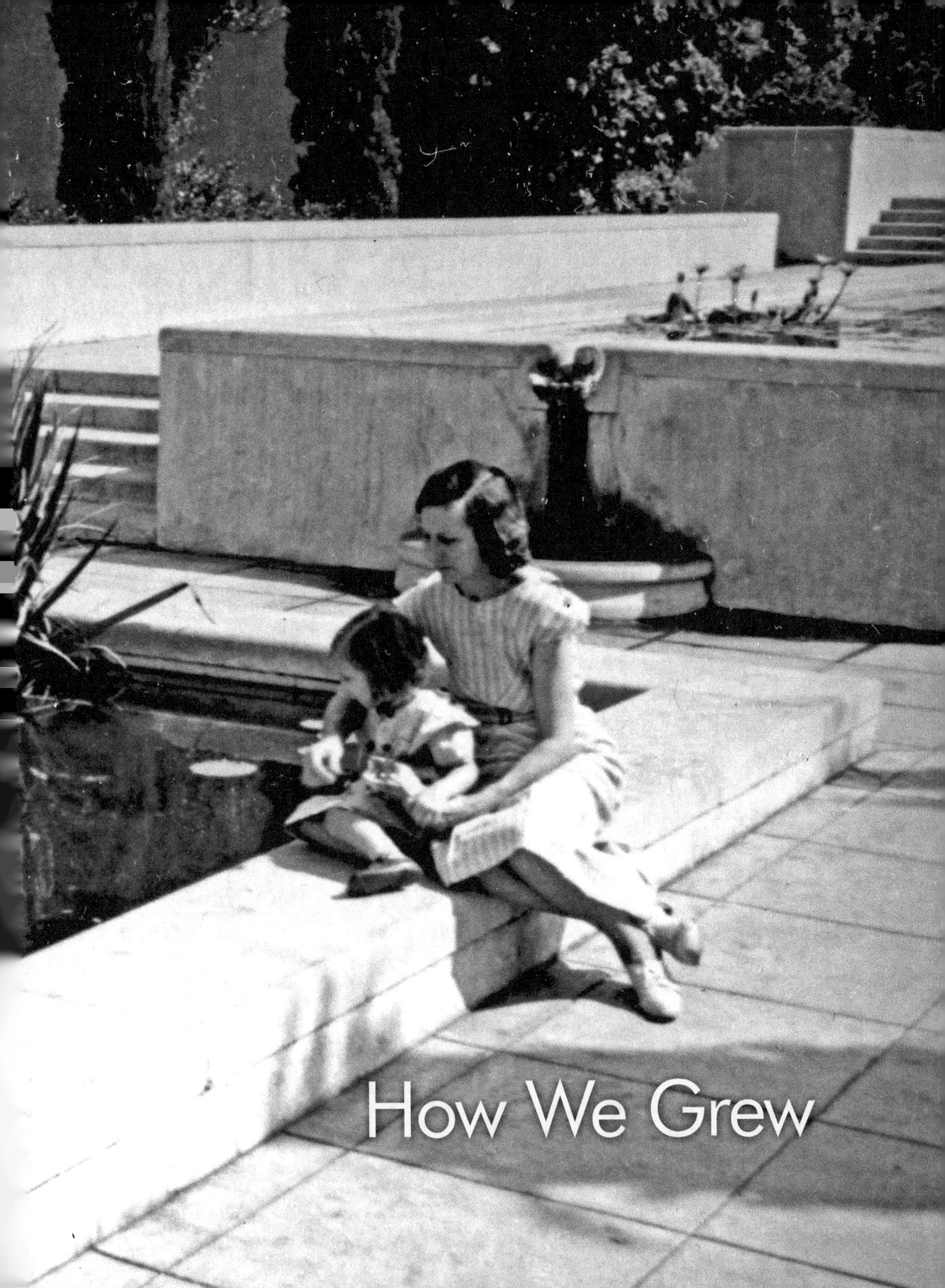

How We Grew

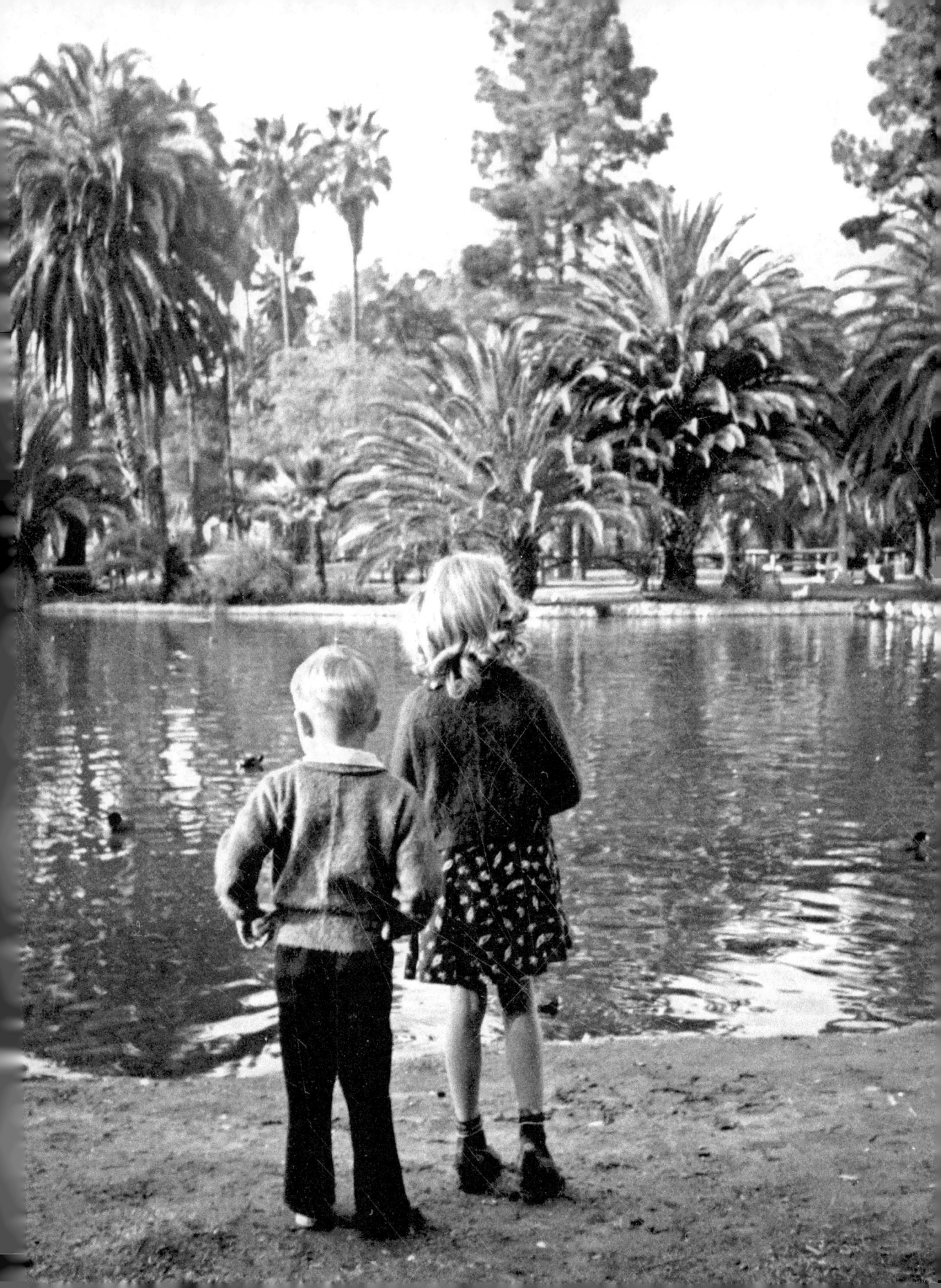

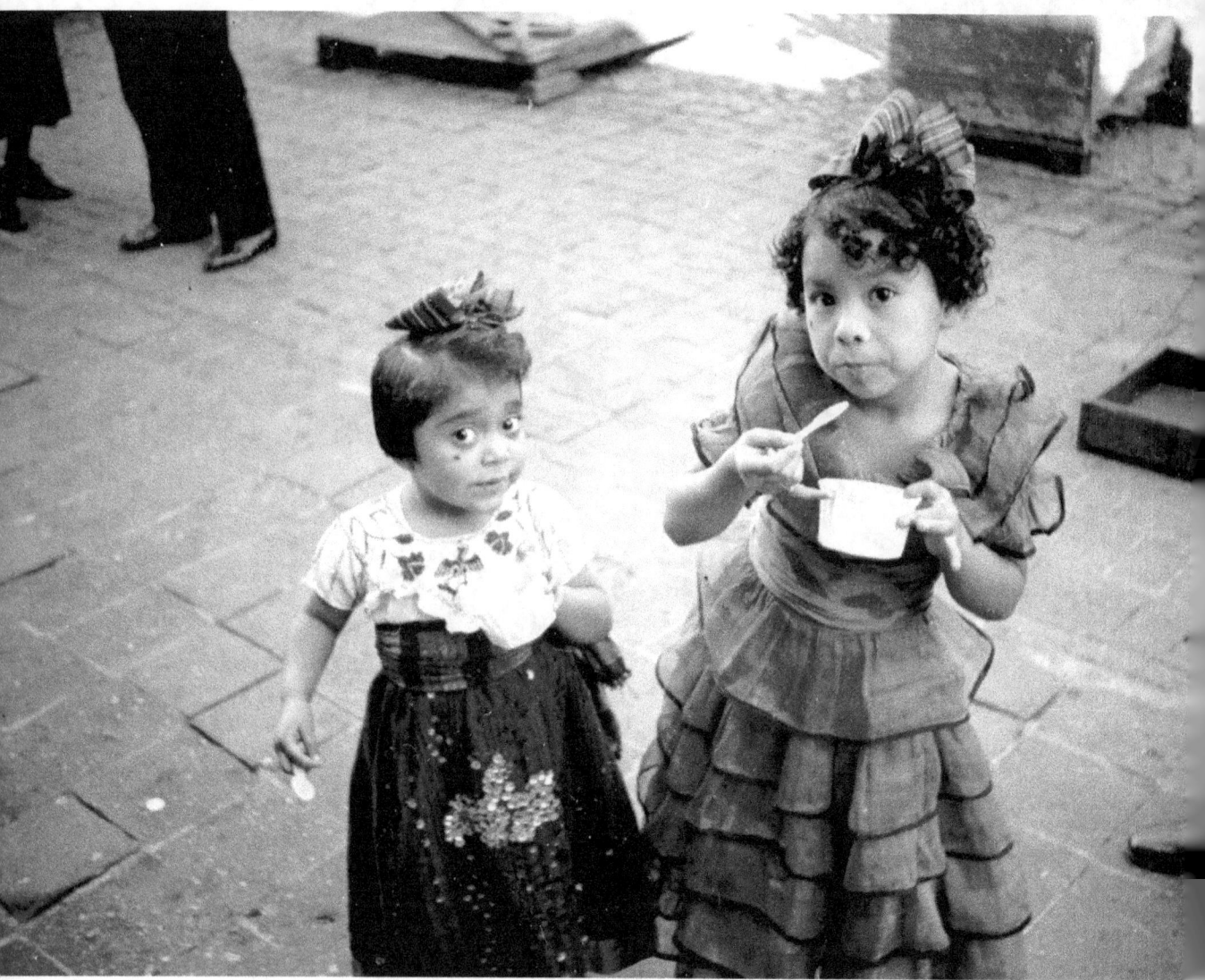

Youngsters enjoy treats on Olvera Street, ca. 1937.
(Order #00008464)

Opposite: Three boys converse near Olvera Street, ca. 1937.
(Order #00008495)

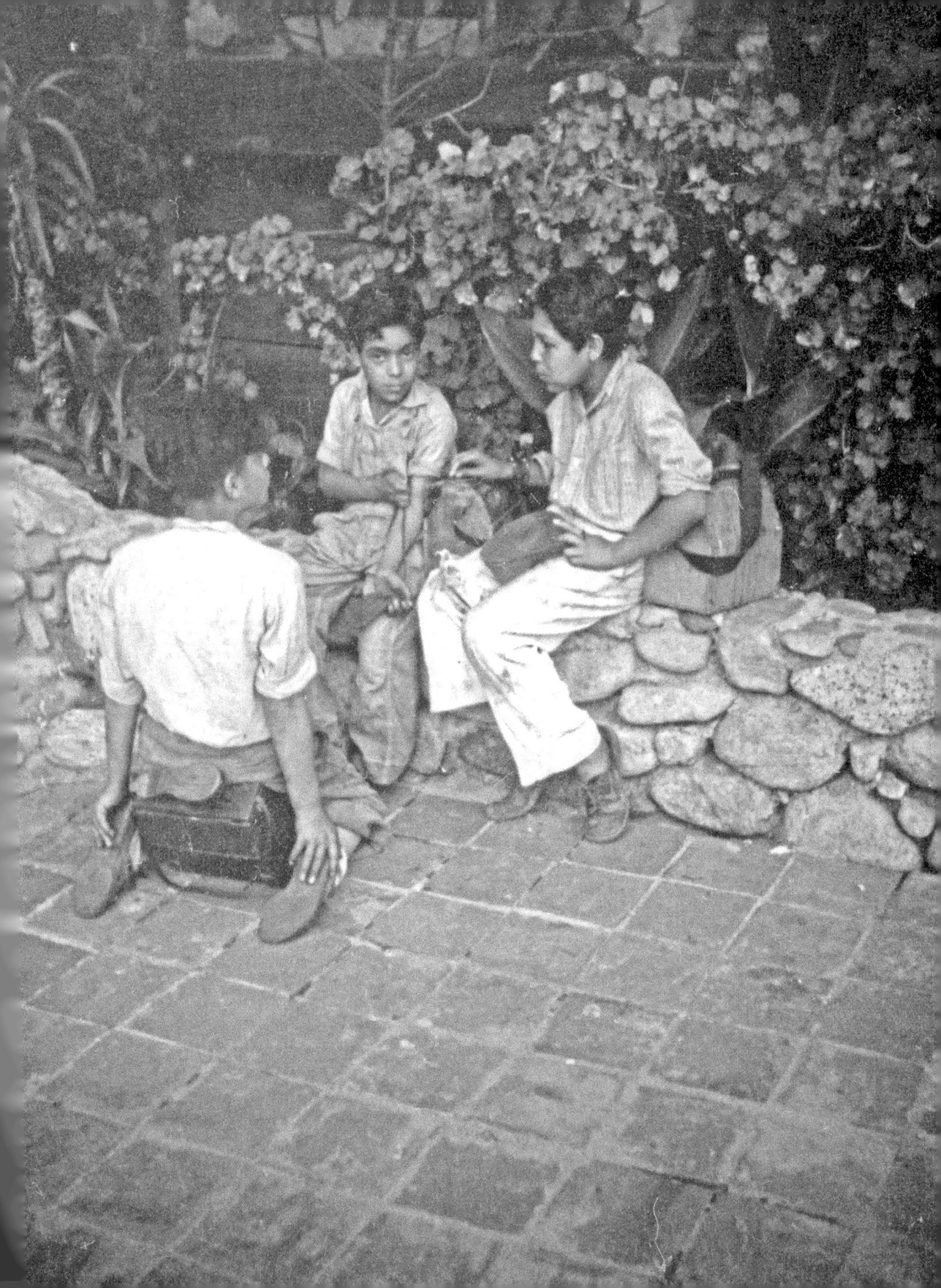

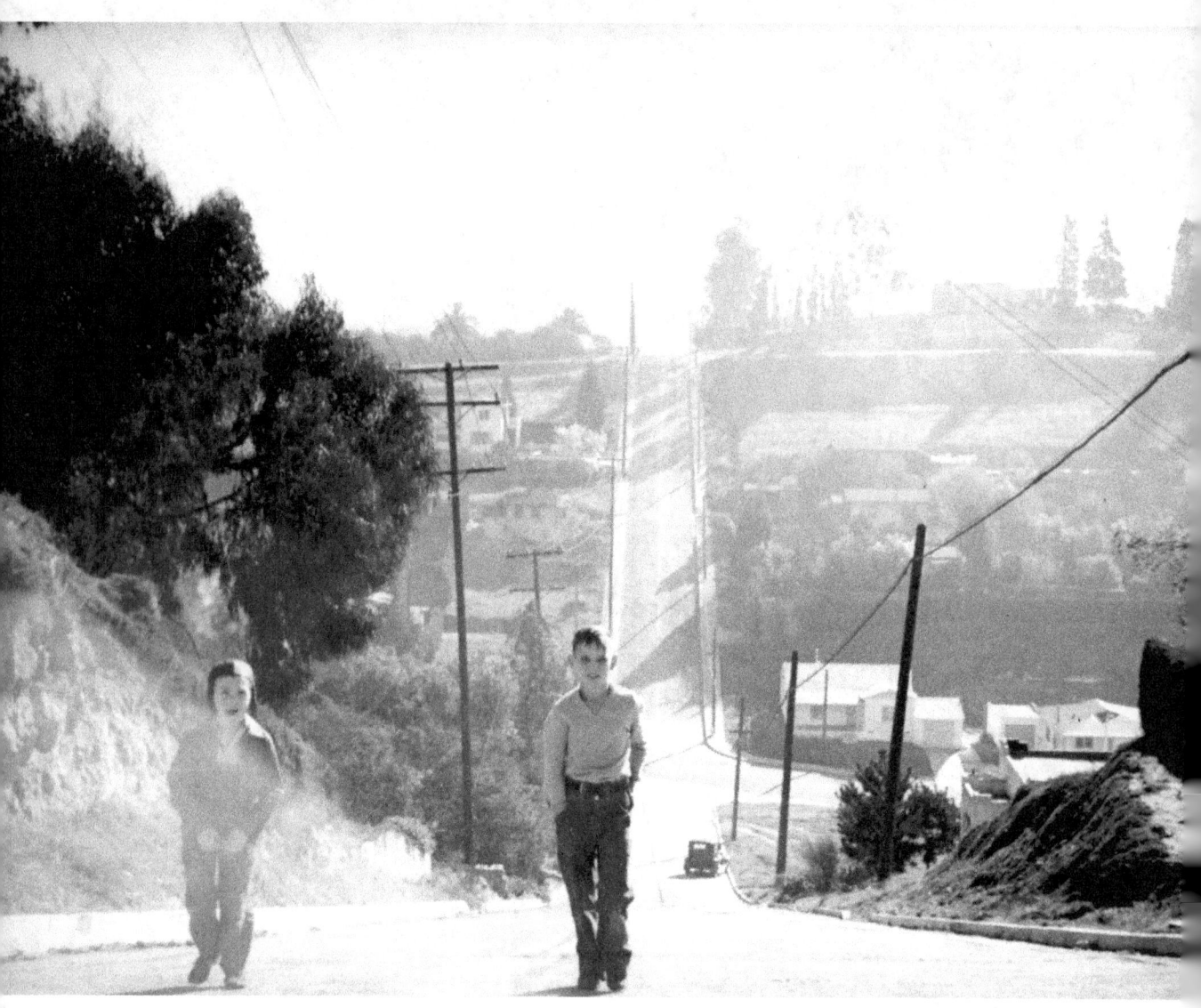

Two children traverse Baxter Street, one of the steepest roads in the city, ca. 1937.
(Order #00067275)

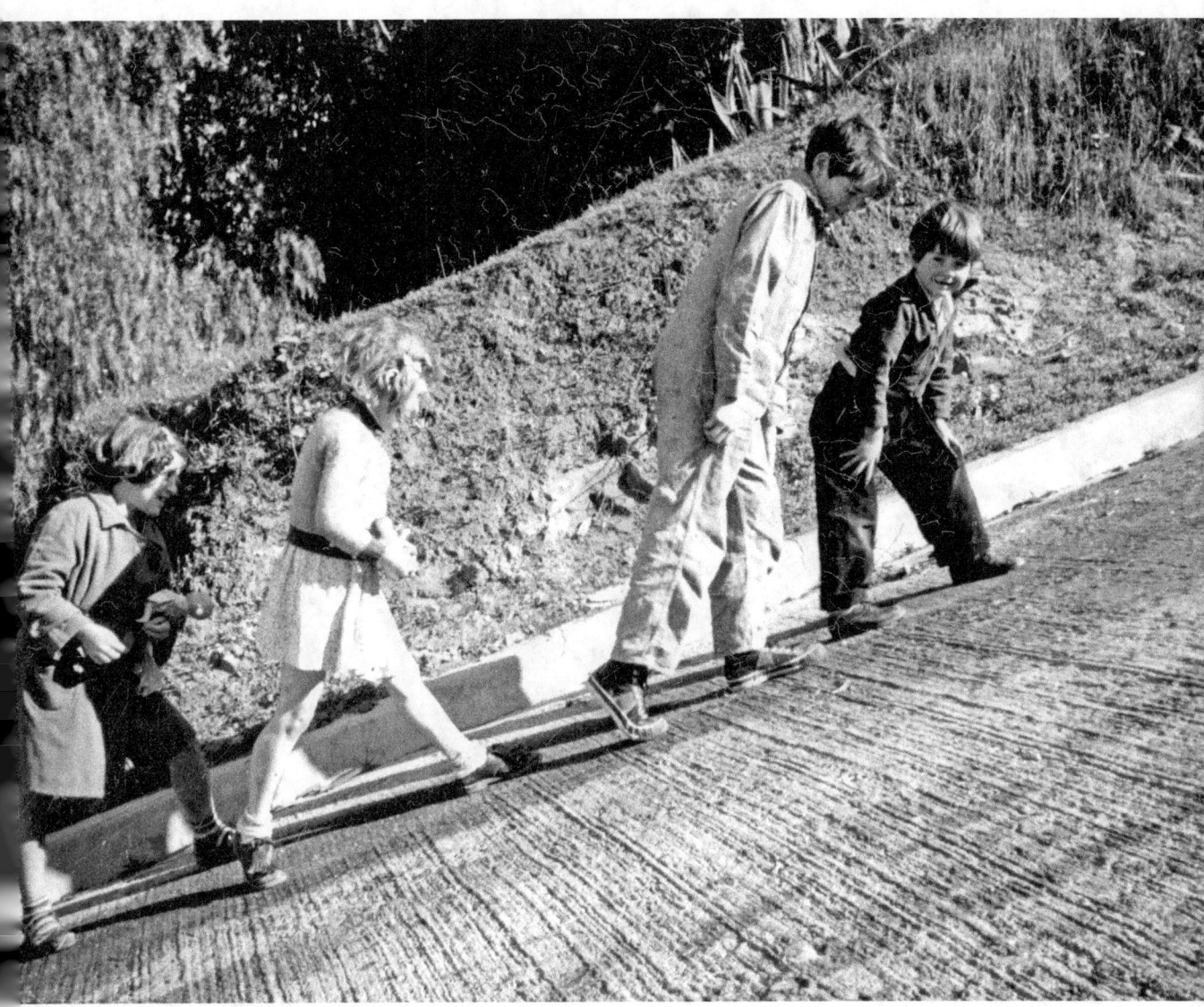

Four tots trudge up Fargo Street, ca. 1937.
(Order #00067281)

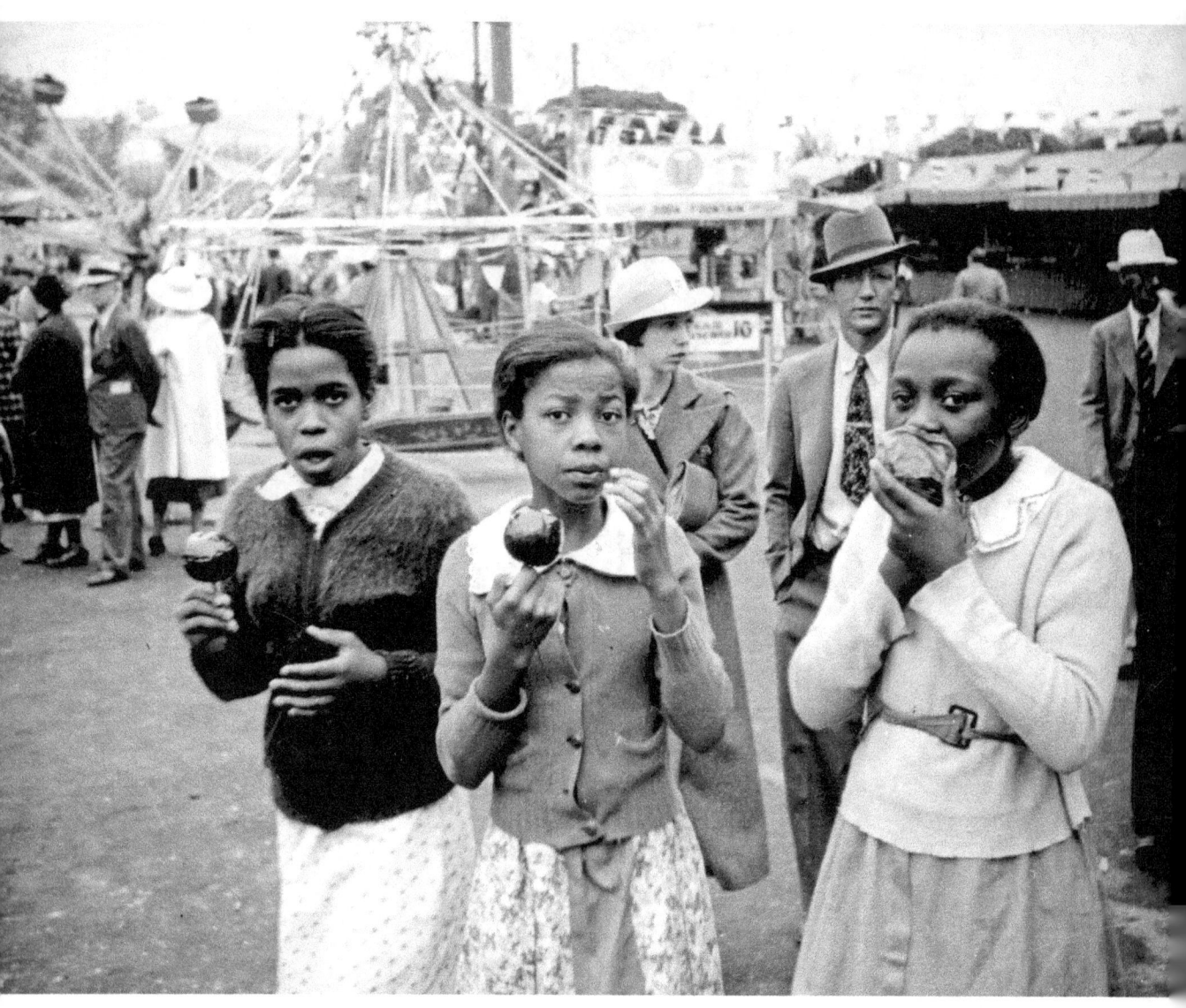

Young ladies enjoy candy apples at the annual Los Angeles County Fair in 1937.
(Order #00081987)

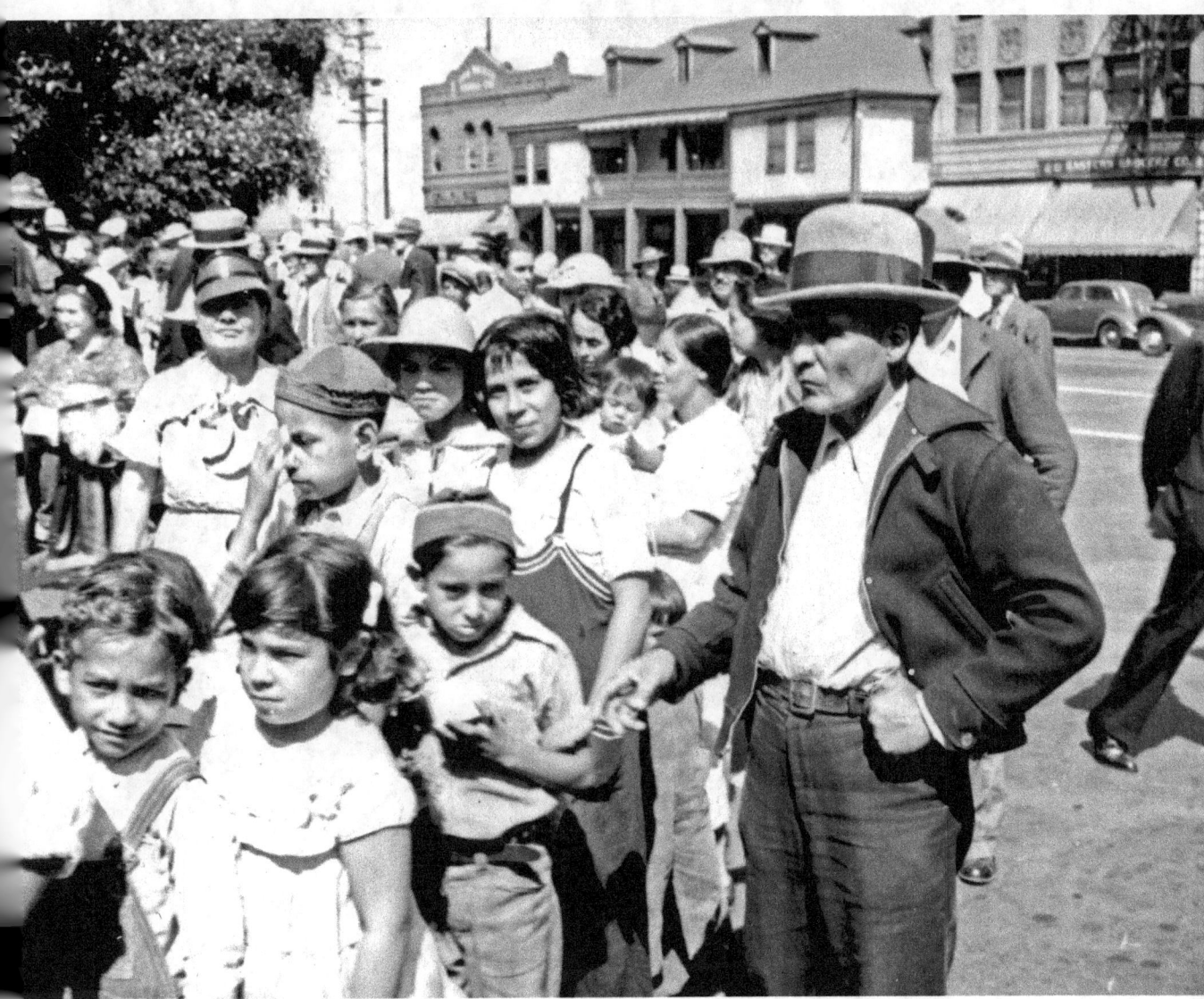

Children stand with adults looking south on Los Angeles Street from
the Los Angeles Plaza toward Arcadia Street. Buildings visible in the background
include the Vicente Lugo Adobe and the Eastern Grocery Company in
the Lee Shing Building, all of which were demolished by 1955, ca. 1938. (Order #00096731)

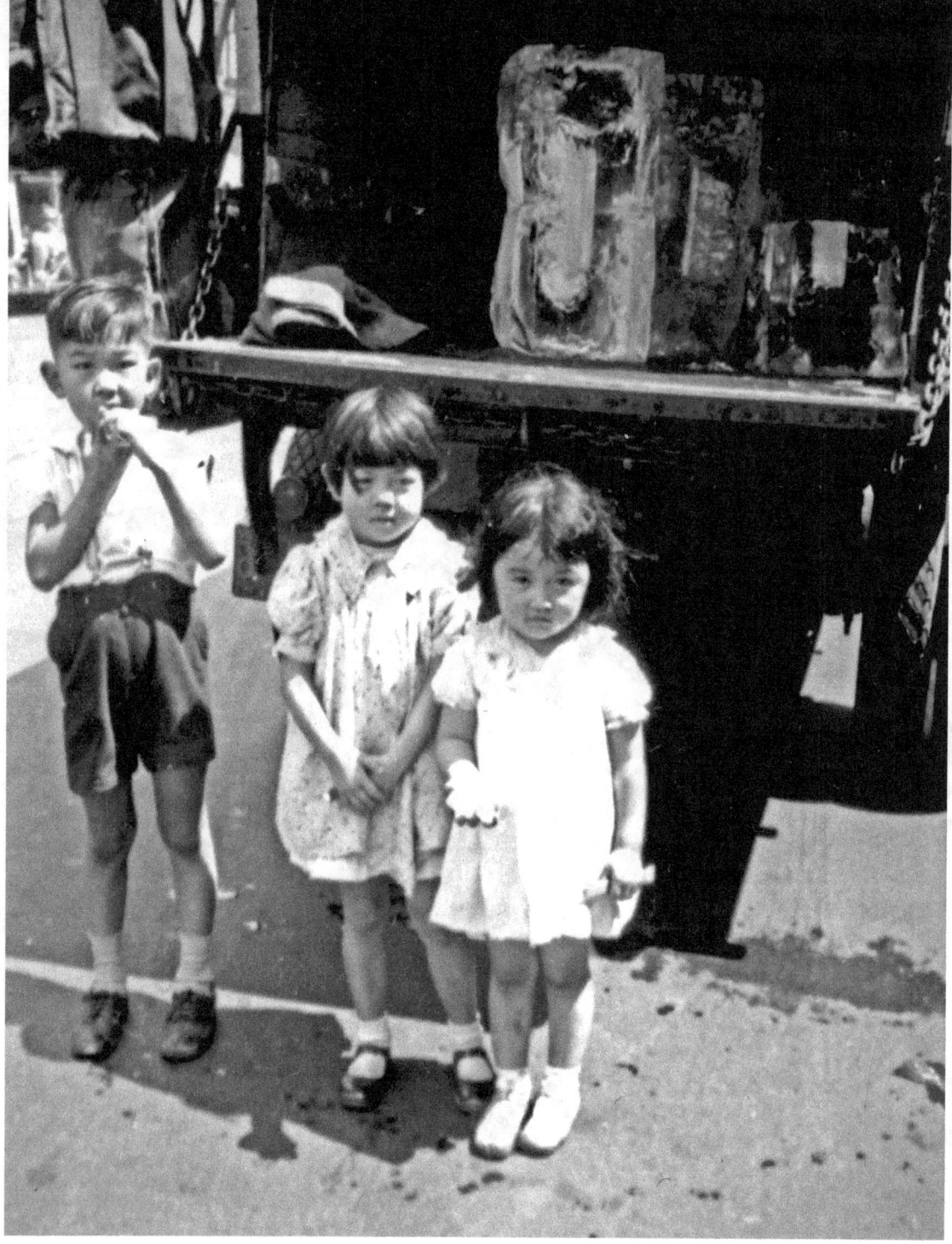

Three children stand by an open ice truck in Little Tokyo, ca. 1937.
(Order #00096776)

Opposite: A youngster tastes pumpkin at Fall Festival/County Fair, held October 27–30, 1937,
at the Farmers Market. (Order #00097726)

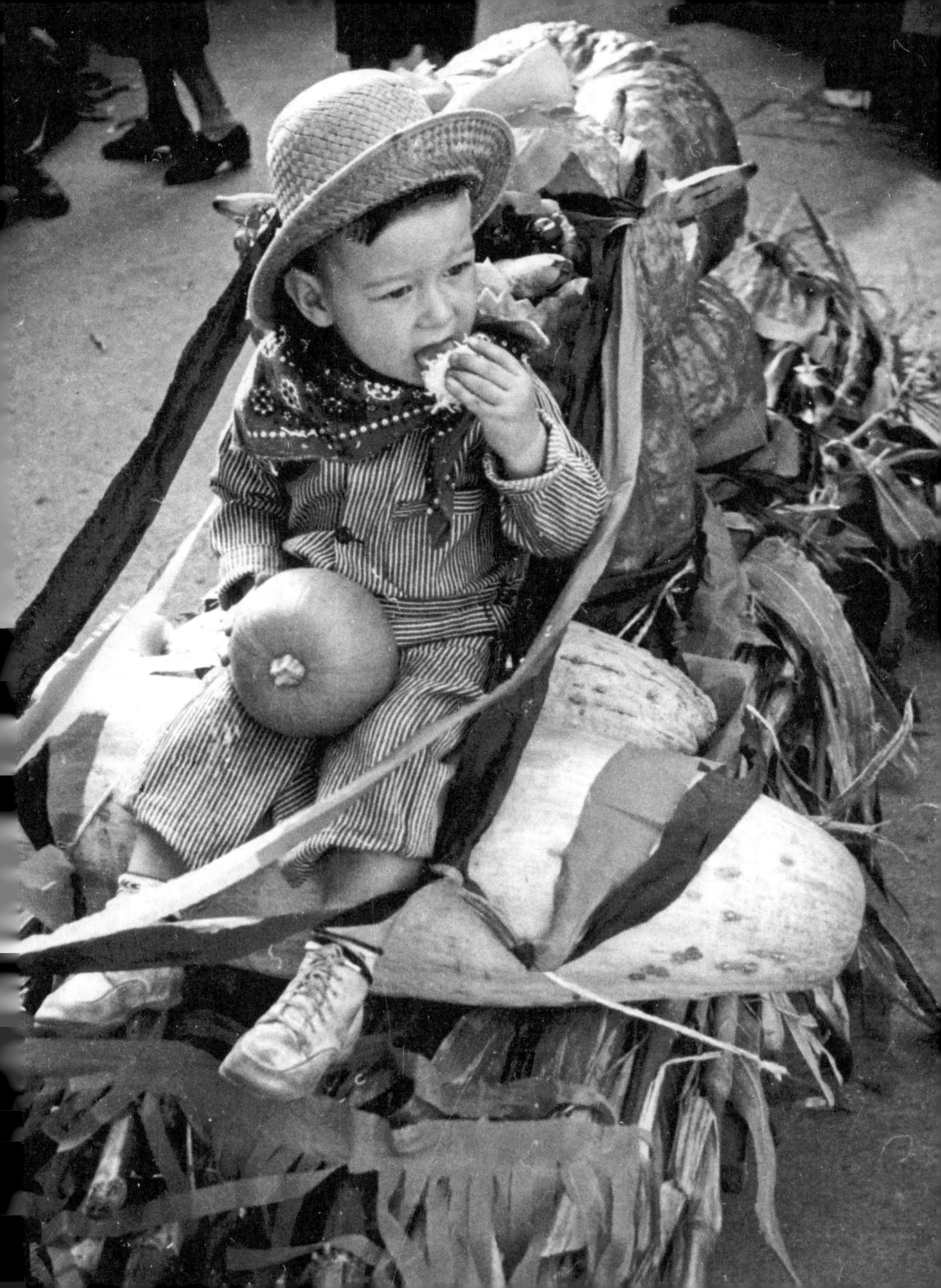

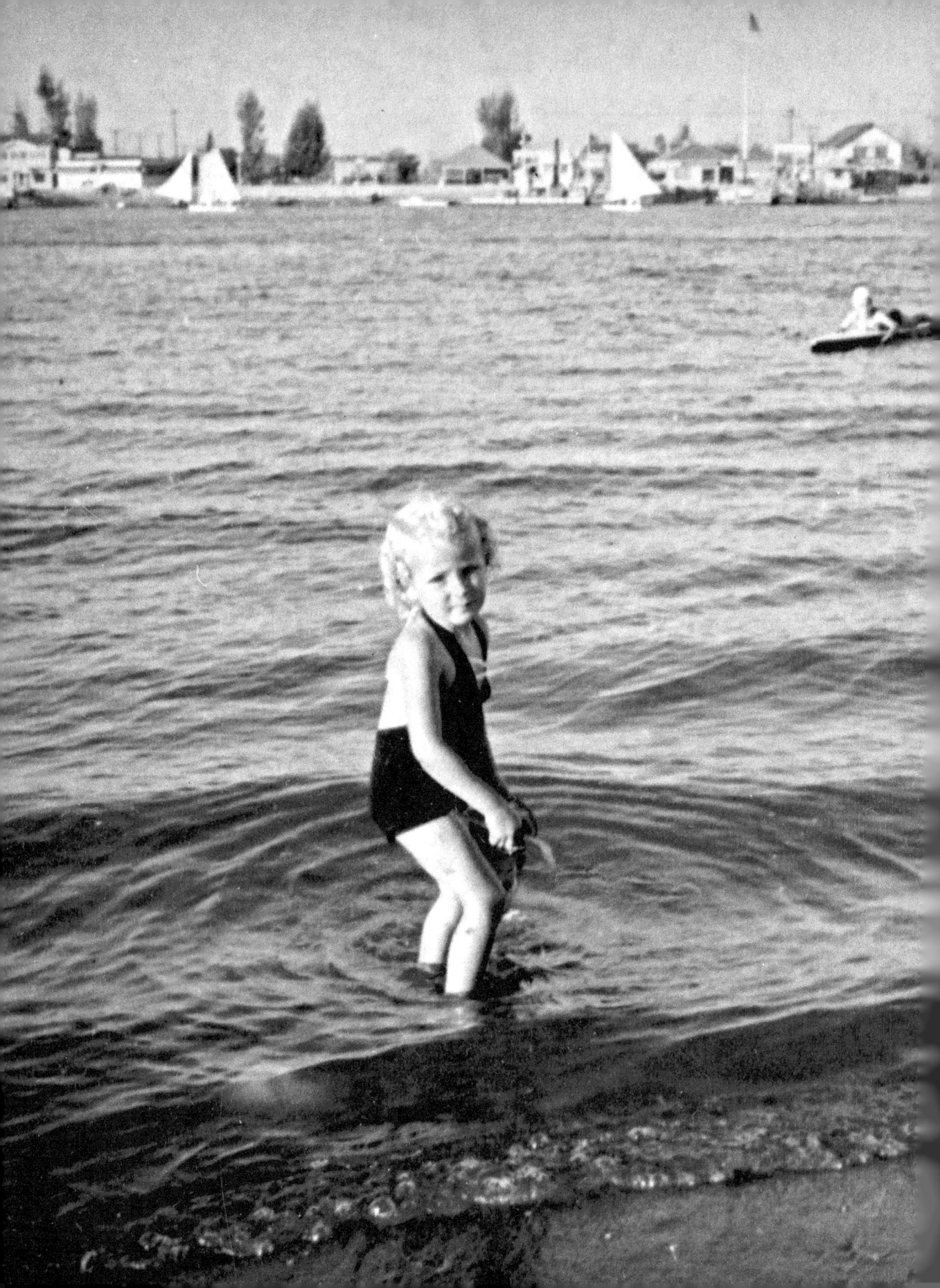

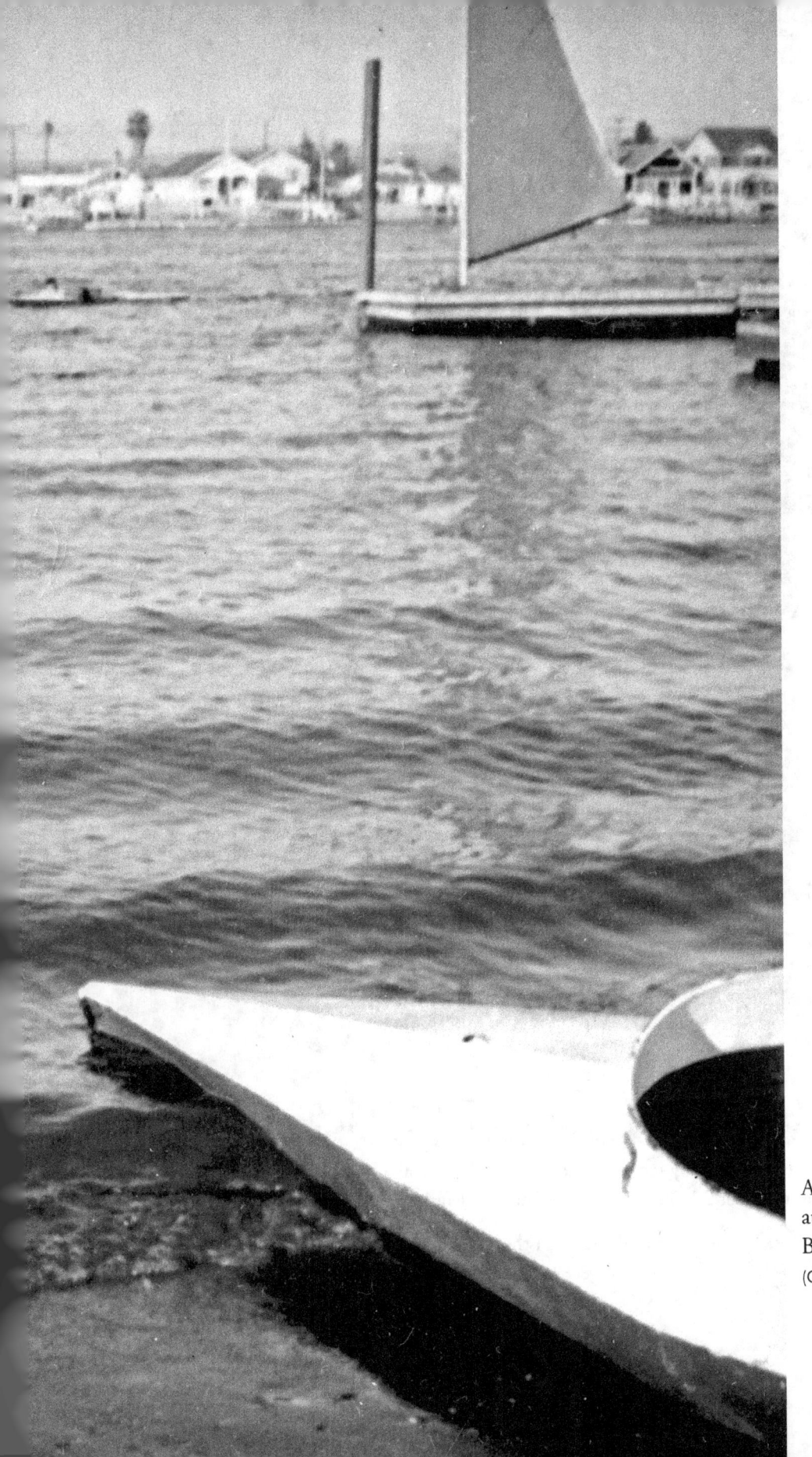

A little girl plays
at the shoreline of
Balboa, ca. 1937.
(Order #00096858)

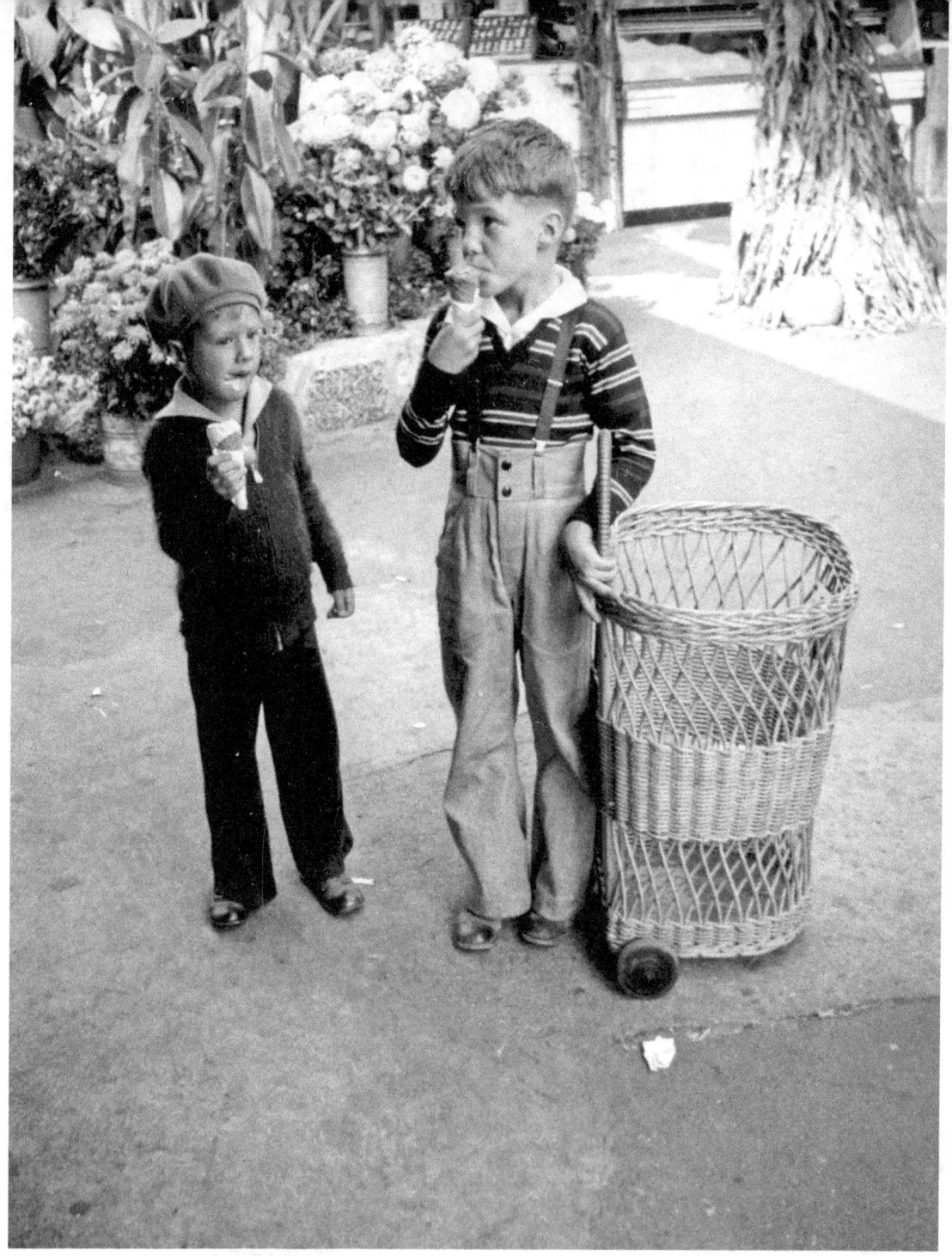

Two lads enjoy ice cream cones at Fall Festival/County Fair,
held October 27–30, 1937, at the Farmers Market. (Order #00097742)

Opposite: A young gent kills time in the San Fernando Valley, ca. 1937.
(Order #00098483)

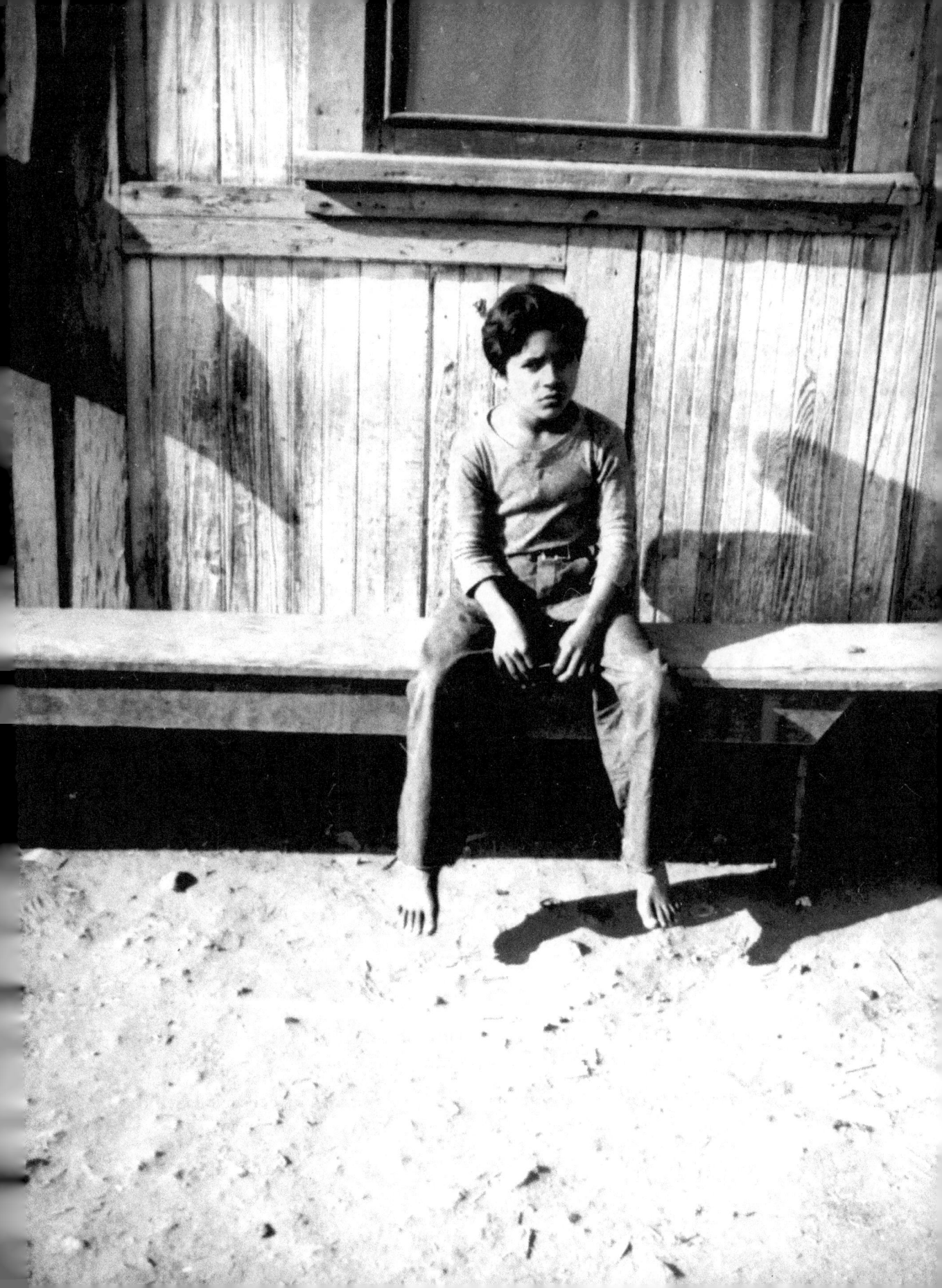

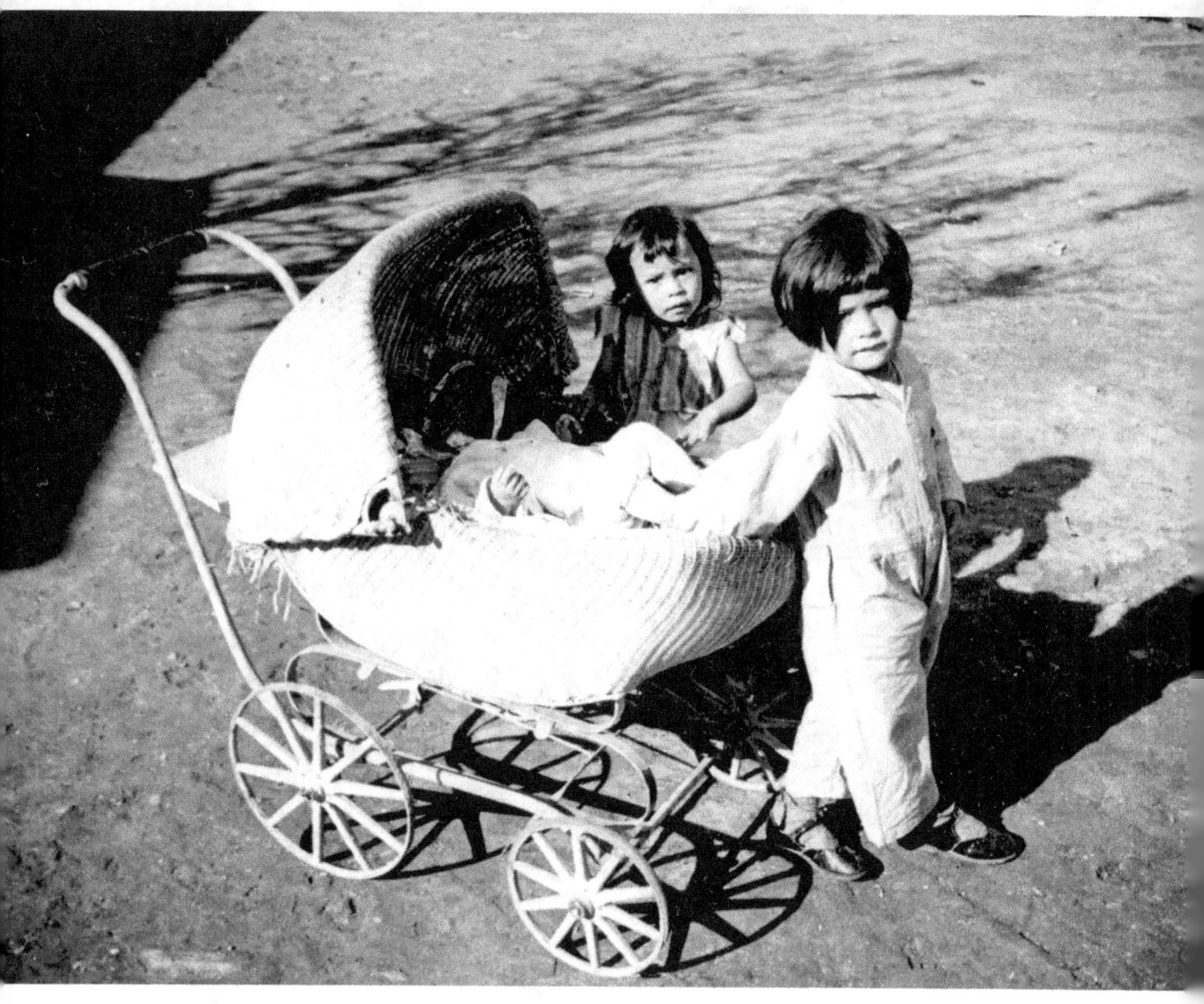

Two girls and a doll carriage in the courtyard of the Santa Cruz Adobe,
located at 641-643 North Broadway. (Order #00098727)

Opposite: A little girl climbs up to peer at the plants growing inside the fountain
in front of the Mission San Luis Rey church, ca. 1938. (Order #00100097)

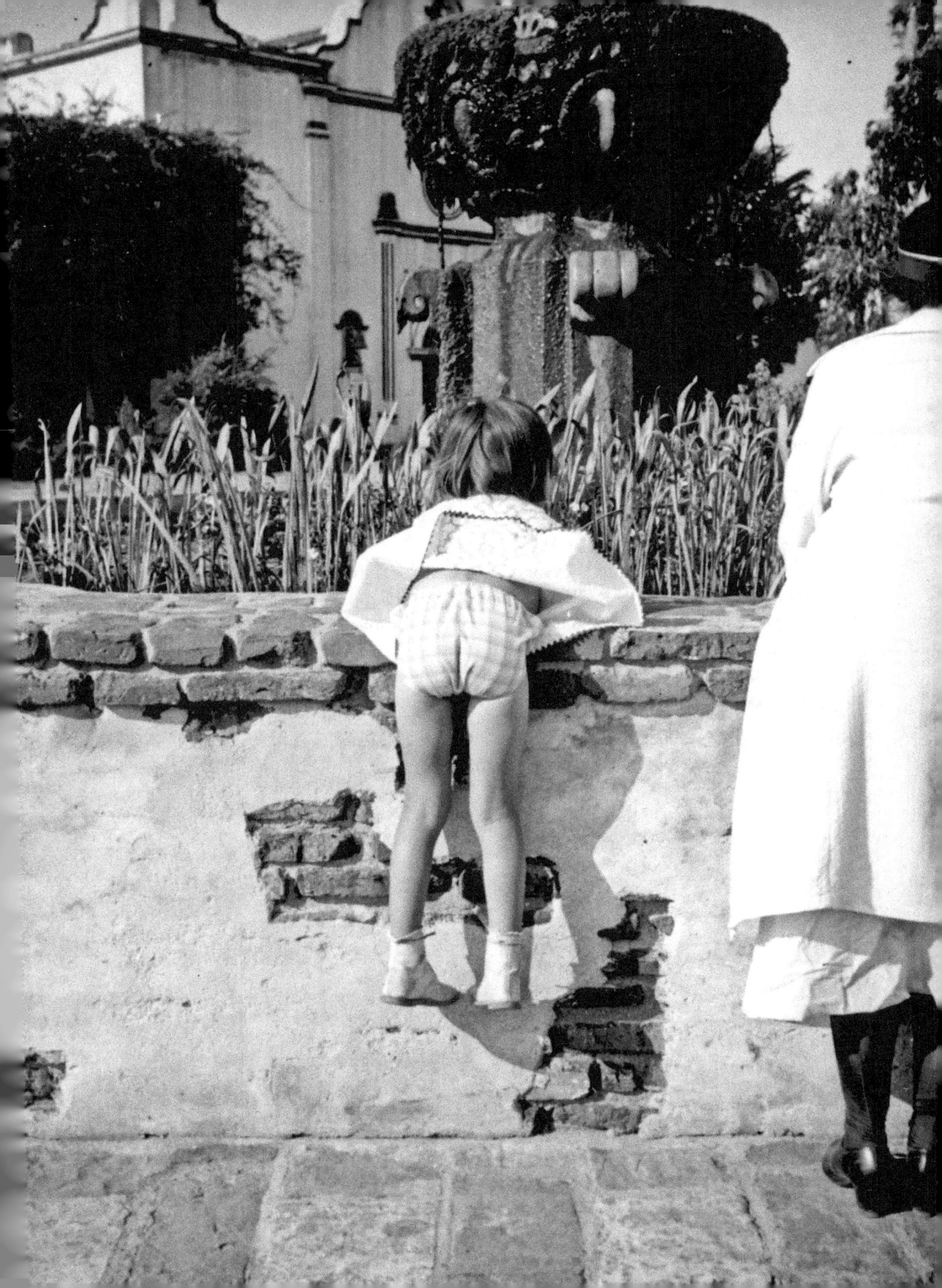

About the Photo Collection

The Los Angeles Public Library (LAPL) began collecting photographs sometime before World War II and had a collection of about 13,000 images by the late 1950s. In 1981, when Los Angeles celebrated its 200th birthday, Security Pacific National Bank gave its noted collection of historical photographs to the people of Los Angeles to be archived at the Central Library. Since then, LAPL has been fortunate to receive other major collections, making the Library a resource worldwide for visual images.

Notable collections include the "photo morgues" of the *Los Angeles Herald Examiner* and *Valley Times* newspapers, the Kelly-Holiday mid-Century collection of aerial photographs, the Works Progress Administration/Federal Writers Project collection, the Luther Ingersoll Portrait Collection, along with the landmark *Shades of L.A.*, which is an archive of images representing the contemporary and historic diversity of families in Los Angeles. Images were chosen from family albums and copied in a project sponsored by Photo Friends.

The Los Angeles Public Library Photo Collection also includes the works of individual photographers, including Ansel Adams, Herman Schultheis, William Reagh, Ralph Morris, Lucille Stewart, Gary Leonard, Stone Ishimaru, Carol Westwood, and Rolland Curtis.

Over 110,000 images from these collections have been digitized and are available to view through the LAPL website at **http://photos.lapl.org.**

About Photo Friends

Formed in 1990, Photo Friends is a nonprofit organization that supports the Los Angeles Public Library's Photograph Collection and History & Genealogy Department. Our goal is to improve access to the collections and promote them through programs, projects, exhibits, and books such as this one.

We are an enthusiastic group of photographers, writers, historians, business people, politicians, academics, and many others, all bonded by our passion for photography, history, and Los Angeles.

Since 1994, Photo Friends has presented a series called *The Photographer's Eye,* which spotlights local photographers and their work. These talks are presented bi-monthly. In 2011, Photo Friends inaugurated *L.A. in Focus,* a lecture series that features images drawn primarily from the Photo Collection. We have presented programs on L.A. crime, the San Fernando Valley, Kelly–Holiday aerial photographs, and L.A.'s themed environments, among others.

With initial funding from the Ralph M. Parsons Foundation, Photo Friends sponsored *L.A. Neighborhoods Project* by commissioning photographers to create a visual record of the neighborhoods of Los Angeles during the early part of the 21st century (all now part of the collection). To ensure the Library's Collection will continue to reflect such an important part of Los Angeles's history, a generous grant enabled Photo Friends to hire five contemporary photographers to document present-day industrial L.A. These images have become part of LAPL's permanent collection and are available through the Library's Photo Database. Photo Friends also curates photography exhibits on display in the History Department.

Photo Friends is a membership organization. Please consider becoming a member and helping us in our work to preserve and promote L.A.'s rich photographic resource. All proceeds from the sale of this book go to support Photo Friends' programs.

photofriends.org

Thank You!

Kim Creighton, David Davis, Matthew Mattson, Charlene Nichols, Maria Novoa, Katarina Robbins, Library Foundation of Los Angeles, and John Randolph Haynes and Dora Haynes Foundation.

How We Worked, How We Played: Herman Schultheis and Los Angeles in the 1930s
Edited by Christina Rice
Copyright © 2016 Photo Friends of the Los Angeles Public Library
Images © Los Angeles Public Library Photo Collection

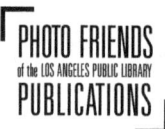

Published by:
Photo Friends of the Los Angeles Public Library
c/o Future Studio
P.O. Box 292000
Los Angeles, CA 90029
www.photofriends.org

Designed by Amy Inouye, Future Studio Los Angeles

Special quantity discounts available when purchased in bulk by corporations, organizations, or groups. Please contact Photo Friends at: **photofriendsla@gmail.com**

ISBN-13: 978-0692700570

Printed in the United States

www.ingramcontent.com/pod-product-compliance
Lightning Source LLC
Chambersburg PA
CBHW081000170526
45158CB00010B/2855